3-12-75

The New Consciousness
in Science and Religion

The New Consciousness in Science and Religion

HAROLD K. SCHILLING

A Pilgrim Press Book
from
United Church Press
Philadelphia

Library of Congress Cataloging in Publication Data
Schilling, Harold Kistler, 1899-
    The new consciousness in science and religion.
    "A Pilgrim Press book."
    Bibliography: p.
    1. Religion and science—1946-   I. Title.
BL240.2.S347   215   72-13792
ISBN 0-8298-0247-9

The excerpt from "The Bird and the Machine" on pp. 153-54 is from *The Immense Journey* by Loren Eiseley. Copyright © 1955 by Loren Eiseley. Reprinted by permission of Random House, Inc. The quotation on pp. 156–57 is from *We Are Not Alone* by Walter Sullivan. Copyright © 1964 by Walter Sullivan. Used with permission of McGraw-Hill Book Company.

The quotations on pp. 187–88 are from *A Rumor of Angels* copyright © 1969 by Peter L. Berger. Reprinted by permission of Doubleday & Company, Inc.

The scripture quotations are (unless otherwise indicated) from the *Revised Standard Version of the Bible,* copyrighted 1946 and 1952 by the Division of Christian Education, National Council of Churches, and are used by permission. Biblical quotations marked NEB are from *The New English Bible, New Testament.* © The Delegates of the Oxford University Press and the Syndics of the Cambridge University Press 1961. Reprinted by permission. The biblical quotations marked PHILLIPS are from J. B. Phillips, *The New Testament in Modern English* (New York: Macmillan, 1958).

United Church Press, 1505 Race Street, Philadelphia, Pennsylvania 19102

TO MY FRIENDS
of the
Science-and-Theology
Discussion Group,
especially those
active in it
while this book
was being written:

Ian G. Barbour
George Bradley
Herman Carr
John J. Compton
Frederick Ferré
Harmon Holcomb
Claiborne Jones
John Ollom
William G. Pollard
Francis O. Schmitt
Roger L. Shinn
Huston Smith
Charles West
Daniel Day Williams

CONTENTS

8

9

10

FORWARD

It may be well to call attention here to several features of this book to which there is no explicit reference elsewhere. First, the primary motivation for writing it has been to present, aside from the specific subject matter indicated by its title, a more general message of hope for our time and for the future. To be sure, there is much about the world that is thoroughly undesirable, very much suffering and terrible evil; and there are times when these seem to dominate the situation, and when discouragement, or even downright despair, seem amply justified. It is my conviction, however, that despite all such evidence to the contrary, the basic character of the universe—or of nature, man, and God—is *for good*, and that it provides more than merely adequate support for a joyously confident, hopeful, and adventurous faith that life is indeed worth living. This above all else is what I have wanted to say herein, and I hope the reader will be able to recognize it as implicit in everything I have actually said.

Second, this book offers a careful analysis of what the contemporary consciousness can, and actually does, discern about the way things are fundamentally, and especially of what the new insights of science and religion can tell us about it. Without the support of such analysis, faith and hope are likely to be no more than empty, wishful sentiments. However, this analysis is not highly technical, and this book is not a "scholarly treatise" in the sense of being designed for the expert. It is intended rather for interested general readers of modest competence, of whom I have had many, young and old, in my classes and in numerous lecture audiences, conferences, and discussion groups all over the country, and who have not found such analysis too difficult.

Next, my experience with such persons suggests also that many of them will want to know where else they can find the kind of information and interpretations I have presented. The liberal number of bibliographic references included in the text are offered primarily as resources for further study by such readers. This is why most of them cite so-called semipopular rather than highly technical books and articles—though this does not mean that they are inferior or unreliable sources.

Indeed, I feel that this book in its entirety should be regarded as primarily a resource book. It deals not so much with its author's own ideas as with those he sees developing elsewhere. Thus it is primarily reportorial and descriptive, calling attention to remarkable new resource material out of which the thoughtful person can build his own experience and thought, his own faith and beliefs, in harmony with what he selectively conceives to be the most meaningful insights of his time. To a large extent it is because I see such resources available in rich abundance and variety, and see also many concerned and able people, of all ages and persuasions, eager to appropriate and profit from them, that my hope is not only utterly confident but excitingly venturesome as I face into the future.

What the nature of the new insights is, and how it derives in general from the new consciousness, will be discussed in Part One. What they are in detail, and what their meaning and significance are relative to science and religion respectively, will be studied in Parts Two and Three.

I am deeply indebted to numerous persons for help they have given during this study—far too many to mention here individually. Those who have read and given their critique of large parts or of all of the manuscript in its later stages of development are Hans Freund and the late Henry Finch (philosophers at The Pennsylvania State University), Ian Barbour (scientist and professor of religion, Carleton College), Curtis Beach (clergyman in Pittsburgh), Herman Carr (physicist, Rutgers), Gabriel Fackre (theologian,

Andover-Newton), Frederick Ferré (philosopher, Dickinson College), John Ollom (physicist, Drew University), Roger Shinn and Daniel Williams (theologians, Union Theological Seminary), and Ernest Hawk (my student), Jacob Wagner (my pastor), and Frederick Schilling (my brother, and a theologian). Their suggestions have been most helpful.

The most potent direct influence upon my thought during the time this book was being written has come from a group of friends, including some of those just mentioned, called the Science-and-Theology Discussion Group, which has met for ten years, twice a year, for a weekend—and to whom I would like to dedicate this volume. The discussions we have had, focusing upon papers and books by members of the group and upon the writings of other workers in our field, have been tremendously stimulating and enlightening. I can't imagine where anyone could possibly get more utterly frank and cogent criticism of his work in "science and religion" than from this group. For this I am most grateful.

Harold K. Schilling
The Pennsylvania State University

part one

The New Consciousness of Man

I. New Sensitivities and Sensibilities

THE "ENORMOUS EXTENSION OF REAL APPREHENSION"

Something is happening to man that is so momentous as to constitute a major emergence in his evolution. He is experiencing a tremendous expansion and transformation of his consciousness—and thus becoming a being with a new mentality. It is to the study of this remarkable phenomenon that this book is addressed, with special reference to science, technology, and religion.

Admittedly the term "consciousness" is suspect these days and in some circles even regarded as altogether meaningless. In others, however, it is an indispensable concept for the adequate portrayal of mankind. I shall be using it in the following sense: *Human consciousness* refers to being aware of, or perceiving, conceiving, knowing, understanding, as well as reacting and responding to reality. We may speak of it as expanding and intensifying when human beings are becoming more sensitive to reality, when they perceive more of its aspects and dimensions, and when knowledge and insight are increasing both horizontally in extent and vertically in depth. We shall speak of consciousness as undergoing transformation when its modes of perception and comprehension, the content of its vision, and the character of its response to the world are changing radically.

This is precisely what many observers see actually transpiring today on a grand scale. And they see it to be attributable in large measure to the impact upon man of contemporary twentieth-century science—now often called *post-modern science* to distinguish it from *modern science,* its predecessor of the seventeenth, eighteenth, and nineteenth centuries, which was in many respects very different.

We shall be studying the contrasting features of modern and post-modern science in considerable detail to see why the latter is so influential in the transformation of human consciousness. Meanwhile, however, the reader should be forewarned about two features of that study: first, that its primary concern is not actually science itself, or its recent development, but its effects upon "human nature"; and second, that when I do speak of science I actually mean in general "science-and-technology."

Post-modern science is the science of relativity and quantum physics; of the new astronomy with its myriads of galaxies, radio objects, quasars, and so on; of creative chemistry, with its utterly new kinds of materials, such as the plastics and "miracle drugs"; of the new biology, with its chromosomes, genes, DNA, genetic codes, and holistic (whole-istic) or organismic emphases; of depth psychology, psychiatry, psychosomatics, as well as its newer "humanistic psychology"; of the powerful social sciences that have added so much to our understanding of the societal and communal behavior of men and women. These are, of course, well known to be tremendous epoch-making developments in the realm of ideas. It is not so well known, however, that they have to do with much more than ideas only. They represent not only additions to *what man knows* but changes in *the way he knows*, and in *the way he feels about, responds and relates to, the known and unknown*. In other words, they indicate profound changes in man himself. Not only are his mental equipment and abilities being modified and extended, but sensibilities that have been lost or atrophied are being restored or renewed, and fresh ones are emerging. The human imagination is being amplified. Men's minds and hearts are being liberated from inhibiting attitudes and conceptions to which they had fallen prey in the modern era, so they are now able to explore realms and dimensions of reality from which they had been blocked until recently. Intuition, properly safeguarded against excesses, has been admitted to scientific respectability. Novel conceptions and symbols are becoming available for investigating the reality and significance of the nonrational or transrational in human experience. In a sense history is repeating itself. The historically pivotal Copernican revolution, which gave birth to modern science, was also characterized by radical changes in man's mentality and general experience. Herbert Butterfield, renowned author of *The Origins of Modern Science*, has described these as "fundamental changes in outlook," "remarkable turns in the current intellectual fashion," a "subtle . . . alteration in men's feelings for things" and "for matter itself," and awareness of a "new texture of experience."[1] It is just this sort of transformation in depth that we are experiencing now, a change in the very "texture of experience"; and it is the kind that inevitably brings with it a crucial turning point in man's history.

The late Karl Jaspers found remarkable similarities between the present situation and that of the ancient so-called "axial period" of history, from about 800 to 200 B.C., the time of Confucius and Lao-tse, Buddha, Zarathustra, the great Hebrew prophets, the remarkable Greek sages. This was the time which, to quote Jaspers, "gave birth to everything which, since then, man has been able to be, the point most overwhelmingly fruitful in fashioning humanity"; when "man becomes conscious of Being as a whole, of himself and his limitations" and "asks radical questions. . . . In this age were born the fundamental categories within which we still think today, and the beginnings of the world religions, by which human beings still live, were created. . . . Religion was rendered ethical. . . . This overall modification of humanity," Jaspers suggested, may be termed "*spiritualisation*. . . . The unheard-of becomes manifest. Together with his world and his own self, Being becomes sensible to man, but not with finality: the question remains. . . . For the first time *philosophers* appeared."[2] What tremendous advances these were for the human spirit—and for the transformation of human consciousness! And Jaspers felt that nothing at all comparable to it had happened since then—*until now.*

Now, he sensed, man's mind is once more undergoing revolutionary changes, and another axial period is in the making—and, much popular opinion to the contrary, a new spiritualization. But this one is clearly going to be different for at least one reason: because of the presence in *our* world of what Jaspers called "an intrinsically new" causal factor, a new single but compound reality which I shall designate by the hyphenated symbol *science-and-technology* or simply *science-technology*. Science and technology (not hyphenated) are, of course, far from being identical, and in important respects they are very different. Yet they have for a long time been closely related, and today they have become very much dependent upon each other. For the ongoing work of science the perpetual creation of new substances and devices by technology has become an absolute necessity, just as for technology science's ceaseless production of fundamental data, concepts, and modes of thought is now utterly indispensable. Also it has become virtually impossible to distinguish sharply between the concerns and attitudes of science and technology. Many of their purposes and projects are inextricably enmeshed. So-called applied-science or engineering-development laboratories are increasingly doing what would formerly have been regarded as the business of "pure science" exclusively —and vice versa. There are good reasons, then, why science and technology are commonly conceived of as one great enterprise, whose impact upon man can no longer be resolved into two clearly separate components, that of science and that of technology.

Jaspers definitely located the beginning of this second axial period in our time. While, he noted, "Technology, in the sense of the utilisation of implements, has existed as long as men have existed," its character changed radically when "after the eighteenth century" a "decisive leap . . . took place in technological evolution . . . in the technological life-form as a whole."[3] What happened then was its wedding, so to speak, with the new exact science of the modern period. This in turn brought about the birth in the post-modern period of their offspring, the hyphenated science-and-technology, which with its amazingly ingenious devices and processes has amplified technological effectiveness millions of times. We should note especially, however,

that its unprecedented potency[4] is issuing in transformations not only of man's environment, but of himself; and
that this shows up nowhere more obviously than in an
"enormous *extension of real apprehension.*"[5] This has come
about because, for one thing, science-and-technology provides instruments that function as extensions of men's
senses, so they can "see" very much more than formerly.
For another, it provides devices that amplify men's intellectual abilities so they can reason and compute much
more effectively and rapidly, even when the load of variable
factors and complex relationships is exceedingly heavy.

If early in our century persons had appeared who could
analyze and reason through problems thousands or millions of times more difficult than any dealt with formerly,
and could apprehend in seconds what would previously
have required months or years, they would have been
acclaimed as supermen. Had they also been able to trans-
mit their astonishing abilities to their offspring and thus to
future generations, this would surely have been celebrated
as nothing less than an epoch-making new emergence in
the evolution of Homo sapiens. But this is exactly what has
in fact already happened. The present generation of humans—which has at its disposal all the magic powers
created by cybernetic science-and-technology—displays
these unparalleled abilities right now. Men and women of
today have experienced just such an evolutionary leap
forward—by virtue of an "enormous extension of real
apprehension."

Nor is this potent apprehension only of the analytic and
computational variety, for, as we shall see in detail later, the
new media enable men also to perceive and "feel" more
holistically (whole-istically) or systemically, more con-
figurationally in terms of patterns, as well as mythically,
and in depth.[6] In view of all this it seems altogether proper
to say that in our time there has appeared a genuinely new
order of human experience, and especially of real apprehension—and a new quality of life.

THE "NEW CONSCIOUSNESS OF THE WORLD"
The length of time spans and physical distances in commu-

nication has been reduced so nearly to zero that there now reigns on earth a remarkable degree of simultaneity of human experience. Men can participate existentially, and be more fully involved, in what other men experience even at great distances. Thus there has come about a remarkable new development in human relations, which Jaspers spoke of as follows:

What is historically new and, for the first time in history, decisive about our situation is the real unity of mankind on the earth. The planet has become for men a single whole. . . .

From our vantage point, the interlude of previous history has the appearance of an area scattered with mutually independent endeavours, as the multiple origin of the potentialities of man. Now the whole world has become the problem and task. With this a total metamorphosis of history has taken place. . . .

All the crucial problems have become world problems, the situation a situation of mankind . . . nothing essential can happen anywhere that does not concern all. . . .

Technology has brought about the unification of the globe by making possible a hitherto unheard of speed of communications. The history of the one humanity has begun. A single destiny governs the whole.[7]

Doubtless these assertions are meant to be taken as statements of fact and not merely expressions of hope. While Jaspers was fully aware of the disruptive elements of our culture—such as competitive nationalism, racism, classism, individualism, and churchism, as well as the demonic powers of war, economic exploitation, organized crime, genocide, and despotism—he was aware equally of its unifying and cohesive forces that have been drawing human individuals and groups together into a genuine, though as yet far from perfect, global community in which increasingly they share the good and suffer, and endeavor to ameliorate, evil and misfortune *together*.

It is important to recognize also that this has been an experience not only of outer coalescence but of profound inner unification as well. Many men are being united not only physically, by being brought into close neighborly proximity, but "spiritually," by truly global concerns and ideals, by increasing mutuality of understanding, and by a feeling—not only reasoned conclusion—that all men are indeed governed by a common destiny. Jaspers spoke of this as "a new consciousness of the world,"[8] and he considered it to be *the* evolutionary emergence par excellence that makes the present period of radical metamorphosis[9] truly axial in history.

Actually, however, "consciousness of the world" denotes much more than simply awareness of the nascent solidarity of mankind, significant though that is; for after all "the world" is more than "mankind." Furthermore, if postmodern science has taught us anything with absolute certainty it is that man is in no sense separate from nature, as he was once thought to be, but is rather an integral part of it, deeply embedded in its cause-and-effect system. Contemporary man is coming to sense keenly that the world is an all-inclusive community of beings—such as the earth's matter and energy; its soil and mineral deposits, atmosphere and waters; its plants, animals, and human beings; its things, as well as personal and social realities; its many relationships and events—all of which together constitute an integrated systemic whole rather than merely a loose collection of essentially self-sufficient, independent entities. As everybody seems to realize now the world is an ecosystem (ecological system), all of whose parts are so potently interrelated, interdependent, and interpenetrating that none can be said to exist in genuine isolation, or without affecting, and being affected by, all the others, as well as the system as a whole. So efficacious are these systemic relations that they determine to a large extent the very nature of the individual parts of the whole.

To illustrate, consider the contemporary conception of "human nature." Contrary to earlier understandings, man's *humanity* is not something fixed, as though it were an intrinsic, character-determining essence which he possesses without reference to the rest of the world; it is, rather, nature-dependent, and therefore derivative and contingent, arising in large part from the impact of his environment upon him. Take, for example, a person's mind or intellect, i.e., his ability to think and reason. It is not an organ of the body, like the heart or brain, but a function or process, an aspect of the whole person that develops during his or her lifetime in reaction to external stimuli. So far as we know, a normal newborn baby has no mind at birth, though he does have the capacity for it. If he were isolated permanently in an enclosure where no light or sound or other such stimuli could penetrate, he would grow into no more than a non-human mass of protoplasm, becoming what is commonly called "only a vegetable."

Hence we have come to see that man is completely in, rather than separate from, nature and the world, and that his very personhood and humanity are nature-dependent as well as culture-dependent. As the world changes, so inevitably does human nature. Were nature to degenerate, so would we. Of course, this must be said in principle also about all of man's fellow creatures, be they animate or inanimate, human or nonhuman. They too are system-dependent. Therefore to be "conscious of the world" in our time means to realize that the world is a unitary, integrated whole and to be aware of the systemic interdependence, solidarity, and common destiny of *all* its inhabitants and components.

AWARENESS OF THE "NATURE" OF "PHYSICAL REALITY"

Clearly, in view of the preceding paragraph our next subject must be man's radically new understanding of the basic nature of reality—here taken to be that which impresses itself upon the human consciousness coercively, which exists whether it is perceived or not and is not therefore merely imagined. As William James once said, reality is what we *must* take into account and dare not disregard or deny. Our question is: What is the fundamental character of reality so conceived? What has man learned recently about its basic structures, dimensions, and attributes? More especially, in this section we shall be concerned with that segment of reality which we come to know verifiably through the natural and social sciences, and which I shall designate as *physical reality*. And I begin with that component of it which is commonly called *matter*.

It would be virtually impossible to exaggerate how truly revolutionary man's contemporary scientific conception of matter is. Almost everything once said about it is now being denied. To illustrate, matter was assumed to consist of atoms that are unchangeable, indestructible, without internal "parts," and to consist of primordial substances whose "properties" are inherent and in no sense derivative, and in terms of which all the objective characteristics of the world may be explained. To ask what something *is* was to ask what it is made of fundamentally. Table salt, for example, was said to be that particular form of matter whose molecules consist of an atom of sodium and one of chlorine; and the atom of sodium *is* simply a bit of the cosmic stuff called sodium, and the atom of chlorine a bit of that called chlorine. Nothing more could or needed to be said, because nothing more simple or fundamental was known or, according to current thought, conceivable.

Now, however, we feel differently about all this, for matter has shown itself to have a remarkable hierarchical structure with levels and depths (see chapter III), and atoms are by no means its most fundamental units. We now know that atoms are exceedingly complex, and dynamic rather than static, with both particle and wave properties. Contrary to earlier views, they do have internal structure and consist of much smaller entities, such as electrons, protons, neutrons, and still others, among which occur very strange happenings. Were we to ask what these sub-atomic entities are "made of" we would be told that this sort of question has become inappropriate these days, since it represents a way of thinking that is no longer useful. As science has explored the micro-world within the atom it has not found there anything to which the traditional notion of substance might be applied usefully.

On the other hand these explorations have led to the remarkable insight that the most fundamental realities of matter, and more generally of physical reality, are relationships, processes, and events rather than bits of substance. From this point of view, to say what an electron or neutron *is* is to say what it is by virtue of its behavior, and not of its material content. Thus, to be specific, an electron is conceived of as that micro-entity which behaves in certain specifiable ways in the presence of other entities; and similarly a proton or neutron is defined by a uniquely different behavior pattern. It follows that its properties must be regarded not as intrinsic essences but as consequent characteristics deriving from relationships disclosed in its behavior. Thus man has become keenly conscious that fundamentally *matter is relational,* much more like a delicate fabric of dynamic interrelationships than an edifice of hard building blocks.

It is its relationality that confers upon matter the exceedingly interesting qualities we shall look at next. For one thing, the nature of matter's internal relationships is such that the so-called "elementary particles," as well as other "parts," are *gregarious,* i.e., they display a tendency to aggregate or unite into larger and more complex structures. Thus protons and neutrons tend to join, producing atomic nuclei; these with electrons form atoms; atoms with atoms make molecules; molecules congregate, producing matter in bulk, i.e., large objects, from crystals to rocks to mountains, planets, galaxies. There is then in our universe much coming together and sticking together—gregariousness.

Next, aside from mere joining together, there is also much building together, of the kind which in temporal perspective is seen to be *historically developmental and evolutionary.* According to the post-modern vision there has been an evolution not only of the biological species and of the geological features of the earth but also of inanimate matter itself. Long ago there existed only its elementary particles, or at most its simplest kind of atoms, those of hydrogen. The many species of other atoms and of molecules came on the scene later, and the combinations of molecules, such as crystals and rocks, rivers and oceans, planets and galaxies, still later. In other words, to begin with there were no complex structures of matter, and later there were. The dynamism of its relationality is such that matter displays remarkable developmental drives, so that matter itself may be said to be constructive and developmental—it builds.

Another important aspect of this relationality has come to light through the momentous discovery that matter is *transmutable* into energy and vice versa, and that therefore neither matter nor energy may be regarded as the completely autonomous eternal reality it was once thought to be. The two traditional conservation laws, one for matter and one for energy, have become one, for *matter-energy* (chapter IV), proclaiming that it is the single compound reality, matter-energy, that is conserved. How much of the matter-energy may in a given situation show up as matter or as energy will depend upon the physical relationships prevailing at the time. It would seem that neither matter nor energy is "the basic stuff" of physical reality. It is matter-energy that plays that fundamental role. Matter and energy are simply two different states of matter-energy, very much as water and ice are different states of the one substance, H_2O. Actually, then, what has been said thus far about the nature of matter applies as truly—and more fundamentally—to matter-energy. Matter itself is relational, gregarious, and developmental because this is the case for the more inclusive reality, matter-energy—and indeed for physical reality in general. Certainly the complex structures we have considered are structures not only of matter but of matter-energy.

Matter-energy also *creates*—*de novo* or *ex nihilo*. Not only does it build new structures out of older parts (when, for example, it builds molecules out of existing atoms or subsequently builds material structures out of those molecules), but it actually creates entities of a quite different kind, such as have no preexisting parts in the usual sense. These are the qualities that characterize the new structures as wholes and emerge as products of their systemic wholeness and holistic (whole-istic) drives. Thus when material objects (matter in bulk) appeared on the scene there emerged with them a vast array of formerly nonexistent qualities, such as solidity, fluidity, malleability, elasticity, temperature, color, electrical conductivity, and magnetic polarity. These are physical realities as truly as the material objects whose attributes they are, though not of the kind that have "parts." Nor did they exist on earth prior to the genesis of matter in bulk or of complex physical

systems, for individual molecules do not have such qualities. There is no such thing as a hot or cold molecule, or a
malleable one, or an electrically conducting one; there
never was. Such attributes are exhibited by systemic
wholes only, not by individual parts or constituents.

It seems, then, that physical reality has been evolving by
virtue of at least two holistic drives: from simple relationships and structures to increasingly complex ones (chapter
V deals with the notion of simplicity-and-complexity in the
universe), and from qualitative poverty to qualitative richness and luxuriant variety (chapters III, VII, IX). Without
the latter the world would have been terribly drab and
without charm—or much meaning. And it is here that the
concept of the creativity of physical reality seems especially
meaningful, for it is within this advance toward increasingly significant quality, which becomes possible only in
wholes, that there occurred the remarkable evolutionary
emergences or burstings forth successively of life, mind,
and spirit, each of which itself exhibits a unique aspect of
physical reality's creative powers. What happened apparently was this: When in its structural development inanimate matter-energy reached the stage of the very complex
"giant molecules" (polymers), its correlative qualitative
development also took a mighty step forward, since at that
point in the history of nature certain kinds of molecules
became self-replicating and therefore alive. Thus animate
matter-energy appeared on the scene, and with it in due
time a vast array of bio-organisms having the amazing new
qualities of "life." In this way physical reality attained
another dimension and became matter-energy-life. Much
later, after structures had developed still further and animals appeared, another critical degree of complexity and
wholeness was attained, and another range of qualities
emerged—at least in the higher animals and mankind—
those of mind. These then prepared the way for the emergence of spirit (to be defined later), and physical reality
became, by virtue of these creative thrusts, matter-energy-
life-mind-spirit. Finally, we must note that when human
beings did appear on the scene life, mind, and spirit
attained added dimensions; physical reality came to in-

clude the complex relationships, structures, and processes of human social existence; and evolution came to include social as well as biological evolution.

Admittedly, this has not been the traditional way of conceiving life, mind, and spirit and their many varied manifestations; but I believe it to be in complete agreement with what the new consciousness senses regarding the nature of reality, from both a scientific and religious point of view. It takes life, mind, and spirit, as well as social existence, to be manifestations of the holistic character of physical reality and therefore to be relational rather than substantive in character and thoroughly indigenous to nature, coming into being by nature's own developmental and creative processes. This understanding will be expounded more fully in chapters VIII and IX.

In that context we shall note also some very different realities. On the one hand, there are nature's ambiguities, inconsistencies, and unpredictabilities; it exhibits not only a reign of fundamental lawfulness but an equally fundamental reign of randomness and chance—and, with these, prodigal wastefulness, ugly perversions, stark brutality, tremendous cataclysms, evolutionary dead ends, disease, and vermin, as well as the horrible evils perpetrated by mankind. In view of these we must recognize that physical reality not only builds but destroys, not only enriches but impoverishes, and that it causes a vast amount of suffering and tragedy. Not only is there life and growth but decay and death. On the other hand, there are also process-realities that are transformative and remedial. Though nature does wound and hurt, it also heals and soothes and often transforms for good. Out of tragedy and wreckage there do come forth new life and more desirable patterns of existence. The "nature" or quality of things is not fixed but changes, and can be changed, often remedially. It seems, then, that physical reality is such that its historical development, or evolution, is brought about by both constructive and destructive processes, by both holistic and antiholistic drives—and that among the fundamental characteristics of physical reality we must count its creativity and remediality.

SENSING THE MYSTERY OF REALITY

Another fundamental quality of physical reality—and indeed of all reality—is its mystery. In considering this I shall first ask what "mystery" means and then show that physical reality does have that characteristic. Then we shall examine reality in general, with special reference to the new consciousness of mystery.

The former is a bit tricky, because, while many writers do refer to mystery, they seldom say explicitly what they mean by it. However, a contextual analysis of usages in the literature have revealed that there are at least seven distinguishable major meanings of it that are significant for our subject. For introductory purposes the general features of these findings are presented here and in the next chapter. Most of the details, however, are relegated to the Appendix. Judging from the reactions of numerous audiences on campuses and elsewhere, many readers will want to study this appendix (which is not unduly technical or difficult); this is not necessary, however, since my overall argument does not presuppose it.

So, what is meant by the assertion that reality is fundamentally mysterious, as truly mysterious in essence as we have noted it to be relational, developmental, creative, and remedial? There seem to be two basic meanings: first, that it is not, and cannot be, known or understood or controlled fully; and second, that its character is such as to evoke a strong sense of wonder and awe, as well as a feeling of enchantment or fascination, and sometimes even of fear (*Ehrfurcht*). Thus the term *mystery* as used here emphatically does not denote an as-yet-unsolved problem or puzzle, or a gap in our knowledge, or simply the unknown. Rather it refers to what is sensed to be unknowable, and incomprehensible, and inexplicable, or even inaccessible *in its fullness* to the human mind. In this first sense the term *mystery* refers to what Jaroslav Pelikan has called "the quantity of the unknown." In the second sense it connotes, as he suggests, "the quality of the known." What we do know has a glory quality. It is sensed to be ineffable in that we are aware of more in it than we can talk about adequately or can fathom by strictly rational analysis. It has nonrational elements that can only be intuited rather than reasoned out rigorously. According to this understanding, the coming of knowledge does not diminish or eliminate the sense of mystery but intensifies it. The more that is known about something genuinely mysterious, the more—not less—wondrously mysterious and enchanting it is sensed to be.

It is in this dual sense that nature is now seen to be mysterious: much of it is unknown, unknowable, and unfathomable; and what is known evokes endless wonder and awe. As I shall explain in subsequent chapters, the evidence for this lies in the depths of the interior of matter-energy and in the character of life, mind, and spirit; in the quality and extent of nature's systemic interrelationships and interdependencies; in its lawfulness and randomness; its dynamism and evolutionary holistic creativity; its transmutability, transformability, and remediality; its limitlessness and openness to the future; in the structure and depths of space-time; in the infinite variety of its qualities; in its drives toward the social wholes we call communities; and in still other fundamental features.

With this awareness comes the realization that nature has also dimensions other than those directly perceivable and conceivable by science. For example, as Alfred North Whitehead remarked so perceptively, "When you understand all about the sun and all about the atmosphere and all about the rotation of the earth, you may still miss the radiance of the sunset."[10] Surely he was thinking of something other than physical light or luminosity, perhaps something like beauty, or charm, or glory, or majesty, or magic—or in any case something about which one can communicate much better with the expressive depth-language of art and poetry than with the reportorial steno-language of the sciences. There must be many such extrascientific dimensions or realms of nature, and in our time one is not nearly as hesitant as formerly to declare them to be real—as real as the snowflakes, waterfalls, flowers, birds, and human beings whose attributes they are.

Then there is the mystery of nature's ambiguities, noted in the preceding section, of its horrors and its glory—in short, the mystery of "the good" and "the evil" and of their coexistence and interaction, as well as of the processes by which misfortune, tragedy, and suffering are in time transformed remedially for good. Thus we become aware that mystery may evoke not only wonder in the glory sense but wonderment in the sense of wondering, anxious perplexity, and profound concern, or even traumatic anguish.

Finally, the mystery of physical reality is such that it perpetually evokes questions that point beyond the realm of proximate realities toward ultimacy, questions about ultimate meaning and value, ultimate purpose and goal, ultimate good and evil, ultimate creative and redemptive power, ultimate origin and destiny. Thus nature has again become for the human consciousness a window open to the transcendental and immanental reaches of reality, whence come intimations of creative-redemptive divinity transcendent to and immanent throughout nature or the cosmos. This is mystery that evokes more than wonder, namely worship. It is the ultimately mysterious reality commonly called *God*. The meaning of this for the new consciousness will be considered in Part Three. Here I only point out that there has recently been much radical thinking about "God" —radical in going to the roots of meanings—and suggest that some of its strains are utterly in accord with contemporary scientific and biblical insights about the character of reality and the world. It has been proposed that the key to such accord lies in recognizing that God is, like all other reality, holistically relational, rather than absolute and substantive, as traditional theism has conceived him to be. This is my view also.

THE NEW CONSCIENCE;
"REVOLUTION BY CONSCIOUSNESS"

An exceedingly important—and gratifying—outcome of the new consciousness is the growing new conscience among men. Many are deeply disturbed by the all too obvious fact that to a large extent our Western culture is tragically out of harmony with the basic character of the universe. They sense that there is something very wrong about men's compulsive preoccupation with material values, when the universe is fundamentally not materialistic but relational. If it is true that even matter itself, not to speak of the world as a whole, is more like a delicate fabric of meaningful and vital interrelationships than an edifice of hard, inert building blocks, wouldn't it seem at least appropriate, if not morally imperative, for men to be concerned much more with relational values? Furthermore, if it is indeed the case that the quality of the universe, as well as of individual and communal life, mind, and spirit, depends so crucially upon wholeness and holistic drives—from which alone meaningful quality derives—shouldn't our highest values be those of unitedness, mutuality, conscious interreliance and cooperation, and "individuality in community" rather than separateness, complete independence, cutthroat competition, and "individuality for its own sake"? Can there be any doubt that, though the unity of mankind with nature is very real, as noted in our discussion of "the consciousness of the world," there do exist among men malignant attitudes toward nature and vicious structures of human self-interest that threaten to disrupt that unity and even to destroy our planet as a place fit for genuinely human habitation?

Perhaps nowhere do these concerns show themselves more sensitively and urgently than among those of our youth—and elders too—who are calling so vigorously for a renewal or transformation of our culture,[11] and for the reversal of the unfortunate and evil influences and trends so dominant in it now. Their general views and hopes are, of course, well known.[12] I wish to comment, however, on certain elements of their consciousness and insight that seem less well understood but are especially pertinent for present purposes. Consider, for example, the symbols chosen by the so-called "flower people" for calling attention to their message forcefully, though not violently: flowers (in their hair) and bells (at their ankles or waists). Why not hurled bricks and swinging clubs? What were they—and many others who did not actually wear flowers—trying to say that could not be symbolized by the use of violent force and explosive sounds?

This, I think: The basic character of the universe, to

which human life should conform, is revealed much more in the gentle might of its tender elements than in the irresistible power of its coercive and violent ones. Indeed, it is not only revealed but actually determined far more by the delicate processes of life, such as operate in the lowly daisy and buttercup, than by the tremendous forces of the violent hurricane or exploding atomic bomb. Also, the flowers and gently tinkling bells, and many other lovely things like them, possess typically a kind of strength the harsher ones never have, namely, the enchanting and transforming power of their radiance, glory, and mystery. This is, of course, the message not only of our youth today but also of that remarkable young Nazarean Jew who lived two thousand years ago and who said, with consummate sensitivity and wisdom, "Consider the lilies of the field, how they grow; they toil not, neither do they spin: And yet I say unto you, That even Solomon in all his glory was not arrayed like one of these (Matt. 6:28–29, KJV)." And who said further (in the language of the *New English Bible*): "How blest are those who . . . are the sorrowful . . . [and] of a gentle spirit . . . [and] who hunger and thirst to see right prevail . . . [and] show mercy . . . [and] whose hearts are pure . . . [and] are the peacemakers . . . [and] have suffered persecution for the cause of right; *the kingdom of Heaven is theirs* (Matt. 5:3–10, NEB, italics added)."

Let it not escape our notice that, aside from the invitation to "consider," all these sayings of Jesus are direct statements of present fact, not assertions or promises of what might be the case if certain conditions were met, or certain ideals were actualized. Nor are they, at face value, commands or injunctions. They simply state that those who are sorrowful, or are of a gentle spirit, or are peacemakers, or suffer for the right, and so on, are in fact richly blessed; and that the kingdom of Heaven *is*—not will be— theirs. This is the kind of universe we live in, so these passages declare. It is one in which tenderness is supreme in power and meaning. And not the least insight about it may be derived from considering the lilies, which grow unobtrusively and without compulsive striving and yet are seen to be arrayed in an order of glory that is quite beyond any attained by the Solomons of the world. It is this sort of world to which the human way of life must somehow be made to conform, and to which it would conform—and which it would enhance—if it were a flower style of life.

It is, of course, obvious that this poses many difficult questions and issues which we shall want to face squarely. We begin with a consideration of "revolution." Indubitably our present culture is incapable of either accepting or adequately supporting a flower style of life. This is because it is still dominated too much by the old consciousness, which has at least two serious flaws: It has almost completely lost sight of the reality of mystery and its charm, and of the potency and crucial significance of tenderness in the overall scheme of things; and it is preoccupied excessively not only with the feverish pursuit of materialistic gains but with megapower and megatechnics—as is the case so much in big business and industry, in power politics and the military establishments, and in our virtually instinctive resorting to massive force and violence as means of "solving" problems and "resolving" disputes. This calls for radical change and revolution. And, our young protesters of the flower persuasion insist, it must be not an overthrow by violence but a "revolution by consciousness," to use Charles Reich's very apt expression.

The point of this phrase is that there can be no genuine revolution unless it springs out of, and is supported by, radical change in the way human beings think and feel habitually. No amount of forcible tinkering with or overturning and altering the visible and tangible features of a culture will suffice. There has to be a fundamental change down deep in the hearts and minds of men and women, i.e., in their consciousness. Now it is one of the main themes of this book that such a revolution-by-consciousness is already under way and that, much popular opinion to the contrary, both science-technology and religion in some of their contemporary forms are contributing mightily to it. Especially is this the case, I feel, in the rehabilitation and intensification of human sensitivity to mystery and tenderness—

without which there can be no culture consistent with the fundamental character of the universe.

The next chapter will indicate in an introductory fashion how contemporary science and religion can, and do, so contribute to the shaping of a new consciousness and a new culture.

II. Sensitivity to Mystery
in Science and Religion

SEEING MYSTERY
"THROUGH THE EYES OF SCIENCE"

Underlying my argument is the assumption, which I shall try to justify, that science has changed radically in the twentieth century, and in such a way that it can now be said that mystery is discernible through its eyes. Admittedly any such suggestion must seem farfetched, if not downright nonsensical. For the sciences certainly have no "teachings" on mystery. Each of them is highly selective in its concerns and deals with only a restricted area of nature. None has chosen to study the subject of mystery per se or developed methods appropriate to it. Nor is the concept of mystery needed to explain or predict anything of direct scientific concern. We cannot expect, therefore, to cite scientifically derived conclusions about it.

Does this mean that we are already stopped? No, I suggest, because there is much to be learned from science aside from its direct teachings. In trying to understand how this can be, let us be reminded of an important difference: between the *study of nature* and the *study of science*. Science itself is an enterprise in the study of nature. To study science is therefore to study that enterprise, to investigate, from the meta-viewpoints of history, sociology, philosophy, and other disciplines, how science "is done." Nevertheless, it reveals also much about nature that the gaze fixed upon it directly misses. For nature reveals itself in part through the way scientists react or respond to it, i.e., through the procedures they feel compelled to adopt in order to investigate it successfully and through the characteristics of their experience of nature. Surely if nature were different all these aspects of science would be different. Scanning nature for manifestations of mystery through the eyes of science is thus a potent kind of dual seeing— through the study of nature itself *and* of science—and, by the way, includes the reflections of philosophy upon both. Also it should be said that "science" and "scientific" actually connote much more than is commonly supposed, and that if we take too narrow a view of their meaning we shall miss far too much of what science in its fullness has to offer. Its total vision and power of discernment do not arise exclusively from its technical ideas and procedures but often from its less formal character as a personal and social enterprise.[1] Recent remarks by John Compton are very much to the point here, that

there must be an understanding of science as a human activity; and to this end, there must be comprehension of the total, historic phenomenon of "doing" science. Prevailing intellectualist philosophies of science, however, analyze the sciences outside this human context of development and meaning. Science is treated as a body of propositions, terms, operations, . . . or as a process of experimental manipulation, of theory construction. . . . A phenomenological philosophy of science, on the other hand, should be expected to take seriously the incarnation of scientific work in the historic-personal-perceptual life of its practitioners.[2]

What is commonly lost sight of, in other approaches to the understanding of science, is that it is intensely human and personal, in many respects like the arts, and that imagination, intuition, and creativity are extremely important in its life and thought. Through them there come to many of its practitioners, as they experience nature, profound insight and understanding about it that transcend those derivable only by formal experimentation and theoretical analysis. After all, scientists are typically human. They are not mere cold intellects or logic machines, grinding out purely syllogistic deductions or making experiments conforming to strict methodological prescription. It is doubtful that many of them would be in science professionally if all it yielded were the kinds of precisely verifiable propositions that eventuate from such formal methods. The most prized insights of science are generalizations that go far beyond such limited conclusions and concepts and require for their inception a high order of imagination and aesthetic intuition. Often profound philosophic reflection is called for, and overarching synthesis becomes necessary, quite as much as detailed analysis. The ability to "sense" what is scientifically valuable or significant is indispensable in both research and subsequent exposition, and such sensing is utterly intuitive.

Consider, for instance, science's most basic insight, that the events of nature are interconnected causally in such a way as to be largely predictable quantitatively. This belief did not appear overnight. Until recently, perhaps the sixteenth or seventeenth century, most men felt themselves to be mere pawns in the interplay of seemingly blind forces in a universe beyond their understanding. Perplexing and seemingly irrational tragedy and catastrophe abounded. As far as man was concerned, history just happened to him, much of it making no sense. True, many men attributed its happenings to the will of God, but this too meant for the most part that they simply did not understand nature itself —or history, for that matter. Then science came along, in its post-Galilean-Newtonian manifestations, and with it a marvelously enlightening understanding of nature in terms of cause-and-effect relations. The causality principle that expresses this basic insight is not, however, a conclusion resulting from a particular research project or even a long series of them. Nor is it the outcome of a "correct" sequence of syllogism: because A and B, therefore C and D and E and so on. It is rather the expression of a gradually growing understanding, a coming to sense what is true beyond the conclusions of formal empirical research.

Many of science's most profound insights are of this sort, going far beyond any conclusions required by the data alone, and coming into being by synthesizing leaps of the imagination. In his fascinating book, *Beyond the Observatory*, Harlow Shapley lists what he calls "ten revelations that have most affected modern man's life and thought."[3] Among these are our contemporary understanding of the chemical origin of life, of cosmic evolution, relativity, the subatomic micro-world, the meta-realm of the galaxies. I would say that all of these are of the broad-perspective type that provide both general understanding and precise, detailed technical knowledge. Surely it is not inappropriate to speak of such grand visions as revelations and to regard them as science's finest gifts to man, the best of what it seeks to discover and create, know and understand.[4]

However, to say this is to realize not only what science *does* but what it *is*. It is the whole of it that results in such vision. It is not only an intellectual method and its explicit output but a *way* of life, of thought, of faith, of attitude, of questioning, and of coming to know. It is a communal sharing—of concerns and responsibilities, of dreams and adventures, of successes and failures. It is also, and no less meaningfully, personal integrity and commitment to the common good, and hard work, and great fun.

One comes to sense this keenly, and even to "feel it in one's bones," so to speak, when one exposes oneself to such books as Loren Eiseley's *The Immense Journey, The Firmament of Time*, and *Darwin's Century*[5]; Michael Polanyi's *Science, Faith and Society* and *Personal Knowledge*[6]; and John R. Platt's *The Excitement of Science.*[7] What breaks through to us from these exemplars and portrayals of science is its humanistic and existential character, its social aspects, its affinity to the arts, its sense of mission in the world, its historic and philosophic involvement and significance. This is what confronts one compellingly also in great biography, e.g., in Philipp Frank's *Einstein,*[8] and René Vallery-Radot's *Life of Pasteur,*[9] where one meets great spirits at work, men whose contributions to the life of the world were made in great travail, and whose concerns—scientific concerns—were by no means confined to those of a narrowly conceived science. What we encounter there, as in the lives of many lesser men, is a science that is practiced with deep seriousness and a sense of responsibility but also eagerly, with playful curiosity that feels free to follow every promising lead and does not arbitrarily rule out from its purview any aspect of reality that seems at all open to its exploration.

It is because science is in fact truly humanistic in this rich sense that I can commend it to the exponents of "revolution by consciousness" as a rich resource for the future. The science community does have interests beyond those of a more narrowly conceived science, and it does achieve insights that transcend by far any that are derivable by formal experimentation and theorizing only. From this point of view I now suggest that for an increasing number of scientists the awareness of the reality and significance of mystery in nature is one of those transcending understandings. This is why there are, as we shall see, many references to it in the literature of contemporary science even though mystery is not one of its direct concerns.

Roszak speaks movingly of "the beauty of the magical vision" which "is the beauty of the deeply sensed, sacramental presence," the experience of which "yields no sense of accomplished and rounded-off knowledge, but on the contrary . . . may begin and end in an overwhelming sense of mystery."[10] It is my plea that it is precisely this kind of vision and generalization that comes to a significant number of scientists and followers of science, and that it comes to them "through the eyes of science" as they reflect—intuitively and imaginatively, critically and analytically—about the character of the world they are exploring.

Let it be understood, however, that I do not claim this sense of mystery to be a phenomenon acknowledged by the entire science community. In the first place, it seems—on the basis of much informal evidence—that for most scientists the term mystery denotes no more than an as-yet-unexplained or still-unsolved problem. When, for instance, they say that the mystery of biological life is disappearing, they usually mean only that much of what once seemed strange and mysterious about it now seems familiar and understood. In this sense the history of science has been a remarkable success story in the dissolving of more and more "mystery"—of the problem-puzzle type.

Many scientists actually go farther than this and assert that there is no other mystery. They emphasize especially that science recognizes none that is either impenetrable or forbidden as sacrosanct, not to be invaded by man. It is my opinion, however, based again on informal evidence, that they do not thereby wish to deny the fundamentally mysterious quality of things but only to react against obscurantist taboos. It cannot be denied that hands-off attitudes have been altogether too prevalent in religious circles and have created serious problems for the scientific community. Even today one hears in many areas of the church vigorous objections to certain scientific ventures, such as the attempt to synthesize life in the laboratory, on the grounds that since life is one of God's mysteries man should not try to penetrate it. Moreover, too often this serves as a smoke-screen behind which to escape from the onslaughts of rational thinking and rigorous investigation that might overthrow cherished beliefs. So often have scientists encountered such attitudes among religious men with regard to mystery that they find it difficult to see that the term can have a meaning that does not evoke such attitudes.

This does not, however, tell the whole story. The science community is far from monolithic in regard to these matters. Many of its members know full well that temporarily unsolved problems are by no means mystery's only manifestation in nature. For one thing, they have come to feel that the prospects for continued scientific investigation are unlimited, meaning that though science has in the past solved enormous numbers of problems, there are good reasons to suppose that the number remaining for solution in the future is still unlimited, and they realize that to say this is to speak of much more than a mere problem, namely, of an aspect of genuine mystery.

Furthermore, science has been looking at itself critically in recent decades and is aware of its limitations. It is now humbly conscious that, while its methodology is powerful and extremely successful, it is not all-powerful. It realizes that each science has its own interests and preoccupations, and procedures tailored to those interests. None undertakes to explicate all of the universe; nor do all of them together, as now constituted, cover all of it. Moreover, it just may be that the universe is limitless in an infinity of physical dimensions, in which case it would make no sense to suppose that it could ever be fathomed completely. Surely, then, much of it may indeed be inaccessible to scientific analysis and description—as Einstein believed it to be. Therefore not nearly as many scientists as formerly are ready today to assert dogmatically that there is no ultimate, insoluble mystery. Other recent developments have contributed to the intensification and expansion of what I shall refer to as science's perceptual sensitivities and capacities. These have created a new situation in which the glory and wonder aspects of mystery in nature can be discussed much more freely and imaginatively than would have been possible only a few decades ago. With respect to discernment "through the eyes of science," this has taken on new meaning because "the eyes of science," as well as science itself, have changed—toward an expanded conscious awareness of mystery. This is the change from modern to post-modern science that we shall look at in detail in the next section.

Meanwhile let us remember that for our purposes the fundamental question is not what scientists themselves think about mystery but rather what their work has disclosed about nature and science's experience with it, from which *we* may draw conclusions about mystery.

THE MODERN VERSUS THE
POST-MODERN SCIENTIFIC WORLD VIEW

Strictly speaking, the construction of "world views" is the business of philosophy, science having no competence in that direction. There are therefore objections to calling any world view scientific. Since, however, science has recently contributed much of the basic material out of which such views are built, many writers do speak of one as scientific if it has been derived in large part *from* science, even though not directly *by* science. I shall do likewise, and speak in this sense of a modern and a post-modern scientific world view. In this section I shall contrast these in an introductory fashion.

By way of highlighting their general characteristics symbolically, I offer two figures. The first, representing the modern conception, is merely a circle. The second is a ring of radially directed arrows pointing outward and inward that also mark off a circular area, yet not one with a definite boundary. This symbolizes the post-modern view.

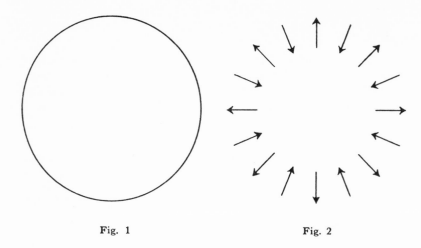

Fig. 1   Fig. 2

According to the former view the world was closed, essentially completed and unchanging, basically substantive, simple and shallow, and fundamentally unmysterious—a rigidly programed machine. The second regards it increasingly as unbounded, uncompleted, and changing, still becoming, basically relational and complex, with great depth, unlimited qualitative variety, and truly mysterious —a restless, vibrant, living, growing organism forever pregnant with possibilities for novel emergences and developments in the future.

The arrows are intended to symbolize the dynamism of the world, emphasizing action, event, and change more than substance, fixity, and eternality. Their alternation in direction suggests a state of perpetual dialectic tension: advance and retreat, depths and heights, simplicity and complexity, order and disorder, outwardness and inwardness, evolution and involution.

While these differences in outlook are pronounced, they should not be taken to represent a sharp historical discontinuity. Twentieth-century science did, of course, come naturally out of earlier centuries, where it had deep roots. Indeed, late in the nineteenth century there was in the air a widespread feeling that something very strange and un-predictable was about to happen in men's conceptions of the world. And yet during its last decade most physical scientists felt that all the significant problems posed by nature had been solved, and that all the fundamental prin-ciples of the physical world were known. The following excerpt from the catalog of the University of Chicago, 1898-99, is typical of that confident yet frustrating mood:

While it is never safe to affirm that the future of Physical Science has no marvels in store even more astonishing than those of the past, it seems probable that most of the grand underlying principles have been firmly established and that further advances are to be sought chiefly in the rigorous application of these principles to all the phenomena which come under our notice.[11]

Moreover, it was thought that since nature was without doubt rigidly deterministic there *could* be no radically new developments or genuine surprises. What a closed-world conception this was (fig. 1)!

But then suddenly surprises did come—in such utterly unanticipated discoveries as radioactivity, X rays, and the quantum phenomena—that simply would not fit into that neat conceptual scheme and required the creation of radi-cally new conceptualities. Thus began post-modern science (fig. 2); and it is important to recognize that it is all of science we are talking about, not just physics. Today's literature about science abounds in references not only to the new physics but to the new chemistry, new biology, new psychology, new anthropology, and still others, imply-ing that a new day has dawned for science in general.

To understand the radical character of this dramatic development one must realize, however, that it had to do not only with new phenomena and new ideas but with "new modes of thought," not only with the conceptual content of science but with its ways of conceptualizing, and with the basic assumptions underlying its experimental and theo-retical operations. Alfred North Whitehead, one of the truly great sages of our time, wrote as follows:

Fifty-seven years ago it was when I was a young man in the University of Cambridge. I was taught science and mathematics by brilliant men and I did well in them; since the turn of the century I have lived to see every one of the basic assumptions of both set aside; not, indeed, discarded, but of use as qualifying clauses, instead of as major propositions; and all this in one life-span—the most fundamental assumptions of supposedly exact sciences set aside.[12]

Robert A. Millikan, Nobel prize winner in physics, recalling this "dramatic introduction . . . to the new period of physics," remarked:

Nobody at that time dreamed . . . what an amazing number of new phenomena would come to light within the next thirty years, or how revolutionary, or, better, how incomprehensible in terms of nineteenth century modes of thought, some of them would be.[13]

This does not mean, however, that science cut all connections with its intellectual past. After all, it has always been cumulative in its quest, and even during times of revolutionary upheaval it builds upon, rather than renounces, its past. While much of the old may pass away, always much of it remains. Furthermore, the earlier (modern) science was by no means inherently stultifying, for in its time it opened up vast vistas of the universe for human experience and investigation, brought forth ingenious methods of inquiry, and produced huge bodies of remarkable knowledge and understanding. It was imaginative and daring. Certainly it was one of the most magnificent achievements of the human spirit.

Nevertheless in time it did lose some of its luster and forward thrust and began to solidify and become a roadblock. What had been gloriously liberating and open became to an unfortunate extent inhibiting and closed. It was not dead, however, and was able to react to the disconcerting new discoveries with self-criticism and self-correction, so that the reminiscing Millikan could say that

we all began to see that the nineteenth century physicists had taken themselves a little too seriously, that we had not come quite as near sounding the depths of the universe, even in the matter of fundamental physical principles, as we thought we had.[14]

Thus there came into being the remarkable qualities of science and its vision that have yielded the insights symbolized by figure 2.

How much more profound and far-reaching man's thinking did become! Nowhere does this show up more than in post-modern man's experience of the depth dimension of things. It is interesting that Millikan, in discussing nineteenth-century physics in contrast to the new physics, pointed first to its inadequate conception or sense of the "depths of the universe." Today we know (see the next chapter) that physical reality has an interior with many recognizably different depths and levels, at each of which there exist distinctive structures and qualities of matter which were formerly quite unknown. The discovery of this interiority and depth turned out to be *like* the opening of Pandora's box in releasing upon the world a host of forces that could never be recaptured and confined again, but *unlike* it in that these forces were great new insights, powerful new modes of thought, and quite new intuitions and feelings about reality, for instance, those about its holistically relational and developmental character, that have expanded and enriched human experience so immeasurably. Before the release the world investigated by science was little more than a thin skin or a shallow surface layer of reality. Now science is exploring reality in depth, and depth has in this way become the key that unlocked or opened to the human consciousness vast regions of reality of which it was until recently quite unaware.

Also it is the key, or at least one of the indispensable keys, to the realm of genuine mystery in nature. Without doubt it was the lack of knowledge of the depth dimension of reality that accounts for the almost complete unawareness of the mystery aspects of nature that prevailed in the modern period. No sense of depth, then no sense of mystery. Now that men have become keenly conscious of the depths in matter-energy, in space-time, in the processes of life, and especially those in the depths of the human psyche, they are again experiencing enchantment, wonder, and awe in their encounter with nature, and thus the "overwhelming sense of mystery" of which Roszak has spoken so eloquently.

Finally, depth is the key that unlocks the door of awareness of ultimacy (mentioned toward the end of chapter I
and to be examined further in the next section), where one
encounters the mystery that evokes not only wonder but
worship. This is, of course, the realm of religion.

THE SIGNIFICANCE
OF MYSTERY FOR RELIGION

We have noted that, while for science mystery is of no more
than peripheral concern, for religion it is central. This is
because religion has to do with the mystery of ultimacy—
and therefore divinity—and may be said to be man's reaction or whole-response to it. I know of no more profound
a statement of this than the following one by Whitehead:

> Religion is the vision of something which stands beyond, behind,
> and within, the passing flux of immediate things; something that
> is real, and yet waiting to be realized; something which is a remote
> possibility, and yet the greatest of present facts; something that
> gives meaning to all that passes, and yet eludes apprehension; some-
> thing whose possession is the final good, and yet is beyond all reach;
> something which is the ultimate ideal, and the hopeless quest.
> The immediate reaction of human nature to the religious vision
> is worship.[15]

Can there be any question that Whitehead is here referring
to ultimate mystery, and to religion's inextricable involvement with it, even though he does not mention it explicitly?
An important role of ritual and liturgy in religion is to keep
alive in the worshiper a keen sense of wonder and awe in
the presence of ultimate mystery, just as one important
responsibility of theology, i.e., the reasoning and conceptualizing part of religion, is to keep it alive intellectually in
the critical thought of the worshiper. No doubt this is why
the language of religion is influenced so much by a sense
of the reality and power of mystery and is to so large an
extent symbolic and mythical in character. The discursive,
technical languages of, say, the sciences are not capable of
adequately communicating the transrational and noncognitive meanings and implications of insights that come out
of man's encounter with ultimate mystery.

It would be a mistake, however, to suppose that *ultimate*

here means *far distant*, or *outside of the natural world*, or only *beyond human existence*. For the mysterious "something" of which Whitehead speaks "stands beyond, behind, *and within* . . . immediate things," and the recognition of this comes close to the heart of religious insight and sensitivity. As evidence of this I point to one of the most remarkable religious books of our time, *A New Catechism* (Dutch, Roman Catholic), a work of uncompromising scholarly integrity yet written with sage wisdom and warm human concern in the language of the common man's everyday life in the real world. I find it most significant that Part I of this profound book is entitled "The Mystery of Existence." It leaves no doubt that the ultimate mystery to which biblical religion responds is to be looked for primarily in the nearby realities and experiences of the common life.

Where are we to find it? It is in our own home. The beings around me—men, plants and even objects—are a mystery which grows as I penetrate their nature. My own thought, my "I", my feelings and the life of other men all escape my comprehension, and every science which explains part of them leaves us with a greater sense of admiration for all that is discovered and described. And the more clearly a thing appears as a living unity, the better it can show itself, the better does it reveal itself as mystery.[16]

These quotations from Whitehead and the *Catechism* suggest why in religious thought the idea of *mystery* is so often linked with those of *depth* and the so-called *vertical dimension* of reality. The presence of ultimate mystery is never sensed through the superficialities of things and events but only "beyond, behind, and within" them. To recognize mystery in "men, plants and even objects" we must "penetrate their nature," i.e., go inside them, vertically downward, so to speak. Profundity and ultimate meaning, that always seem to partake of mystery, are never obvious or directly perceptible in the shallows but only in what William James called the "thickness of life" and in what we are calling their interior depths.

The term *God* that is so central to biblical religion, and is so often tossed about with seeming abandon, stands for a reality that is first of all mystery about which we know almost nothing. Nevertheless, countless men and women, of many times, cultures, and religions, have asserted confidently that this God-reality, however conceived, has somehow broken through to their consciousness out of the depths of cosmic and personal existence, and filled them with wonder, and awe, and holy fear (*Ehrfurcht*), and shaken them in all their dimensions and to the very foundations of their being, and evoked from them a whole-response in worship. They have testified too that out of this encounter, momentary or continuous as it may have been, there have come to them satisfying meaning, ethical demands, and transformed lives. Here is mystery indeed! And it is ultimate mystery since it has to do with that which is sensed to be ultimately real, ultimately meaningful, and ultimately good—in other words, with that which matters most—and is called *God*, however it may be spelled by men of different insights and cultures.

The experience of the biblical tradition has been that the God so encountered is an awesome, terrible, searching and demanding reality from which there is no escape, and to which an adequate response is not only worship in a restricted, cultic sense but worship that includes a complete yielding to its demands. Hear the words of the psalmist:

O LORD, thou hast searched me and known me!
Thou knowest when I sit down and when I rise up;
  thou discernest my thoughts from afar.
Thou searchest out my path and my lying down,
  and art acquainted with all my ways. . . .

Such knowledge is too wonderful for me;
  it is high, I can not attain it.

Whither shall I go from thy Spirit?
  Or whither shall I flee from thy presence?
If I ascend to heaven, thou are there!
  If I make my bed in Sheol, thou are there!
If I take the wings of the morning and dwell in the
  utmost parts of the sea,
even there thy hand shall lead me,
  and thy right hand shall hold me. . . .

Search me, O God, and know my heart! . . .
and lead me in the way everlasting!
—Psalm 139

Surely these are the cries of a soul sensitive to the depths of existence beyond, behind, and within, high and low, in all directions, at all times—and to the searching, demanding, leading mystery-reality to be encountered in them. I suspect that without this sensitive awareness and responsiveness there can be no religion, either as worship or commitment. This is *the* significance of mystery for theology and religious faith. Their very life and health depend upon keen sensitivity to it.

Unfortunately, however, religion has had difficulties in this area of its experience and thought, along a wide front and apparently in all high religions.[17] In no small measure this has been due to science's erosive effects upon those human sensitivities that are so vital to religion, the sense of depth and mystery. Especially was this the case during the modern period. Until that time, and for many centuries, men and women of the biblical tradition felt that there was ample evidence that they could discern ultimate mystery—and the presence of God—everywhere, including nature. With the advent of modern science this ability was largely lost, and one reason for this was that its world view made it virtually impossible for men of a scientific bent to intuit or conceptualize depth and mystery. Religious thinkers had good reason to feel that, as Michael Foster put it:

Modern science is knowledge which eliminates mystery. In contrast to Greek science it does not end in wonder but in the expulsion of wonder.
Modern scientific knowledge does not contain degrees of depth or profundity.
Revealed truth by contrast offers depth after depth to the understanding without being exhausted.[18]

Many people would say that this is an accurate description of post-modern science also, as far as depth and mystery are concerned, among them Roszak, who charges that contemporary science deracinates the human experience of the sacred. I can't help feeling, however, in view of the tremendous differences between modern and post-modern science noted in the preceding section and to be explored more carefully in Part Two, that this kind of charge rests upon serious misconceptions of contemporary science—as well as of man's new consciousness. For if scientists are interested in anything today it is the interior depths of physical and social reality. I dare say that almost all of the most rewarding findings of post-modern science have come out of its explorations of nature's depths. And from these findings it has become abundantly clear that mystery *has* been discerned there "through the eyes of science." No longer can it be said justifiably that religion finds man's basic sensibilities and sensitivities toward nature being eroded and corroded by the scientific vision.

BELIEFS AND THE EXPANSION OR CONSTRICTION OF CONSCIOUSNESS

Whether or not one can sense reality in its vertical dimension and in the ultimate reaches of mystery depends not only on one's physical senses and sensations but also in large measure on one's beliefs, conceptions, or mythical understandings as to the nature of reality. The keenness of our sensitivities is not constant; they can become sharp or blunt, depending on circumstances. Perception is a two-way active process rather than a one-way passive one. Thus seeing involves much more than simply opening one's eyes. It takes place when, on the one hand, the observer, having opened his eyes, receives light from an object, and when, on the other hand, he reaches out to that object conceptually to grasp what can be seen of it. The process is then a receiving and a taking. And knowledge is both a product of perception and a frame of reference or a probe which makes perception and conception possible. In other words, what we *do see* is determined to a considerable extent by what we *have seen and conceived* and by what we suppose or believe *can be seen*. It is amazing how difficult it is at times to see—say, through a microscope—what one does not expect to see, and how easy it is to see what one does expect, even though it may not be there to be seen. This is the case in complex experimentation and long-range re-

part two

Insights of the New Scientific Consciousness

III. The Depth Dimension
of Physical Reality

HIERARCHIES OF STRUCTURES AND LEVELS
Let us now consider more fully the subject of the interior depths of matter,* and begin with the idea of physical reality as a hierarchy of hierarchies of levels and structures. L. L. Foldy, professor of physics at the Case-Western Reserve University, speaks of this as follows, while discussing the prospects for exploring the interior of nucleons, i.e., of the "particles" (protons and neutrons) of which atomic nuclei consist:

... with the examination of the structure of the proton and neutron one is investigating a new hierarchical level in the material organization of the physical universe, related to, but underlying, the now substantially explored level of atomic and nuclear structure.

Elsewhere in the article he speaks of

a hierarchy of organized structures, each level of the hierarchy being characterized by a degree of internal logical structure of its own, in part independent of the hierarchies lying above and below.[1]

There are three key concepts here: first, that of "levels" in "the material organization of the physical universe"; second, that of distinctly different "hierarchies of structure" resident at the various levels; and third, the idea that these hierarchical levels are "in part independent" of one another. If we were to "journey into the interior of matter," as Max Born put it, it would be "like going down into a deep mine. Strata after strata pass by"[2] and succeeding ones are recognizably different and partly independent.

Actually, however, this analogy of the mine is in an important sense misleading. For the levels inside matter

---

* "Interior depth" is not a standard scientific term, though its connotation is well understood.

are not above or below one another in the usual sense, as in a gravitational field. They are, rather, inward or outward of any bit of matter, however it may be oriented in space, and inside or outside of one another. Thus to "descend" into the interior means simply to dig farther into it.

There is, of course, nothing new in the idea that, if we would understand nature truly, we must look behind its façade and in some sense penetrate *into* it. Until recently, however, science was unable to push very far inside, certainly not far enough to give us a keen sense of vast depth or of many levels. Now it can and does. Consider, for instance, how many levels we now recognize in the interior of a sample of matter such as, say, a cat, each one situated inside of all preceding levels in the series. Oversimplifying somewhat, there is, first, what we may call the surface level, that of the entire organism. *Inside* of it we encounter the level of its organs (e.g., the heart and lung). If we *enter* one of these we come upon the level of its various tissues. *Inside* of any of these there is the level of the cells. *Inside* of cells there are the chromosomes, and *inside* of them the genes. Proceeding in the same fashion, always looking farther *inside*, we encounter in succession the molecules and atoms. *Inside* the atoms are their nuclei and the electrons surrounding them. The nuclei house within them the various nucleons. In the modern era no one would have dreamed that the exploration of the interior of matter would disclose so extensive a gamut of levels, each one characterized by a distinctive species of physical structure different from all the others "above" or "below" it. And yet, as Foldy was reporting, right now physics is seeking to investigate still another, more interior, level, *inside* the nucleon, at which, I may add, it expects to find one more kind of elementary particle, to which the theorists have already given the fascinating name of "quark." What a picture! Wheels *within* wheels *within* wheels, so to speak. Depth *within* depth *within* depth!

THE VAST RANGE OF DEPTHS
An especially interesting feature of this picture is not only the existence of many levels but the vast range of their

depths. To understand this we need a way of comparing depths. This is particularly important since in this connection depth does not, I repeat, mean what it ordinarily does. Perhaps this will help. First we can speak of each level as having a *degree of depth* or *insidedness* or *interiority*. It is like the children's toy that consists of a series of boxes inside one another, each one smaller than the preceding one. The fourth box is inside of the first, second, and third, and therefore may be said to have depth or insidedness to the third degree. By the same token, the eleventh level of matter has depth to the tenth degree. To get to it we must open ten successive doors to the next interiors, or make ten successive soundings in depth.

Another way of comparing depths is by reference to the sizes of the entities associated with them, like the sizes of the successive boxes of the toy. The smaller a box is, the farther in it must be. Roughly speaking, the lengths of typical objects at what we have taken to be the first level, such as trees, or cars, or desks, or cats, are of the order of feet; at the levels of, say, cells, their lengths are only thousandths of an inch; several levels lower, at that of the atoms, diameters are measured in only billionths of an inch; and at the very next level, that of the nucleus, millionths of billionths. Clearly, and of necessity, the deeper the level, the smaller the entity encountered there.

But these subatomic particles are not only very small but relatively very far apart, as far apart as the planets in the solar system. If we look at a car from the viewpoint of the first level, it looks like one continuous object that seems to be full of matter. If, however, we could observe it from the perspective of a molecule, it would seem to be only a swarm of billions of billions of tiny bodies (molecules) that are very far apart, and therefore it would seem almost completely empty. If now we could descend to the level of the nucleons, the molecules would be seen to break down into atoms, then these into nuclei, and these into nucleons. This descent would then have revealed the car to be a swarm of swarms of swarms of ever smaller corpuscles, and at the lowest level would seem more empty than at any higher level. Unlike the toy nest of boxes, a sample of matter appears to become both more empty and more populated with increasing depth.

A third index of depth relates to energy requirements. Relatively little energy is required to break the wall of, say, a biological cell, to see what is inside it. To invade a molecule, however, requires much more, and to break into an atomic structure requires immensely more. To smash atoms one needs to bombard them with high-speed projectiles (other micro-particles) with tens of thousands of so-called electron-volts. Entrance to an atomic nucleus demands millions of electron-volts; in the case of nucleons, probably a hundred billions.

Notice that in terms of both the size and the energy index, the lower levels are much farther apart than the upper ones. Near the surface a step from one level to the next lower one involves but little change in either size or energy requirement. In the subatomic depths, however, such a step downward involves a huge decrease of the one and an increase in the other. No wonder nineteenth-century science failed to develop a keen sense of great depth or interiority in matter, or in nature as a whole. The levels to which it was able to descend were all so close to one another as to seem virtually indistinguishable as far as depth was concerned. One could explore everything "in sight" down to the atoms with instruments and amounts of energy that were commonplace in the physical and chemical laboratories of the time. Hence the idea of significantly different levels or depths didn't even arise.

But the picture is not yet complete. For the exploration of the interior of physical reality has been proceeding also in the opposite direction, from the molecules outward toward the stars. There, too, science has encountered discrete hierarchical levels, and structures corresponding to them, that are combinations of more interior ones. Thus beyond the level of the molecules is that of the crystals, rocks, and mountains. Beyond it are the levels of the planets, planetary systems, and those of the various types of cluster-aggregations of stars, then the incredible galaxies, and the metagalaxy or metagalaxies. While at these outer levels science is in a sense exploring outer space, in another it is still probing the interior of physical reality, for the whole stellar system may be regarded as one aggregation or structure of matter, albeit a huge one.

Until this century almost nothing was known about the stellar expanses beyond the solar system and relatively few stars near it. The so-called celestial sphere seemed very shallow indeed. Less than fifty years ago there was a debate that stirred up a lot of dust, between a distinguished astronomer and a young upstart (the now-celebrated Harlow Shapley), about the diameter of the stellar universe, which was a very hot question then. The conservative answer was 25,000 light years,* and the radical one, by Shapley, was 250,000 or 300,000. It was an audacious idea, but it won the day, and because of findings since then we now speak, without intellectual discomfort, about celestial objects billions of light years away. Then there was presumably only one galaxy; now we think there are probably billions of them. Altogether it is a mighty aggregation, and again we see it as a "wheels within wheels" kind of system of levels and structures. And what a tremendous range of depths it includes!

Why has post-modern science been able to reveal so very much? Briefly, here are some of the reasons, all having to do with man's expanding consciousness. First, there was an unexpected breakthrough of completely new phenomena, such as X rays and radioactivity, which invited investigation of vast realms of reality whose existence had not been suspected before. Then the initial glimpse into these new worlds stimulated the creation of new experimental techniques with which to explore them more fully. Thereupon additional strange new entities and happenings were encountered there that called not only for new instrumental devices but for novel conceptual ones as well. New habits of thought, a new feeling toward matter, a new mind-set, as well as a new outlook came into being—not only particular new ideas. This interesting sequence of events in the response and reaction of physical science to the opening up of a new field of inquiry seems quite typical of one

---

* The *light year* is a unit of distance, not of time; the distance traversed by light in a year at the rate of 186,000 miles per second.

kind of scientific discovery, namely, the type that is unexpected, i.e., without initial theoretical prediction. It is this sort of developmental process that has led to the vast body of knowledge about, and keen sensitivity to, the internal depths of inanimate matter that were unavailable to nineteenth-century man.

Meanwhile the sense of depth has become strong in the life and mind sciences also. Indeed, it may be that the first formal recognition of "depth" as a scientific term occurred in "depth psychology." Scientists often speak also of the investigation of life "in depth," i.e., at the molecular level, as in the new genetics, virology, and physiology. Occasionally it shows up in anthropological and sociological discussions. Clearly, Michael Foster's dictum that "scientific knowledge does not contain degrees of depth" is untrue of science today.

QUALITATIVE VARIETY IN MATTER; THREE DEPTH REGIONS

We began this chapter with a study of what Foldy called "the material organization of the physical universe" and were able to recognize within it a large number of discrete levels, each of which was identified in terms of a unique type of physical entity to be found there. The second section considered the distribution of these levels and the vast range of their depths—in the interior of each bit of matter at whatever depth it might be found, as well as of the entire system of physical reality of the universe. Now, in this third section, we must look more intensively at the entities or structures that reside at the various levels, in order especially to see how very different they are qualitatively, and to call attention to their hierarchical interrelationships and characteristics.

Long ago, and until as recently as the beginning of the modern era, Western man believed that there are at least two different kinds of physical reality, distributed in horizontal layers one above the other, namely, terrestrial and celestial substance. The latter pervaded heaven and was the abode of God and his celestial hosts, and it was therefore unblemished and perfect, in contrast to the former, which pervaded the home of man and was imperfect. When dark spots were discovered on the sun—in heaven—this seemed downright scandalous and, for most men, incredible; as did also the discovery of jagged mountains and craters and apparently arid desert regions on the moon. Such "earthiness" in the celestial realm could not be! It was therefore a truly epoch-making achievement of modern science when it demonstrated that celestial bodies are made of the same stuff as are those on the earth, and that terrestrial physics and chemistry apply also to the heavens.

This conclusion still holds, of course, expressing an extremely important fact of the universe, namely, that it houses only one matter, everywhere. And yet in our time it has had to be modified in significant ways. For matter must again be conceived as distributed or organized in "layers"—in depth. However, these newly discovered layers are not like those of a three-storied universe or a mine. The descent into a mine takes one *through* successive strata, i.e., from one into and through the next; whereas in matter each successive stratum is inside, not outside, the previous one; and to "descend" means to dig deeper, i.e., farther, into the same layer, not in any sense out of it. Successive ones are not below or above but inside or outside of one another, and strictly speaking they aren't layers at all but enveloping regions of depth, each one surrounding the next deeper one.

What we must now examine is that in these depth regions matter manifests itself in radically, though not completely, different ways, almost as though in each one there were a different "kind" of matter.

In doing this let us employ Foldy's language about hierarchies. A hierarchy is a series or system of interrelated entities divided or classified in ranks and orders. In this sense the physical universe may be regarded as a hierarchy of hierarchies of structures and relationships. Each of the subhierarchies is to be found in a particular depth region, and each one has a unique logical structure which is in part independent of its "neighbors" inside or outside of it. A "logical structure" I take to be one whose properties can be set forth by a logically consistent system of ideas, or theory. This is what I mean by a different "kind" or "manifestation" of matter.

Let us now speak of the entire matter-component of the cosmos as the major hierarchy under discussion. It includes the whole gamut of levels, from the nucleons outward to the metagalaxy. Within this overarching hierarchical system there are three known subhierarchical depth regions, each spanning a number of levels where, roughly speaking, the same characteristics of matter may be found and the same theoretical ideas apply. These sub-hierarchies I shall call respectively the *micro-world*, which includes the subatomic levels; the *macro-world*, that group of levels lying near one another and constituting the "surface layer" of ordinary things, from the atoms to, say, the planetary system; and the *meta-world* of the stellar, galactic, and metagalactic levels. These must not be regarded as sharply separated, for clearly, despite their pronounced differences, there is both physical and theoretical continuity between them, as well as significant overlap. After all they are "independent" only "in part" (Foldy). Consider now how very different matter is in these three depth regions.

COMPARING THE MICRO- AND MACRO-WORLDS

For the most part in the macro-world matter presents itself to us in its material bulk aspects, and as ordinary objects to which the classical conceptions and laws of mechanics* apply directly. It is here that matter displays its organismic features, the phenomena of life, mind, and spirit, to which the laws of biology, psychology, and the social sciences apply. It is the realm of low temperatures and modest densities, intermediate distances and time intervals, and relatively slow motions. Here is where one encounters solids, liquids, and gases—and combinations of them with forces and motions that make for mountains and plains, rivers and oceans, winds and waves, raindrops and rainbows, planetary rotations and sunsets, burrowing rabbits and soaring hawks, flowers and bells. Thus the macro-

---

* *Mechanics* is the branch of physics that deals with forces and motions.

region of physical reality houses or possesses those qualities that make it suitable for human habitation. It is the depth region from which man looks inward (toward the micro-world), when he wonders about the physical foundations of his existence, and looks outward (toward the meta-world), when he reflects upon the spatiotemporal depths of the universe.

Thus the impressions and conceptions of matter that ordinary experience yields are those that derive almost exclusively from the extended body or bulk aspects with which matter confronts us in the macro-world. In the micro-world, however, it appears predominantly in its particulate aspects, as a world of myriads of tiny separated "particles," in which classical mechanics does not apply directly. At these levels there are no objects consisting of bulk material, no solids, liquids, or gases, and no qualities that emerge from closely knit aggregations of atoms or molecules. There is no heat or temperature here, no color or sound or fragrance, no flowers or bells. Hence we must be prepared to think and theorize differently as we investigate this depth region. Some of the differences will be studied in this chapter, and some in succeeding ones.

The most obvious difference is, of course, that of fullness versus emptiness. The macro-world gives the impression of continuity and solidity. A chair, for example, seems utterly filled with ponderable material, which is supporting and resisting in its effect and can therefore keep its shape virtually unchanged under considerable loads. There are no obvious chinks or interstices in it. It is as though its wood or metal were genuine continua. This continuity feature of matter in bulk would-show up also in the case of a body of liquid or gas. If, however, we could take up residence in the micro-realm inside of an atomic nucleus, say on a proton, our environment would seem essentially empty. During our descent to the nether region the continuum aspect of the chair would dissolve into an atomistic or particulate one. As noted earlier, the chair would seem to turn into a series of successively appearing swarms or particles that are very small and far apart, thus giving the chair an appearance of disconcerting emptiness. This explains the frequent assertion that if a macro-object were compressed by a powerful super-press until its constituent particles touched in some sense, it would be a submicroscopic pellet.

Next, the distinctive characteristics of a so-called particle of the micro-world are very different from any found in the macro-world. Not only is it extremely small but it is so tightly bound internally that tremendous energies are required to break into it. Typical macro-particles are marbles and stones, apples and eggs, wagons and tractors; and these can be fragmented or penetrated with relative ease. To break up or probe into a micro-particle, however, requires the huge energies of the atom smashers noted in the preceding section. This represents an important quality difference between the two kinds of particles. Not only are the micro-structures exceedingly small but their internal tightness and impenetrability may be said to be of a uniquely different kind.

Third, micro-entities exhibit a thoroughly unorthodox and paradoxical behavior. They are *unorthodox* in acting as no ordinary objects ever do: like particles in some situations and like waves in others. They are *paradoxical* in the sense that to ascribe both particle and wave properties to them is to engage in the logically heinous practice of mixing categories—as though one were to say that trees are like houses and operas. For particles and waves are radically (categorically) different in kind. As everybody knows, a macro-particle such as a stone is very different from the waves it generates when it is dropped into a pond. The stone is localizable, whereas the waves are not, i.e., their position cannot be specified definitely in the same sense. The stone keeps its place and size, whereas waves spread out over the pond. The stone consists of specifiable substances, has weight, may be hot or cold, and displays many other characteristics of materials; but none of this may be said about waves. Waves are categorically configurational, not substantive. A wave train is a "shape," not a material thing. It is difficult to imagine how two physical entities could possibly be more different than a macro-particle and a macro-wave train.

Why then talk in this paradoxical way about micro-entities? Why drag waves into the picture? For the same reason that particle imagery was used in the first place. The fact is that when science looks at matter at the levels of the micro-world, the wave phenomena noted there are as real as are its particle aspects. In some situations the former come to the fore, and in others the latter do. When, for instance, a beam of electrons is fired at a slit in a diaphragm (or at a pair of slits, or a grating) it is diffracted (bent around corners) just as in the case of light and sound beams. Since diffraction phenomena are distinguishing features of waves, one must conclude that electrons, as also other micro-matter entities, have wave characteristics as truly as do sound and light. If, on the other hand, such a beam traversed a transverse magnetic field it would be bent just as would a beam of electrically charged water droplets or other charged macro-particles. Electrons, like other micro-entities, are thus seen to have particle properties also. Whether we like it or not, we must accept both sets of properties for the denizens of the micro-world. Matter itself leaves us no choice.

Neither does the reality called radiant energy, or light. In the nineteenth century, physicists came to feel that the corpuscle-wave controversy about its nature, which had persisted intermittently ever since the days of Newton and Huygens, had been resolved once and for all, and that light was beyond doubt waves—and, more specifically, electro-magnetic waves. Then, early in the twentieth, Max Planck and Albert Einstein, with many other physicists, found that, contrary to prevailing conceptions, light sometimes behaves like particles.

Actually the discovery of this utterly surprising aspect of the nature of light came in three steps. First, studies of radiation from so-called "black bodies" showed that the emission of radiant energy occurs not in continuous streams but in discontinuous, discrete spurts, so to speak, each with a certain minimal quantity of energy that came to be called a quantum. Energy is never radiated in less than the amount of such a quantum. Then it was found that energy is also absorbed by a receiver only in discrete amounts, the same quantum. Still later, it became evident, for instance in the investigation of photoelectric phenomena, that light is also transmitted in space, from emitter to receiver, in the same quanta, and that these had some of the properties of discrete corpuscles or particles—which were then called photons. Thus light was seen to be both wavelike or undulatory (which had been known for a long time) and particlelike or particulate (which had been denied for a long time)—and this in turn paved the way for the acceptance of the notion that matter also *must* be dualistic in this way.

The discovery of these quite unexpected and seemingly paradoxical aspects of micro-reality led first to the emergence of remarkably innovative modes of thought and then to the resolution of the paradoxes. This development constitutes one of the truly momentous advances in man's intellectual history and in his understanding of reality, and it is of such epochal significance for our subject that we must soon look at it in some detail.

THE META-WORLD

For the present, then, let this comparative account of the two lower hierarchies of matter suffice, though much remains to be said about them. Consider now the meta-region of the stars, of high-temperature bodies of plasma, the fourth state of matter, and of huge amounts of radiant energy. Here too we have had many surprises that contribute to man's sense of the uniqueness of each hierarchy, as well as of the vastness of the range of quality differences spanned by physical reality as a whole. We can here mention only a few of these surprises. Space and time, once regarded as separate realities, have been found to constitute a single continuum: space-time.[3] Physical geometry is now known to be non-Euclidian; and out of this came the interpretation of gravitation as due to curvature in space-time.[4] After these came the discovery of "nebulae running away," interpreted as the continual expansion of the stellar universe, as indicated by the so-called Doppler shift in stellar spectra.[5] Later came the daring idea of the "continuous creation of matter-energy in space-time,"[6] which, though now considerably modified still has to be reckoned with. Especially exciting recently has been a series of discoveries of very strange stellar objects, among these the so-called quasars (short for quasi-stellar radio sources), that put out prodigious amounts of energy, as much as 10,000 times the brightness of a billion suns;[7] and still more recently the so-called pulsars, that emit seemingly regular radio signals, being spoken of in terms of "gravitational collapse."[8]

Our knowledge of the stellar world has grown also along somewhat different lines; for instance, with reference to the basic nature of stars. First, we now know something about their internal temperatures, something not available to nineteenth-century astronomy, namely, that they run up into billions of degrees. Since the stars are, of course, very massive, it seems therefore that by far most of the matter-material of the universe exists at temperatures immensely greater than any found naturally in our macro-world. Without doubt there are also myriads of cold planets interspersed among the stars, but these probably constitute only an exceedingly small fraction of the total mass of matter in the universe.

The enormous output of radiant energy by the stars can now be accounted for in terms of nuclear reactions,[9] a continual "nuclear cooking," in which nuclear reactions occur spontaneously and atomic synthesis is achieved on a large scale.[10]

Another rather obvious feature of this meta-region is its radically different structuring of the aggregations of its basic entities, the stars. Certainly in terms of present knowledge it does not look like the structurings of the micro-world, such as the atomic aggregates of elementary particle-waves that make up atoms or the combinations of atoms that constitute molecules. Nor is the meta-structuring similar to the macro-structuring of crystals, or rocks, or steel, or plastics. In the stellar case we have seemingly loose aggregations of huge extent in space-time and of ill-defined shape, one fundamental characteristic of which is their lack of rigidity and their unceasing change both internally and externally, as noted in the preceding discussion. Examples of such structures—or perhaps one should say quasi-structures—are the multiple stars, the globular clusters, the spiral nebulae or galaxies, and the meta-galaxy. Here is a large range of bonding or structuring, from the rather tight double stars to the seemingly very loose swarm type of aggregation of the galaxies. In classical cosmogonies and cosmologies it was customary to regard these aggregations by analogy as cosmic bodies of unconfined gas subject to kinetic theory. Thus celestial mechanics was not much more than Newtonian terrestrial theory writ large. One wonders how long this will be regarded as at all valid. For it is hard to fit nonclassical phenomena—such as "big bangs," the explosions of novae, the universal red shift expansion, the phenomena pertinent especially to relativity theory, the pressure of the huge amounts of radiation traversing space-time, and the unceasing evolutionary changes (see later) experienced by stars, planetary systems, and stellar aggregations—into the early simplistic cosmic-kinetic-theory schemes.

Perhaps scientific history will repeat itself. In the not too distant past we learned that classical mechanics of the macro-world was not adequate for use in the micro-world —because, to use Foldy's language, each of these worlds, or aspects of matter, had "a degree of internal logical structure of its own, in part [though not completely] independent of the hierarchies lying above or below." Surely it must be admitted that the meta-hierarchy also is very different and in part unique, with many aspects that seem strange indeed when contemplated in terms of micro- and macro-experience. In the case of the micro-world its uniqueness was taken care of theoretically by the invention of a second kind of mechanics designed especially for it— quantum mechanics. May it not be that in the future, the perhaps not too distant future, still another, third, kind of mechanics will be needed to handle the uniqueness of the stellar realm—galactic mechanics? This would then be recognizing formally the relative independence of three large hierarchies of levels, three basically different aspects of matter and vast ranges of qualitative variety in nature.

I have not intended to give the impression that the differences among these hierarchies are complete, without any common factor or interrelatedness and unity. There is, after all, only one matter. It is like the situation in the electromagnetic spectrum, where the color varieties of light are certainly different in many ways yet are all light, with common basic features in addition to those that are unique and different. It is in this sense that there is also but one reality called matter, though there are many varieties or aspects of it. Moreover, the principles of quantum mechanics are now seen to be applicable in the macro-world also, even though for most practical purposes Newtonian-Laplacian mechanics is more useful there. The independence of these two logical structures is not complete. In fact the one, classical mechanics, may be regarded as a special case of the other, quantum mechanics. This kind of theoretical relatedness and coverage may, we hope, some day be extended to include all three hierarchies—and others that may put in their appearance.

Let us now recall by way of summary that this chapter has dealt primarily with a newly discovered variety of quality aspects of physical reality. For a long time science has been investigating such characteristics of nature horizontally, i.e., at the levels of the macro-world of ordinary experience. Post-modern science, however, has made us conscious of a large variety of unexpected kinds of quality to be found in the vertical direction, inward and outward, associated with the various levels of the hierarchical organization of matter.

MYSTERY IN THE DEPTHS OF MATTER

What may now be said on the basis of scientific experience and knowledge about mystery to be discerned in the interior depths of matter? I suggest that from the contents of this chapter we may conclude at least this much: First, there is the *glory-mystery, or the wonder, of the many levels and the vastness of the range of depths* in the interior of physical reality. Second, there is the mystery of *the immensity of things known*, the immensely large and the immensely small, the immensely distant, beyond, and the immensely near, within; as well as the immense pressure toward, and achievement of, aggregation and combination. The recognition of these comes from the pursuing of nature itself. A third comes from reflecting upon science rather than nature directly. What I refer to is the fact of history, that from time to time science experiences unexpected breakthroughs into its consciousness of great realms of reality that have apparently been in existence a long time and yet remained unnoticed. This is the *mystery of the as-yet-unencountered*, of that which may actually exist, even though as yet men have no inkling of it.

Man has certain organs, or "senses," that are directly responsive to some realities, which he can therefore perceive directly, e.g., eyes that are sensitive to light, ears to sound, skin to heat and cold, and so on. He has no physiological equipment for detecting and identifying directly such other realities as magnetism and electricity. No doubt this is why science was completely oblivious of the existence of the latter before the sixteenth century. Not until then was it known that there was "electricity" and that it was as all-pervasive as we now know it to be—and to have been before its breakthrough to human consciousness. The spontaneous disintegration phenomenon, radioactivity—with its various radiations—remained unknown even longer, until the twentieth century. So did Roentgen's X rays and other "invisible light" in the electromagnetic spectrum, beyond the red and violet. They too are all-pervading. X rays, for example, are now known to come to us "naturally" and in a steady stream from both the micro-world and the astro-world.

To suppose now that there are not still others just as pervasive, yet still beyond our ken, would be foolish indeed; and a breakthrough of one of them may occur at any time, with momentous consequences for our understanding of the world. For it must be remembered that such happenings are always upsetting, since major breakthroughs always cause major revolutions in science. Certainly it must be said that the revolutionary changeover from modern to post-modern science was caused primarily by the breakthroughs that occurred early in this century. And the end thereof has not been "the expulsion of wonder."

Indeed the possibility that, however much may be known at any time, there may exist other all-pervading realms or dimensions of physical reality not yet encountered, together with the impossibility of knowing whether or not this is the case, constitutes an abiding mystery of nature. And it is a *mystery of both the glory and the unfathomability* of existence.

IV. The Symphonic Character of Matter-Energy: Its Particle-Wave Features

FROM SEEMING PARADOX TO PROFOUND UNDERSTANDING

When both light and matter were seen to be at once undulatory and corpuscular it became apparent that in some sense paradox had to be taken seriously as a significant aspect of man's understanding of the world. For a while, of course, physicists were jokingly accused of going irrational. Sometimes, it was alleged, they talked of matter and light as particles and at other times as waves—without rhyme or reason. Nevertheless, physicists went merrily on their way, not worrying about it, knowing full well that nature does not lie and feeling confident that their experiments don't either. The particle and wave phenomena of the micro-world *were there* plainly to be seen, and some day, somehow, the paradox would disappear. And it did.

We should be very clear about what this experience can teach us. It is that, for one thing, paradox arises not from intransigent incongruity in the nature of reality, of, say, the electron and photon, but from man's far too rigid and unyielding habits of thought and from the character of his language, which in turn result from his limited experience and from his reluctance to accept unconventional implications of new experience. For another, it is that the encounter with paradox may be exceedingly fruitful of new and unexpected insight.

When the electron was first discovered it seemed only natural to call it a particle. This had been, for good reasons, the conventional way of imaging the fundamental building blocks of matter. Why not then also the electron? No other imagery came to mind. Indeed, as Donald H. Andrews,[1] distinguished chemist of Johns Hopkins University, explains:

Up to the time of the third decade of our present century, about the year 1923, scientists agreed almost unanimously that everything in our universe was made of particles . . . and this *particulate* image dominated most of scientific thinking in the first half of our present century.

Particle ideas had been remarkably successful in explaining Ernest Rutherford's celebrated experiments in atom bombardment, and in yielding the epoch-making Rutherford-Bohr model of the hydrogen atom, which pictured it as a miniature planetary system governed for the most part by classical mechanics. Scientific treatises as well as popular expositions abounded in impressive diagrams depicting a variety of atomic structures in terms of particles and their orbits.

At that time, however, science's experience with micro-entities was still rather limited. Only the particle features of matter had been encountered. Then the apple cart was upset. Andrews says that

only fifteen years elapsed between Rutherford's experiments pointing toward a mechanical explanation of the inner nature of the atom and a new series of experiments in the mid-1920's pointing toward a *completely new and different picture* (italics added).

The undulatory, wave aspects of matter broke through to man's consciousness. Even molecules and atoms, that had for a very long time been assumed to be corpuscular—and axiomatically so—suddenly turned out to be wavelike also.

Unfortunately, however, physics was rather unprepared for this kind of happening. Particle conceptions had been so spectacularly and uniformly successful in handling the theoretical problems of chemistry, and even the early ones of physics in the field of atomic structure, that they had created the impression—more as an unconscious feeling than as a reasoned conclusion—that they were accurate, pictorial representations of the interior of atoms, in one-to-one correspondence with theory. Electrons quite as much as atoms and molecules really were particles. This was a rather too firm, even though unintended, assignment of electrons and their likes specifically to the category of particle; and this is what later caused the perplexity in regard to the mixing of categories, when the wave characteristics of matter put in their appearance.

In retrospect we can now see that it might have been wiser to be more noncommittal in the beginning with respect to particle imagery, and to speak of electrons only as in some ways analogous to, rather than as really like, particles in the old familiar sense. Then with the advent of wave imagery this could have been incorporated into the same analogical discourse without the disturbing implication of paradox. It is not paradoxical to assert that an entity is at once somewhat like (analogous to) a particle and somewhat like waves. It *is* paradoxical to say that it *is* both particle and waves. Some micro-entities are even more strange. Mesons, for instance, are triply analogous, being like particles and waves *and forces*—forces because their role is in part to hold protons and neutrons together in atomic nuclei.

This then is, at least in part, the way the paradox was resolved and profound understanding emerged: The empirical findings pointing to paradox were taken to mean that the newly discovered strange phenomena and entities (those of the micro-world) differ so fundamentally and categorically from the more familiar ones (of the macro-world), known earlier, that no theory can possibly describe the newcomers adequately if its concepts and imagery are taken exclusively from the realm of the old. More than that, it became evident that theory in general could no longer be expected to describe reality pictorially, or in one-to-one correspondence with it. Therefore the role of theoretical imagery was assigned to that of analogy and symbol, which provide "partial description" through admittedly imperfect analogies—without any implication of pictorial or categorical accuracy. Thus the way was paved for more adequate symbolization and resolution of paradox, later, as further knowledge became available.

In the case of the particle-wave paradox this was

achieved finally by the adoption of purely mathematical symbols (those of quantum mechanics) and, in general, by eschewing pictorially suggestive concepts wherever possible. This was an exceedingly important and fruitful step forward that led to a genuine expansion of human consciousness and insight—as well as momentous and sophisticated refinement of scientific methodology.

It is not suggested that the picturing of micro-entities is undesirable always, but only when the theoretical picture is taken to be descriptive of their actual features in detail. To picture things by analogy, when one is aware that the picture will necessarily be inadequate and may even be misleading in important respects, can be very helpful. Indeed, most physicists and other scientists seem to think habitually by means of pictorial models and symbols, even when these are not brought out into the open or postulated explicitly in their theories. To solve physical problems without such thinking aids as models seems to be extremely difficult. Models can suggest ideas that might not come to mind otherwise. Often it is advantageous even to employ alternative models with regard to the same reality. This discourages dogmatic commitment to one only and makes for a more critical attitude toward them all. Also it helps to keep the mind open to the coming of new experience and new interpretations.

WAVE IMAGERY; ACCENT ON "THE SYMPHONIC" IN PHYSICAL REALITY

While the imagery of this "completely new and different conception" of quantum mechanics certainly has powerfully transformed both the content and method of scientific thought in our time, and has mightily affected human consciousness, its new symbolism has not yet become common property—even after its magnificent success for several decades. Many people find it much more difficult to think in terms of waves than of particles. Since, however, this conception has been so fruitful, no thoughtful person should remain unfamiliar with it.

A book that seems unusually helpful for this purpose is Andrews' book, *The Symphony of Life*, from which we have already quoted twice. The title's reference to music is obviously symbolic and invites us to study the world with an accent on its dynamism and holism as well as its harmonies, as these may be visualized by wave patterns. To give us a feel for such patterns he provides an interesting exposition of certain aspects of sound and music, helps us to apply them analogically to matter, and then to reality and life in general.

Let us now accompany him on a tour of a calcium atom in his finger, while he tells about it in the language of wave imagery. En route let us consider how, in the light of what we are seeing, our earlier notions of the micro-world—for instance, that of its emptiness—may need revision.

As you approach this atom . . . [it] looks like a great ball of luminous fog . . . filled with waves and ripples. . . . [The] atomic nucleus, the tiny particle at the center of the atom that was like the sun in the atomic planetary picture . . . you [now] see as the center of this . . . fog . . . surrounded by layers where the fog is somewhat more dense, layers very much like the concentric skins of an onion.

We see that [in this new imagery] the atom has lost a certain aspect of its simplicity; the electrons are spread out in these fog patterns that merge into one another and make the identity of the electron difficult to define, and any idea of precise location for an electron almost meaningless. . . . [T]he more attenuated parts of these electron-fog balls not only spread out into other neighboring atoms, but also extend far beyond what we had thought of as the original single atom; in fact, not only is my finger [containing the calcium atom we are exploring] one total mass of intermingled atomic fog, my whole body is a mass of these intermingled electron-fog waves.

It is obvious that according to this conception the micro-world is not at all empty. Neither is an atom an empty space within which widely separated tiny particles (electrons) revolve in discrete orbits around a central-point particle (the nucleus). An atom is rather filled with a diffuse "fog" of varying degrees of density, and the fogs of neighboring atoms extend into one another. We must not suppose, of course, that this fog, as Andrews calls it, is some kind of subtle, imponderable substance; it is simply the composite of the wave patterns of the electrons in the atom. It is a pulsating fog, for these electron-wave patterns are not static but perpetually undulating, like the sound-wave patterns in a concert hall. Not only is the atom as a whole fundamentally kinetic rather than static (as was the case also for the particulate Bohr atom),[2] but so are its individual constituents (unlike those of the Bohr atom). On the other hand, in this foggy atom individual electrons are lost sight of.

Indeed, it follows that when electrons are conceived in this way the idea of their individual identity loses much of its meaning, and the possibility of their precise identification, or localization, must be abandoned. Just where—to what point in space—could one point to indicate the position of an electron at a given moment, if it is taken to be wavelike? And how meaningful is it to talk of its size, or of where it ends and its neighbor begins? The fact is that almost none of the fundamental concepts that have been so potent in macro-mechanics—such as size, or position and distance, or time and time interval, mass, velocity, momentum—can be used with respect to the micro-world without radical modification of their meanings and of the rules for their use.

More than that, however, with the adoption of wave imagery there is a shift of interest, and of what one regards as important. As Andrews puts it:

We are now more interested in the symmetry of the wave pattern and far less concerned with any specification of the points of location of the wave. We have *delocalized* the electron and are less interested in its location than we are in the character of its "shape." We are far more interested in the pitch of the note it is singing than we are in where it is. We are far more interested in the kind of harmony its tone forms when merged with its neighboring electrons than we are with its space relations in respect to its neighbors. We are more interested in its music than in its motion. We are far less interested in *drawing* a picture to show where the electron is and far more interested in writing the music of its song.[3]

This talk about music and harmony is, of course, metaphoric, but it does illustrate how interest has changed and, with it, our vocabulary and nuance of understanding and feeling. Note also the language of the citation for the 1968 Nobel prize in physics to Professor Luis Alvarez: "for your decisive contributions to elementary particle physics, in particular the discovery of a large number of resonance states made possible through your development of the technique."[4] While the Nobel committee uses particle language in referring to Alvarez's field of research, "elementary particle physics," it uses wave or music language in speaking of the entities he has discovered, namely, "resonance states." The search for particles is a search for resonances, and the search for resonances a search for particles.

This represents a revolution not only in reasoning thought but also in consciousness. Contemporary man can now sense the symphonic character of physical reality and hear metaphorically the music of the spheres within the atom. He is now far more fascinated by the melodic quality and dynamism of its singing than by blueprints of its mechanical structure.

Music has always, I suppose, been counted among the tender elements of life, and as such it has always been one of the most powerful forces in human existence—non-coercively. It says a great deal about the fundamental quality of the cosmos that in speaking about it objectively, i.e., in terms of what one actually knows about it, one must accent the symphonic quality of matter.

CERTAINTY AND UNCERTAINTY; DETERMINACY AND PROBABILITY

One of the most consequential discoveries of post-modern science has been that we may no longer think of atoms as being essentially mechanical systems that are precisely specifiable and predictable. There is something elusive and tantalizing about them, and they are predictable only in terms of statistical probability, with some degree of uncertainty. What is involved here has been formulated in the celebrated Heisenberg's uncertainty principle. As is well known, there has been much controversy as to whether the uncertainty it speaks of is to be ascribed to nature itself or to inherent limitations of man's ways of investigating and communicating about it.

While for our purposes this controversy need not be

resolved, it is important for us to understand that the principle does represent established empirical knowledge. The fact is that in our time nature *has* been found to have an aspect not noticed before, namely, indeterminacy. Thus, for whatever reasons, nature's micro-entities *cannot* be specified or measured without uncertainty. Nature simply is this way vis-à-vis man as its observer. Always heretofore "error" or some degree of "inaccuracy" was thought to be avoidable in principle, if not always in practice. Now we know that this is not the case. And what Werner Heisenberg did, more specifically, was to show that this quality of nature has quantitative features indicated by a lower limit below which the uncertainty cannot be reduced.

But why? Why are inaccuracy and uncertainty inevitable? What is there about atoms and electrons and the like that makes utmost precision in their specification, measurement, and prediction impossible? For our purposes there are two simple but cogent answers that complement each other, one referring primarily to the wave nature of micro-entities and the other primarily to their particle characteristics. Both take observation, measurement, and description to be operations for determining such data as the position, size, velocity, and momentum of objects at specifiable times. It will be helpful to consider both answers—in not too technical a manner.

As to the first of these, the point is simply that for entities conceived in terms of wave imagery—of balls of "fog," of electron-wave fog patterns, of spread-out, intermingling layers of such patterns, using Andrews' metaphoric language—it is meaningless to speak of defining identities precisely or of measuring anything like size or position with certainty. They are simply too fuzzy for that. And, of course, the prediction of future data regarding them is equally problematic and subject to uncertainty. The nearest one can come to quantitative prediction is by means of statistical probabilities. Andrews describes the process this way:

When one of these electron waves interacts with another wave, we cannot predict with exact certainty what the outcome will be.

We can only say that there is a certain *probability* that one result will be found, another probability that another result will be found, and still another probability that still another result will be found. We can catalog all the possible results and assign to each the probability that it will be found; but we cannot say with certainty *which* result will be the answer, although we may know that, among all possibilities, the end result must be in a clear-cut fashion one of these possibilities.[5]

What is predicted, then, in the case of the interaction between micro-entities, is not the certainty of an occurrence or observation but the probability of its happening. Interestingly enough, the same conclusion follows from consideration of the particle aspects of micro-entities, and this brings us to the second answer to the *why?* asked a little while ago.

In the modern era classical mechanics taught that *if* the position and momentum of a particle could be measured accurately at one time, *then* its positions and momenta for all future times could be predicted with certainty. This must now be denied, because of what we know today about the nature of measurement. To measure something about an object is to interact with it instrumentally in some way, and this inevitably alters that which is to be measured. This is because such interaction is always dynamic and introduces forces into the situation, so that the *measured* and the *measurement* affect, and to some extent actually change, each other. To illustrate, suppose we wished to determine the position of a "free" electron by means of a powerful measuring microscope. To detect the position of the electron relative to the measuring scale in the instrument, light must be reflected into it by the electron. But reflection is a collision process, collision between the electron and the successive photons of the illuminating beam of light, and collision introduces forces of reaction and recoil. When a single photon collides with a massive stone consisting of billions of electrons and other particles, the stone is virtually unaffected. But if a photon collides with a single electron, the effect is momentous. They recoil, as in the celebrated Compton effect,[6] somewhat as billiard balls do; both are displaced or deflected from their positions or motions. The very first photon might knock the electron out of position so that the next one coming along in the beam would miss it and not be reflected. In other words, the collision radically alters the position to be measured; and the same conclusion would follow if it were the momentum of the electron that is to be measured.

One reason why the effect of such interaction in measurement is inconsequential in the case of macro-objects—and why modern science was unaware of it—is that they are relatively so massive that the weak forces of measurement change them only negligibly. The micro-particles, however, are so small in mass, and usually so loosely positioned, that even the smallest possible interacting forces affect them significantly. Therefore, for them we must say that indeterminacy in measurement is inevitable and not negligible. It was the quantitative analysis of this that led to the Heisenberg principle mentioned earlier, which asserts that there is a quantitative limitation upon the accuracy of measurement. Thus we have also, as David Bohm puts it, "a quantitative estimate of the limitations on the possibility of giving a deterministic description of the world."[7]

Because of this discovery that uncertainty, or indeterminacy, is a basic feature of the world, it has been necessary to revise our conception of the so-called "laws of nature" and of "causation." Since it is possible to predict probabilities only, the laws by means of which predicting is done must be probability laws, and the term "cause" must refer to a causing of probabilities. This does not mean that the idea of a causally determinate character of nature's events has been abandoned. For post-modern science the world is quite as "deterministic" as ever, though its determinateness is now known to lie in the realm of the predictable probability of events rather than of their predictable certainty. Neither does it mean that all claims of certainty have been renounced. For we can be certain of this, that whatever is caused to happen, and does become actual, represents in principle one of a predictable set of probabilities, as was stated so well by Andrews. Post-modern science is confident that nothing happens that is not predictable in that sense—as a probability. It regards the world as closed to any happening that does not fall within the range of such caused probabilities.

THE PERPETUAL DANCE: STRANGE HAPPENINGS IN DEPTH

Thus far we have studied the micro-world largely with regard to the subject of *structure*. Thus chapter III dealt for the most part with hierarchies and varieties of structure, and the present one, up to now, with the peculiarities of wavelike and particlelike structures. Even the subject of uncertainty and indeterminacy was introduced by analyzing the dynamic interaction of micro-entities from a wave and a particle point of view. Actually this is a back-door approach, which misses much that can be seen only from the front door.

The point is that the exploration of the interior depths of matter has disclosed not only strange structural entities but quite as strange happenings or types of events. (If unorthodox structure, then unorthodox behavior!) Moreover, no discussion of the uncertainty features of physical reality is at all complete if it fails to call attention to such realities as randomness, instability, transience, and transmutation—those that are implied by Max Born's term, *The Restless Universe*,[8] and by what others have called the "lawlessness" of nature, in contrast to its "lawfulness."

The notion of randomness and chance as scientifically recognized aspects of the world seems to have come to us first, with convincing force, through biology, and more particularly from Darwin's daring idea of "chance variation" as an indispensable causal factor in evolution. This is where the tight grip of mechanistic determinism was first loosened. L. Charles Birch, distinguished biologist, in commenting on this, remarked that

it is essential that any philosophy or theology of nature take account of what seems to be sheer accident, random or chance events. They exist. . . . In his excellent history of evolutionary thought, the historian Greene points out that the element of chance in the Darwinian theory appealed to the American philosophers Charles Peirce and William James "as a means of deliverance from the mechanical determinism of nineteenth-century physics and chemistry."[9]

Actually, however, these physical sciences came to give even more recognition to the role of chance and probability in nature by developing its implications mathematically in the kinetic theory of gases and, more generally, in what is called statistical mechanics. At the time, still in the modern era, this represented a new kind of theorizing that was concerned with explaining and predicting the probable behavior of large numbers of molecules rather than with the definitive, determinate behavior of individual ones. For our purposes the point to be emphasized is that it accepted the randomness of molecular motion in gases as fact and postulated it as a basic assumption of the theory. And a highly successful theory it turned out to be!

Now it has been the good fortune of post-modern science to discover many other phenomena and strange kinds of happenings in nature, especially in the micro-world, which apparently cannot be understood adequately except statistically, i.e., on the assumption that randomness *is* one of the fundamental realities of nature. As we go into the depths of matter and encounter the molecules and atoms, we find them to be engaging in what Born calls a "thermal dance." This is the molecular agitation just considered in connection with kinetic theory. Then, to quote Born further, as we "penetrate into the atoms . . . far from finding a state of greater rest, we find still wilder motion." When we enter the nucleus of an atom, we "have hopes of greater rest, firmness, and solidity—but we find none. . . . What goes on in their interior . . . does not promise peace or repose."[10]

Some species of micro-entities are very stable, existing unchanged apparently for very long times, millions of years or longer, and then one of them may suddenly "explode" or eject pieces. This is the radioactive phenomenon. Others have only a transient existence, their "lifetimes" never exceeding a ten billionth of a second. They come and go in great numbers, never remaining on the scene longer than the briefest of moments. Still others, while existing stably for a long time, put on during that time very peculiar "disappearance" acts. Thus an electron may under certain circumstances be "moving along a line" and put in its appearance successively at two different "places" without showing up at intermediate points.[11]

Then there are the phenomena of annihilation and "creation" that result from collisions. To understand them requires heretical thinking, as judged by conventional macro-world conceptions. For example, one must make the "bold assertion," as Born puts it, that "matter does not persist from eternity to eternity, but can be created or destroyed," as when "a positive electron and a negative electron may annihilate one another, their energy flying off in the form of light," or when "they are born, with the annihilation of light energy."[12] This is the phenomenon of transmutation of matter into energy, and of energy into matter. It is this interchangeability and equivalence of matter and energy that has led scientists to speak of matter-energy as a continuum of physical reality, as mentioned in the introduction and indicated in the title of this chapter.

Perhaps the most spectacular of all the micro-world happenings, and one that breaks through into the macro-world on a large scale, is the chain-reaction transmutation of matter into energy that occurs in the explosion of bombs (according to the celebrated formula: $E = mc^2$, where E stands for energy, m for mass of matter, and c for the speed of light). Oversimplifying this, one has before the process a specimen of material consisting of molecules, and afterward only an equivalent amount of energy consisting of photons. Finally, we note the more specific happenings requisite to such chain reactions: *fission* and *fusion*; on the one hand the breaking up of atomic nuclei into fragments with the discharge of energy, on the other the combining of parts to produce whole nuclei, also with the discharge of energy.

THE HORIZONTAL VERSUS VERTICAL EXPLORATION OF REALITY

Let us now recall that this chapter and the preceding one have dealt primarily with a newly discovered, large variety of quality aspects of physical reality, qualities of both structure and event. For a long time science has investigated nature horizontally, i.e., at the levels of the macro-world of ordinary experience. Post-modern science, however, has made us conscious of a tremendous variety of quite unexpected kinds of quality to be found in the vertical direction, inward and outward, in the interior depths of matter. Some of these qualities are: the quantum aspects of matter and light; the particle-wave duality and complementarity of entity and of event; the fundamental uncertainty, indeterminacy, and unpredictability of events; the inevitability of dynamic interaction between a measurement and the measured; the continuity and equivalence of matter and energy, symbolized by the hyphenated term, matter-energy. The fact that these are basically qualities of reality is often lost sight of because of the prominence of quantitative considerations that must necessarily enter into any complete scientific explication of phenomena.

These discoveries have led us to modify our conception of the determinateness of nature, by conceiving its laws and cause-and-effect relations to be statistical and probabilistic in character, so that we now see both determinateness and randomness as basic qualities of nature. They have also led to revisions of our conception of the nature and role of scientific theory. It is not accurate picturization of reality but symbolic explanation and interpretation that describe, explain, and predict—but not completely. To meet the theoretical needs of the micro-world there has been devised a new kind of mechanics, quantum mechanics, in contrast, though conceptually related, to the classical mechanics of the macro-world.

To see things in nature profoundly is to discern the vast wealth of reality in its interior depths beneath its surface features. It means also coming to understand the directly visible, at least in part, through the indirectly discernible depths within. To see in depth is also to see both quality and quantity, and to see them in balance as inseparable and complementary aspects of reality. It means being prepared to accept the utterly novel and unexpected, and even the seemingly incredible or paradoxical, and to think about them imaginatively and even unconventionally if necessary.

Post-modern science has contributed more than a little to man's doing just such seeing and thinking—profoundly and in depth—in our time and for the future.

V. Complexity and Simplicity
in Nature and Science

"THE SIMPLICITY HAS DISAPPEARED"
It is but a short step from the subject of qualitative diversity to that of complexity and, by contrast, that of simplicity. My thesis here is that the post-modern discovery of the vastness of diversity, especially in the vertical dimension, has led to a new awareness and understanding of the scientific significance of *complexity and simplicity as fundamental complementary aspects of both nature itself and of scientific thought about it.*

During the modern period science, as distinguished from technology and the crafts, was little interested in complexity, for it was regarded as an aspect of materials more than of matter. In the latter, the ground-constituent of materials, complexity was thought to be of secondary importance. One of the primary tasks of physics was the search for an underlying order of simplicity, in terms of which matter could presumably be understood and by which the myriads of complexities of materials and phenomena might be explicated. The complexities themselves were not important; what counted was the simplicity by which they could be dissolved. Matter itself was simple. Without doubt, the search for such an order of simplicity, and of a correlative understanding of matter, was dominated—at the time for good reasons—by the attitudes and conceptions of atomism.

This is to say that the sought-for order of simplicity was assumed to be one of simple elementary corpuscles, governed by simple principles, that function as the basic building blocks of matter and therefore as the carriers of the fundamental properties of matter. When all chemical substances came to be classed as compounds or elements (or mixtures of these), and all materials could thus be regarded as combinations of but ninety-two kinds of simple, indestructible, and unchanging atoms, the basic order of simplicity was thought to have been identified and the essential simplicity of nature verified.

This conception was, of course, just what was to be expected from the prevailing Newtonian billiard-ball conception of the world. There was no reason to suppose that the atoms did not obey the simple classical laws of motion and that therefore their behavior was not completely predictable. Why then, it was reasoned, shouldn't it be possible, at least in principle, to understand all so-called secondary qualities—and complexities—in terms of this atomic conception alone? And why shouldn't the order of atoms be regarded as the basic order of simplicity? Toward the end of the nineteenth century it became clear, however, that the complete explanation of things was after all impossible in terms of atoms alone and that nonmaterial fields of force had to be reckoned with also. Nevertheless the huge success of Maxwell's celebrated electromagnetic-field theory, devised to meet that need, seemed to support confidence in the idea of fundamental simplicity—expanded to include both particle and field.

Clearly, however, this particular conception of simplicity in nature is no longer tenable. The atoms of chemistry are not the simple eternal corpuscles of atomism, and the field situation has become much less simple because of the discovery of additional kinds of field forces that must now be taken into account. Not a few writers are saying, therefore, that the simplicity of nature must now be reconceived. Notice, for instance, this assertion by C. P. Snow:

Not too long ago one took it for granted that the final scientific picture of the world would be beautiful, orderly and simple. As it continued to be sketched in, we have had a number of surprises. The beauty is there, but not of the sort to damp down our questions. The simplicity has disappeared.[1]

Apparently Snow feels that we must frankly admit that "the simplicity has disappeared." This is, of course, so sweeping a statement that one wonders what it can possibly mean. Surely not that there is no sense at all in speaking of simplicity in nature; the fact that the immense number of different kinds of molecules (chemical compounds) in the world are all combinations of only a few kinds of atoms (elements) represents genuine simplicity in nature, and it has not disappeared.

What seems to have disappeared is not simplicity itself but the simplistic notion that the chemical atom represents an ultimate kind of simplicity that can itself resolve all physical complexity. What has had to be relinquished is the idea that the level of the atom is the lowest level of physical reality, and that this is where the ground order of simplicity is to be found. That which seemed to be ultimate physical simplicity, namely, the atom, has dissolved into great complexity. Simplicity has disappeared in that sense.

Nor is there good reason to suppose that it can be found elsewhere, say at a lower level. The reason for this is given by the physicist Ralph Lapp, the senior author of the book in which Snow's challenging assertion occurs. He begins:

In June 1962, physicists at the 33-billion-electron-volt atom smashing synchrotron at Brookhaven, Long Island, fired atomic particles through 42 feet of armor plate and discovered the existence of . . . a mysterious and elusive particle as close to nothing as anything can get, and so penetrating that it can shoot through 100 trillion miles of lead like a bullet through a cloud.

Then, after enlarging further on how much of such strange and utterly novel knowledge contemporary research has brought forth, he comments, "Yet, for all we have learned about matter . . . the more scientists probe, the greater complexities they encounter."[2] This statement is, of course, even more startling than Snow's. It shifts the focus of attention from simplicity to complexity and asserts that what further probing discloses especially is complexity, and that it actually increases with depth.

"THE WONDERFUL DIVERSITY OF MATERIAL"
In order to clarify the little-understood distinction between matter and material, and to lay a more adequate foundation for the study of complexity in depth, let us insert here a discussion of the meaning of "material."

To speak of matter-in-bulk is to speak specifically about materials rather than simply matter. One of the most important post-modern developments in science proper is the revival of interest in a subject that for quite some time had been regarded as belonging exclusively to technology, namely, the study of the nature and qualities of various substances and the production of new ones with specifiable useful properties. Among the so-called pure sciences, chemistry was the first to develop a general interest in specific materials—actually long ago—but this interest was accentuated and became more pointed when four or five decades ago this science entered upon the "creative chemistry" phase of its development, and its major preoccupation passed from analysis to composition. This was when it began to bring into existence the utterly new wonder substances, the numerous synthetic solids and liquids, fibers and membranes, plastics and metals, food and drugs. For the most part, it seems, this interest centered for quite some time upon the atom and molecule; the main problem was to synthesize new molecules.

Physics got into the act somewhat later, and from a different point of view, via an interest in the solid state as such and, to a lesser extent, in the liquid state as well. It conceived—and investigated—these states from the very outset primarily in terms not of their constituent particles but of the gross physical properties of particular materials: their electric, magnetic, thermal, mechanical, optical, and still other qualities. In the case of crystalline solids, the kinds of properties the ancient ceramicists, metallurgists, and even the alchemists—as well as their modern successors—were concerned with, such as ductility, malleability, elasticity, temper, brittleness, refractoriness, surface texture, and optical reflection, took on great interest and were seen to have genuine scientific, and not only technological, significance. For their study with post-modern techniques revealed that the qualities of solid matter-in-bulk could not be understood truly in terms of only the properties of constituent particles. They are the properties exclusively of large aggregates of molecules. No individual molecule is ever malleable, or ductile, or hot, or electrically conducting, or smooth to the touch. Therefore, when a substance *is* soft or hard, smooth or rough, this is not because its individual molecules are like that. What is decisive here is structure, the structure not only of the molecule but of the aggregate, of the single crystal, or of the polycrystalline aggregate, with its many crystal orientations, interfaces, domains, lattice perfections and imperfections, purities and impurities, order and disorder, and so on.

Thus ordinary rock specimens, or ancient blocks of metal, as well as the beautiful single crystals produced by ultramodern techniques, came to be seen as wholes that are much more than the sum of their parts, and whose properties are not mere extensions of the properties of their constituent particles. When many molecules aggregate to form a macro-object, there emerge formerly nonexistent relationships and qualities. The object as a whole achieves its own energy states and levels, its own quantum-mechanical symmetries and wave patterns. Here the term hierarchy really comes into its own, for a specimen of such material (matter-in-bulk) truly behaves as an hierarchical whole whose characteristics are determined in part by the unique contribution made by each constituent and partly by the contribution they make together as a system. Thus out of matter-in-bulk there emerge vast arrays of new realities, of material and quality. An immense amount of knowledge has accumulated about such realities themselves, and about the laws in terms of which they can be understood and can be produced technologically with prescribed characteristics.

This understanding of materials as one aspect of the macro-world would not have been possible, however, without profound knowledge derived from the micro-world. As Ralph Lapp puts it:

By every canon of common sense, the solid should have been the easiest form of matter for man to learn to know. Unlike gas it makes its presence plain; unlike the liquid, it stays readily at hand. Firm, compact, cohesive, it is by far the most satisfying to deal with. . . . Yet, astonishingly, it was not until 50 years ago that the actual structure of the solid was confirmed beyond doubt.

Until this breakthrough, it was thought that the *content* of a solid was what determined its characteristics: what made diamonds hard, leather tough, iron magnetic and copper conductive. Vary the content and you could change the substance, said the classical chemists. . . . Today we know that many of the properties of a solid are determined by its *structure*: by the way the material's basic building blocks—its atoms—are ordered, and by the way they join together.[3]

What happened fifty years ago was that X rays were seen to be useful for the investigation of crystal structure, and this revealed a remarkable aspect of the micro-world in solids, namely, that the basis for their shapes lay in the spatial arrangements of atoms.

Considerably later came the further surprising discovery that there are two classes of molecules, the small or light-weight ones, and the heavy giants, called the polymers.[4] The small ones, the monomers,[5] make up the inanimate objects, such as air, water, rock. Animate things, on the other hand, are composed for the most part of the giant molecules, which in turn are built up of many small molecules joined together in repeating structural patterns. Some of these giant molecules consist of hundreds of thousands of small ones. Here again, structure is a primary consideration. Once this was understood, a whole new branch of chemistry was born, polymer chemistry, and it in turn gave birth to an immense array of completely new giant molecules and thus the amazing synthetics (plastics) that have revolutionized so much of contemporary life. In this field man has become a creator in the best sense of the word, for here he has not only analyzed, or copied, or altered, or manipulated what was already in nature but has greatly enlarged it, by the production of many completely new substances and qualities that simply were not there before.

This development represented also an important aspect of post-modern man's experience in depth, and therefore of the expansion and intensification of his consciousness and sensitivities. He has rediscovered through science the reality and significance of one of the fundamental components of life: material. Prof. Cyril Stanley Smith, metallurgist, historian, and philosopher of M.I.T., has some profound observations about this, as follows:

Histories of philosophy are full of discussions of the development of the concept of matter, yet hardly at any point do they touch on the nature and properties of materials. Atoms and the qualities that accompany their aggregation became pure exercises in thought, with the significance of monism and pluralism more important than the visible, tangible aggregations that, in the craftsman's hand if not in the philosopher's mind, were directly relatable to useful properties. Through most of history, matter has been a concern of metaphysics more than physics and materials of neither. Classical physics at its best turned matter only into mass, while chemistry discovered the atom and lost interest in properties.

Speaking of certain past periods of the history of philosophy and of science, Smith remarks further that

sensitivity to the wonderful diversity of real materials was lost, at first because philosophical thought despised the senses, later because the more rigorous experimentally verifiable thought patterns of the new science could only deal with one thing at a time. It was atomistic, or at least simplistic, in its very essence. . . .

Only in the last few decades was it possible for solid-state physics to mature and to merge with a growing technology as attention turned again to materials and to qualities.[6]

Surely to have regained long-lost sensitivity to the "wonderful diversity of real material," in both its internal structural aspects and its more external visible, tangible, and marvelously varied qualities, and then to have imaginatively and creatively brought forth a vast range of other such realities for the enrichment of life that were theretofore nonexistent, is to have had genuine experience in depth.

So real and consequential has been this experience that Professor Smith sees it as an indication that

science [is] reversing the trend toward atomistic explanation that has been so triumphant in the last 400 years, and I predict a more human future based on the symbiosis of exact knowledge (which is by its very nature limited) and experience.[7]

He sees here a development that is parallel in a sense to what is happening in the fine arts.

Through most of European history, since the Renaissance, both connoisseurs and historians of art have reserved their highest praise for painting and sculpture, and the most marvelous artistic uses of materials have been designated "decorative" or "minor" arts. However, the recent trend toward nonobjective art has been accompanied by a new appreciation of the esthetic richness in textures, colors, and other physical properties of materials. Such properties and the technologies derived from them have been appreciated far more in the Orient . . . [where] craftsmen in stone, wood, clay, and metals have sensitively used the subtlest properties of plastic and viscous flow, of crystallization, surface tension differences, and color changes resulting from ions in various stages of oxidation and polarization. They have enjoyed the beauty conferred on a surface by chemical degradation and the irregularity that comes from fracture, deformation, and sectioning of polycrystalline materials.

Thus "sensual awareness of the properties of materials" is, Smith feels, again coming into its own.

The scientists' laudable striving to eliminate the evidence of the senses has sometimes produced a senseless result. But if exact science is used to illuminate empirical experience, and if experience is used to temper the extrapolation of the simple ideal systems of the scientist, then indeed we have real knowledge.[8]

We can now add several items to the summary presented in the preceding chapter. The rediscovery of the importance of material, and its study by science itself, has had momentous consequences. First, it has established the importance of structure, rather than only atomic content, in determining the qualities of aggregates of atoms such as crystals or large molecules (polymers), i.e., of solids and of plastics. With this has come a sense of the wholeness of things as being indeed more than the sum of their parts, and as requiring for complete understanding both analytic and holistic approaches. Second, science is coming to recognize and appreciate the glory of man's senses and intuitions and the fact that he can learn much about physical reality directly through sensual experience—when it is combined with rigorous thought. This is operating toward what Professor Smith calls a symbiotic relationship between pure science and the crafts and arts that is making for a new and more human kind of science. Third, these developments have helped man to become more imaginative and genuinely creative with regard to physical reality. For the first time in his career man has been able to bring forth new substances—for instance, the new "miracle" materials —that certainly did not exist before.

To see things in nature profoundly means also not to neglect perceiving in their exteriors the full significance of their sensually discernible practical and aesthetic glory. Seeing them in depth is also to see them holistically, with sensitive awareness of both their parts and their wholes.

THE GREATER THE DEPTH, THE GREATER THE COMPLEXITY

In what sense can it be said that complexity increases with depth in matter? And does such an assertion refer to physical reality itself or only to what we think about it? The interpretation I shall offer will be developed from the point of view of critical realism,[9] as I believe it to be espoused by most scientists.

According to this view science actually investigates nature itself, not just its own ideas. It achieves much reliable knowledge about it. This knowledge is communicated through systems of theoretical symbols. The descriptions it develops do depict reality, but not in pictorial detail. To illustrate with reference to matter, it really does have an interior, and in it there really are hierarchies of strange and complex entities within one another at different depths or levels. And we do know some of their features rather well —even if only partially. Science's descriptions of these are therefore to be taken as "true," though not literalistically so in detail.

Now then, from this stance of critical realism, what can it mean to say that with increasing depth complexity increases rather than decreases, as is commonly supposed? For a long time only the macro-world was known, and its lowest observed levels were those of the chemical compounds and elements. The existence of lower levels, of the molecules and atoms respectively, was only inferred, not directly verified. In our time, however, individual atoms have been spotted photographically; one of my colleagues at The Pennsylvania State University, Prof. Erwin

Mueller,[10] has magnified metal surfaces two-million-fold with his remarkable ion emission microscope and been able therefore to pinpoint atoms on the surfaces. Thus the direct verification has been achieved. Had this been done a century earlier it would undoubtedly have been hailed as conclusive proof that the ground-level of matter had been found and, with it, the long sought for order of ultimate simplicity.

Today this would not do, because we now know that each one of the atoms identified by Mueller is itself a microcosm of tremendous complexity—and anything but the incarnation of ultimate simplicity. And so is every particle-wave entity encountered within it. Each descent to a lower level has therefore disclosed another order of complexity. And historically speaking, each such descent has added to the sum total of known complexity science has had to deal with before. To put it a bit more graphically, if physical reality is indeed a hierarchy of hierarchies, of structures within structures, or wheels within wheels, it must be that, every time another subset of structures or wheels is discovered, the total set is seen to include more complexity than before. And this is exactly what has happened with each descent to a lower level. This is, I think, what the Lapp assertion means.

It seems clear, then, that it is no longer legitimate to equate any level that happens to be the lowest (most interior) one known at any given time with the hoped-for ground level. While traditionally complexities at one level have always been assumed to be resolvable by the simplicity of a lower one, thus far each such lower level has turned out to be complex itself—and has had then to be resolved by reference to a still lower one. Every discovery of a lower level tempts men, almost irresistibly, it seems, to suppose that the ground level has at last been found. This has been said even in our time, when, having again and again been forced to dig deeper, we should have known better. There is not a shred of evidence to entail, or even only to suggest, the assumption that the lowest level known at any time, or the next one to become known, houses an order of ultimate simplicity in the atomistic sense. It may happen some day that such an order will be found, but there is neither historical precedent nor empirical evidence to support such an expectation. In the meantime it seems necessary to say that, whenever there is in prospect the disclosure of yet another (lower) level, what should be expected there is more, not less, complexity.

THE SIMPLE AND THE COMPLEX
AS COMPLEMENTARY REALITIES

This discussion, intended to represent critical realism, must seem more realistic than critical. For I have blithely counted simplicity and complexity among the actualities of the micro-world, and of nature in general, without giving due recognition to the difficult problem of distinguishing between the "simplicity (or complexity) of the world" and the "simplicity (or complexity) of scientific theory" or thought pertaining to the world. This is, however, of crucial importance for our subject, and we must now look at it carefully.

Let us begin with the following remarks by the philosopher of science, Prof. Nelson Goodman of the University of Pennsylvania:

Philipp Frank has said that without simplicity there is no science. If we add that likewise without science there is no simplicity, we are on the way to understanding a good deal about science and simplicity and the relation between them.

The search for simplicity in science is sometimes questioned on the ground that the world may actually be complex. This betrays a curious perversion of ideas. Rather than the simplicity of science being limited by the simplicity of the world, the simplicity of the world is limited by the simplicity of science. I do not mean that the world is complex until we simplify it. It is neither simple nor complex except relative to—as organized under—a given system. The world has as many different degrees of complexity as it has many different structures; and it has as many different structures as there are different true ways of describing it. Without science, or some other mode of organization, there is no simplicity or complexity. . . . The world, indeed, is as simple as any true system; but it is also as complex as any true system.[11]

It seems to me that on the whole this statement makes good sense. I take it to mean that the world is seen to have two actual aspects that we refer to as simplicity and complexity—when seen with the aid of some organizing principle furnished by science or, say, the arts. The terms have little definable meaning without an organizing principle, and the qualities of nature which they connote are not discernible without one. But neither would they have operationally definable meaning unless they referred to actual realities. If they did not exist they could not be found and observed, for they would not then generate percepts from which the organizing principles could create concepts.

Like all scientific concepts they derive in part from discovery of what is the case in nature and in part from invention—conceptualization or imagery for communicating about it. There have been many arguments about whether electrons are discoveries or inventions. Whatever others might assert about it, the critical realist affirms that the term electron comes out of both processes, discovery and invention. There really are electrons, just as there are ideas about them. Similarly, the insight that the electrons actually do have both particle and wave properties results from both processes. I would make this assertion about complexity and simplicity also, as I believe most scientists would.

It is, however, extremely difficult to define these terms or to say precisely what scientists (as distinguished from professional philosophers of science) mean by them. Moreover, I suspect that most of them employ the terms intuitively rather than with logical rigor. They "feel" that a cubic crystal that is inanimate is simple compared to a living cell, and that a tree is in turn more complex than one of its cells. A tone with a fundamental only is simpler than one with many overtones. When physics learned that space and time, formerly regarded as separate realities, constitute for the observer a single continuum, space-time, this was the product of the discovery of a simple aspect of nature itself, as well of the creation of a unifying and simplifying theory.

There are certain key ideas that do loom importantly in the minds of scientists when they speak of simplicity and complexity, e.g., order and disorder, perfection and imperfection, uniformity and nonuniformity, oneness and multiplicity, though none of the paired realities are sharply distinguishable. One suspects also that, according to some usages, simplicity and complexity refer simply to different degrees of the same quality, for instance, the number of variables in a situation. Thus when the phenomenon or entity requires many variables for its adequate description and prediction it is felt to be more complex than if fewer were required. On the other hand, usually sheer multiplicity is not taken to be synonymous with complexity. What seems important in complexity is the number of its interrelations, especially causal ones. If it must be represented by a network rather than, say, a single chain of causal factors, it is regarded as complex more than simple.

Virtually everything we have studied about the hierarchies—their many levels, their structures within structures, the particle-waves duality, their uncertainty and probability aspect, the many strange events, and the great qualitative variety of nature in both its horizontal and vertical dimensions—contributes to the sense of complexity of physical reality, while at the same time adding to the sense of its being amenable to theoretical unification and simplification.

In this connection we should consider an important, though usually unnoticed, aspect of scientific theory, that Clifford Geertz, anthropologist, speaks of as follows:

In a recent study . . . the French anthropologist, Lévi-Strauss, remarks that scientific explanation does not consist, as we have been led to imagine, in the reduction of the complex to the simple. Rather, it consists, he says, in a substitution of a complexity, more intelligible for one which is less. So far as the study of man is concerned, one may go even farther, I think, and argue that explanation often consists of substituting complex pictures for simple ones while striving somehow to retain the persuasive clarity that went with the simple ones. . . . Scientific advancement commonly consists in a progressive complication of what once seemed a beautifully simple set of notions, but now seems an unbearably simplistic one.[12]

Can there be any doubt that science's ideas are typically

far more complex than those of "common sense?" Thus the latter's conception of the setting sun as an obvious descent of the sun is surely less complex than that of science, with its sophisticated idea of an ascending horizon due to the rotation of the earth. And isn't it true that as science discovers and endeavors to correlate and explain more and more phenomena and natural laws, its theories do become progressively more complex?

Certainly the Newtonian theory of motion was far more complex than that of Aristotelian physics. It dealt with many more features of motion, and therefore it had to employ more precisely differentiated concepts and formulate more logical and mathematical interrelationships among them. Later, relativistic mechanics (Einstein) was even more so, necessitated by its more sophisticated look at the relativities of motions and at a greatly extended range of masses, distances, times, and velocities. One crude though meaningful measure of such theoretical complexity is, I take it, the volume, variety, and ramifications of the knowledge and understanding it symbolizes and the amount of intellectual effort required to master it. Still later, quantum mechanics exhibited even more theoretical complexity, in this sense—and for the same basic reasons. Thus in general science's discovery of more and more complexity in nature is paralleled by more and more complexity in developing theory. And yet as scientists reflect upon such developments they come to feel, almost unanimously, that in this way their overall conception of nature has been enriched *by simplification*; and what they mean, I think, is *simplification by unification*.

I feel that, in view of our present knowledge and understanding, it is necessary to regard both complexity and simplicity as basic—and polar—aspects or qualities of nature, neither being more fundamental than the other. If so, this means that man's consciousness and sensibilities have expanded in another important direction, through the discovery of the importance and actual reality of complexity and simplicity in nature and of their proper complementary relationship.

Again I would like to quote from Professor Smith:

I see in materials engineering the germ of a new and broader kind of science, an attitude of mind, a method and a framework of knowledge applicable to many areas. . . .

The materials scientist has in large degree recaptured in more definite form many of the discarded intuitions of the past. He has returned to a direct and intimate concern with the qualities that fascinated man from the beginning, and the explanation of these properties is now seen to depend directly upon structure. . . . But significant structure is a mixture of perfection and imperfection. . . .

The whole story of man's relation to materials involves the interaction between the simple and complex. . . .

Science now relates to the two extremes of elementary atomistic physical chemistry on one hand and averaging thermodynamics on the other. But why cannot science develop a new approach encompassing the whole range? . . .

I predict the development of some new principles of hierarchy that will enable the effective resonance between molecule and organism to be explored. . . .

This approach would bring together fields that because of their special complexities have been unrelated; it would minimize the difference between the scientist and those who try to understand the human experience. It would incorporate the historian's interest in the past as the basis of the present and the artist's feeling for the complicated interrelatedness of things.[13]

What then is the bearing of all this on our conception and consciousness of mystery in nature? Is complexity more mysterious or incomprehensible, or more wonderful and glorious, than simplicity? Possibly, but not necessarily. My point is, however, that in the post-modern period complexity has come to be seen as an important basic aspect of concrete reality, whereas in the modern period it was largely disregarded as unimportant or at most as of secondary importance. What I find to be especially meaningful is not only the sheer existence and reality of complexity, but the fact that it increases with depth. As we shall see in the next chapter, this suggests unfathomability—and mystery.

There is also simplicity in nature, but its great significance for science lies in its meaning for theory. Simplicity has not disappeared, but it has become desirable to relinquish the notion of ultimate, all-explaining, atomistic simplicity. The significance of this newer understanding of the reality, and of the roles, of both complexity and simplicity in nature is psychological more than logical—and not inconsiderable. It seems that a belief in an ultimate building-block-and-field type of simplicity tends to block the sensing of mystery by tempting men to suppose that nature is ultimately fathomable, encompassable, and completely explicable. It tends to inhibit the imagination by foreclosing other possibilities of thought and thus seems to eliminate mystery and expel wonder. On the other hand, when such belief is relinquished, as I think it must be today, the imagination is freed to roam in reflection among the obviously manifold possibilities and wonders of complexity. The next chapter will bear directly on this problem.

VI. Nature's Reality Open or Closed?
   Its Relationality

THE GREATER THE DEPTH,
THE GREATER THE STRANGENESS

Our next question comes up invariably, it seems, whenever one reflects upon how unexpectedly many levels of depth have already been uncovered. Are there others still hidden? How many are there, all told? Is there a ground or bottom level—or, for that matter, a top one—beyond which there are no others? Is physical reality closed in depth or open?

The answer is, of course, that *science does not know and has no way of knowing* with certainty. For one thing it has no method for demonstrating that something supposed or imagined does not actually exist. It can show, as it has, that there are levels, and a large number of them, but not that the lowest one known is the lowest that exists, or that there is or is not a lowest one. This stubborn fact, that it can never be sure that there is nothing beyond its horizon at any time, constitutes for science a basic *unknown, and unknowable,* and is therefore an aspect of nature's genuine mystery.

On the other hand, scientists do have opinions on this subject, and reasons for these opinions. For some it is an article of "scientific faith" that a ground level must exist. Witness the following creedal affirmation by Prof. A. Pais in an article entitled "The Particles Jungle":

Finding these new forms of matter is exciting. It is also disquieting. Things are not nearly as simple as they seemed in the late 1940's. It is a basic creed of physics, as of other sciences, that Nature's ultimate design is simple. If something does not look simple it usually means that we have not reached the bottom of it. No one can *prove* that Nature must forever be simple, but this drive to simplicity has been an unfailing guide for 300 years. . . . We must continue to follow its lead.[1]

Many scientists agree, feeling with Pais that science's success amply verifies the assumption that has been so central in its thought: Nature is basically simple.

However, not all scientists subscribe to this alleged creed, for instance Snow and Lapp, who, as we have seen, point to recent findings as evidence against it. Consider also the following statement by Gerald Holton, professor of physics at Harvard:

In particle physics today one no longer believes that there are one or two or three very simple laws at the bottom of all this turmoil of spontaneous disintegration and creation of particles. On the contrary, a more correct view is that at the bottom of our simple laws there is a vast· sea, a flux of chaotic disorder in which these particles continually change and rearrange, a whole zoo of "virtual" particles that for small intervals of time disobey all the classical laws. A nineteenth-century physicist would find this view . . . intolerable. It may be that here is a warning to us that when things get very interesting, one has to give up these naïve harmonies and simplicities and must, as it were, face complexity on its own terms.[2] *

Realizing that it is not proper in either scientific or theological discussion to use statements out of context as proof texts, I have presented these simply as evidence that scientists do have diverging views on this subject. If, however, the view reported by Holton were to prevail it would be tantamount to abandoning the idea of a lowest level. For it is doubtful that "a vast sea of chaotic disorder" at "the bottom of our simple laws" can qualify as the *ground level* —where "ground" connotes in the classical sense an ultimate foundation on which all else rests and depends for its explication.

David Bohm, distinguished physicist and philosopher, suggests that not only does nature exhibit great qualitative variety—as we have already noted—but that its variety may possibly be unlimited, "infinite." As he puts it,[3] "Nature may have in it an infinity of different *kinds* of things, . . . an unlimited variety of . . . properties, qualities, entities,

---

systems, levels, etc., to which apply correspondingly new *kinds* of laws of nature" (italics mine).

One aspect of this limitless variety could be, he suggests further, that with increasing depth the nature of things becomes increasingly strange, and eventually so different from anything known elsewhere, that the very notion of level might have to be exchanged for another. He says that "it is evidently quite possible that as we penetrate further still, we will find that the character of the organization of things into levels will change so fundamentally that even the pattern of levels itself will eventually fade out and be replaced by something quite different."

This idea of increasing strangeness is not inconsistent with that of increasing complexity, and neither suggests convergence toward a ground of ultimate simplicity. Nor does the Holton observation that the "bottom" may be "a vast sea" or "flux of chaotic disorder."

Prof. John A. Wheeler, physicist at Princeton University, has also had some significant things to say along somewhat similar lines, in an address before the American Physical Society late in January of 1967. To avoid much of the technical idiom, I shall quote from the interpretation of it by Walter Sullivan, science writer of the *New York Times*, as follows:

He told them that, in the exploration of "elementary" particles, they were nowhere near the most fundamental level of matter. Coming dimly into view, he said, is a never-never land of the utterly small. . . . He pictured this ultra-small arena as alive with interactions of "stupendous" energy and said they take place not only within matter but in what we naively call a vacuum.

In an interview he pointed out that long ago, back in 1899, Max Planck had spoken of a basic unit of distance that came to be called the "Planck distance"

that was utterly small—100 billion billion times less than the width of an electron . . . [and] in Dr. Wheeler's view, it is on the scale of the Planck distance that enormously exciting things are taking place.

The events are so preposterously tiny, in their wave-like behavior, that incredible energy must be involved. This follows . . . from the well-established rule which says: the shorter the wavelength of light or other such radiation, the more energy in each wave.

One can say that in a thimbleful of vacuum there is more of this energy than would be released by all the atomic bomb fuel in the universe. . . . Thus even a total vacuum is the scene of "lively physics," he said.

On such a small scale time can have no meaning. . . . Hence Dr. Wheeler entitled his talk: "The End of Time."[4]

Before commenting on the general implications of these remarks, let us try to understand where this "well-established rule" comes from. There is a simple equation, $E = hn$, which expresses the established fact that the energy content (E) of a photon (a particle-wave of light) equals a constant (h) times its vibratory frequency (n). The greater the frequency of the light, the greater the energy content of the photon. But the nature of waves is such that as their frequency increases their wave length decreases. Thus it follows that the smaller the wave length, the larger is its energy content.

This rule or relation applies not only to photons but to other radiation and other micro-entities as well. The smaller one of them is, the shorter the wave length of its internal wave pattern must be (since small bodies can house only small waves), and the larger must be the amount of energy compressed into it. This is why an atomic nucleus, which is exceedingly small, has exceedingly much energy compared to that of a much larger molecule; and why a still smaller proton must have still more energy. This is why a micro-micro-entity as small as a Planck distance—100 billion billion times smaller than an electron— must be very strange indeed, with "incredible energy" and participating in "enormously exciting" types of events. En route toward greater depths, science has thus far encountered only increasing—not decreasing—strangeness.

IS THERE A LOWEST
AND A HIGHEST LEVEL?

What Wheeler is suggesting, then, is that very far below the levels of physical reality now known there may exist a never-never world of "levels" and "events" that is so utterly strange that in it even the fundamental concepts of distance and time lose all operational meaning, and it may be regarded as "empty." At such incredible depths the "empty" space (physical vacuum) of the interior of physical reality may therefore be conceived as having locked up in it stupendous amounts of energy, such that "in a thimbleful" of it "there is more of this energy than would be released by all the atomic bomb fuel of the universe." (By way of parenthetical side remark, it may turn out that some day man will be able to unlock some of this subnuclear energy, just as he was able to unlock nuclear energy. And it is not unlikely that nature itself is unlocking it in some parts of the meta-world, and that this may account for the incredible outpouring of energy by such celestial objects as the quasars, referred to in chapter III.)

What bearing does all this have on the main question of this chapter: Is there a bottom (innermost) level and/or a top (outermost) one? Is the universe bounded or unbounded in its vertical dimension? My thesis is that it is becoming disconcertingly difficult to reconcile the traditional notion of such bounding levels of matter with the recently discovered facts about the character and extent of its interior—and that this calls for radically different ideas.

It was but natural to suppose that there *must* be a fundament characterized by ultimate simplicity, when descending into matter yielded a sense of decreasing complexity there and increasing simplicity, and the feeling that the bewildering perplexities and diversities of materials and kaleidoscopic phenomena were being dissolved by the apparent unity and simplicity of atomistic matter. Now, however, when it is being said that the seemingly fundamental "simplicity has disappeared" and that the interior vistas of matter yield a sense of *increasing* complexity and strangeness, the idea of such a lowest level seems far from compelling. All this may be said also in principle about any possible upper boundary, for going outward also evokes a sense of increasing strangeness, as was mentioned earlier in the discussion of the meta-world.

The question now is not so much whether a given level may legitimately be designated as the lowest or highest one as it is whether there is a last level at all. Moreover, this becomes even more problematic in the face of indications that at great depths physical reality is so very strange that the very idea of discrete levels may not apply there and may have to be replaced by a radically different concept. Certainly this would be the case if the hierarchy of levels did at very great depths actually dissolve into "a vast sea, or flux of chaotic disorder," in which utterly strange events are commonplace and in which one encounters "the end of time."

There is another reason why the atomistic conception of a ground level is no longer so appealing, namely, that it conceived that ground to be essentially substantive— whereas for the post-modern scientific consciousness the traditional idea of substance has lost most of its value. In the past that idea served a most useful function, especially in connection with the question of what things *are made of*. It was a mighty advance in human understanding of the world when it was discovered that water is made up of two presumably primordial substances, hydrogen and oxygen; that table salt consists of the substances sodium and chlorine; and that indeed all physical things are combinations of a limited number of such elemental substances. Today, however, when we know how complex and strange these substances are in their interior, it serves no useful purpose to ask what the fundamental substantive content of their constituents is, and it leads nowhere except into blind alleys.

Science has learned to ask other kinds of questions, about what is much more important, namely, the dynamics of such entities as protons and neutrons, i.e., about the relationships, processes, and events in which they participate. Indeed, the only way micro-entities can be identified and defined meaningfully is in terms of their behavior. Thus a proton is "that" which behaves in a certain way when it encounters another proton, or a neutron, or electron, or photon, or still other entities. A neutron, on the other hand, is characterized and defined by a different pattern of behavior. Metaphorically speaking, what is really significant about such entities is, as Andrews suggested, not the stuff they are made of but the music they make.

This is what is most significant not only of individual

entities but also of whole-systems—of the overall hierarchy of physical reality and of the world as a whole; it is their relational and symphonic character. And, as we shall consider presently, in such a world no substance-ground is required, no lowest atomistic level.

If now, by way of summary, we again ask our principal question, whether physical reality is closed or open in its depth, we must emphasize that we simply cannot be sure one way or the other. But for me—and I am not alone in this —such knowledge as we now possess points rather persuasively to the probability that depth in matter-energy is unlimited and that in this respect physical reality is open. It is not useful, therefore, to speak of a ground or ceiling level. Nor would thinking of the world as open, i.e., without a physical ground—or ceiling, for that matter—be inconsistent with anything we actually know.

FUNDAMENTAL VERSUS RELATIONAL: A BOOTSTRAP CONCEPTION

For many persons, I suspect, the creedal faith Pais speaks of is compelling not only because it has paid off as a guide in the scientific quest but because it satisfies a basic human need. Man is so constituted that he needs not only particular knowledge but inclusive understanding—a vision of the world as a whole-system. He would find it intolerable if, when looking out upon the world, he could discern only unrelatedness, complexity, diversity, and disorder. To keep his sanity he must be able to see interrelations and interdependencies, and patterns of repetitive temporal change, something he can count on predictably and build on, so to speak.

Now this need for a systemic understanding of the world has been met traditionally in science by the classical concept of a materialistic or substantive foundation-and-superstructure type of system; hence the feeling that a "rock bottom" level is absolutely necessary. This is not, however, the only possible option. Reality may be thought of primarily as a cybernetic network of circuits, or an organism, or a society of things, relationships, events, and processes —more like a delicate fabric than an edifice of brick and mortar. In such a case the idea of an indispensable foundation would be very much less appropriate. Such a system could be either bounded or unbounded, finite or infinite.

The one model may appropriately be called fundamentalist in character and the other relationalist. These two opposing approaches are described lucidly by Prof. Geoffrey Chew, of the University of California at Berkeley. (In referring to the second type of model he uses the very suggestive terms "self-consistency model," "bootstrapper's model," and "antifundamentalist view.") I quote:

> Physicists usually perceive their discipline's goal as the reduction of nature to fundamentals, and the high-energy arena has correspondingly been dominated by the search for "basic building blocks." Finding the quark is for the moment regarded by many as the ultimate prospective triumph; failure to find some such fundamental entity is equated with frustration. There exists, nontheless, a 180-degree inverted point of view, which envisions the absence of fundamentals as the ultimate triumph; this is the bootstrap attitude.
>
> The bootstrapper seeks to understand nature not in terms of fundamentals but through self-consistency, believing that all of physics flows uniquely from the requirement that components be consistent with one another and with themselves.[5]

This is referred to also as the "democratic model," since it regards all of the many species of micro-entities as equally basic to the integrity and self-consistency of the whole system; none is *the* fundamental one. Thus the electrons, protons, neutrons, neutrinos, mesons, and all the rest—a hundred or two in number—are seen to constitute a democracy, none of whose members outranks the rest in fundamental importance, and all of which derive their own unique significance from their dynamic interactions with the others and with the total system which they constitute collectively.

In a sense, then, this view is not only antifundamental but antihierarchical, since a hierarchy is often taken to be "a body of rulers disposed organically in ranks and orders, each subordinate to the one above it" (Webster), and because in this proposed scheme of things there are neither rulers nor subordinates. Does this mean that this relationalist view requires disregarding or renouncing the findings of science we have been studying with regard to the hierarchical organization, ordering and structuring of the interior depths of physical reality? No! For according to another standard meaning the term hierarchy denotes no more than a simple ordinal arrangement or ranking of items without any implication of foundational importance. If the existence of various types of micro-entities be granted, and that of interior levels and depths also, then the concept of the hierarchical arrangement of the former relative to the latter is definitely indicated, and from a bootstrapper's point of view quite acceptable—provided this does not carry fundamentalist implications with it. Just because one kind of entity exists within another, or at a lower level in the total scheme of things, this need not mean that it is therefore more fundamental.

Many people have serious difficulty with this conception of reality and the world. "If there is no foundation," they ask, "where do we stand? Upon what can we build to avoid being swept away by storm and flood? Whence comes the solid support for the vast array of structures that make up the micro-, macro-, and meta-worlds that are situated one upon another? Surely they can't simply float on thin air." What they fail to realize is that such misgivings arise from a mode of thought that is appropriate to concern about the strength and stability of stationary structures, such as buildings, bridges, and dams, for which the need of an adequate foundation is of supreme importance; whereas there are many other types for which it is not, e.g., moving structures such as cars, ships, and rockets—and living organisms such as animals and human beings. These are strong or weak by virtue of their internal forces and inter-relationships without regard to any foundation or under-pinning. The former kind of structure is fundamentalist in character, while the other is relational. And it is the latter that is taken as a model by the bootstrappers for interpreting the character of the world. It is the kind of model for which the main emphasis of thought and concern is upon internal interaction and interdependence, mutual support and systemic wholeness and self-consistency. It is the kind of system in which no individual member is more fundamental than any others. It is a democratic system, and in the case of nature or the world it is one in which the meaning and role of each part derives for the most part from its relationships with its neighbors or fellow members and from the whole system.

UNFATHOMABLE AND MYSTERIOUS

What we have been leading up to is the thought that physical reality and nature in general are unfathomable by scientific exploration and analysis—we can't get to the "bottom" or "top" of it. That this is the case is much more than only a feeling or suspicion, for, as we have seen, there is much evidence for it, even though no indisputable proof. It would be most unfortunate, however, if the reader were left with the impression that thought about the openness and unboundedness of the world in the vertical dimension were confined exclusively to the realm of the inanimate. It is probably true that physics and chemistry have done more than any other of the sciences to acquaint us in rather precise terms with the hierarchical organization of physical reality and with the concept of levels. But these sciences do not undertake in their own right to explore all aspects of that reality. It is conceivable—or even probable—that animate physical reality may have organizational aspects, kinds of relationships, structures and events, over and above those toward which physics and chemistry are oriented. At least this is the intuitive feeling of many scientists working in biology, psychology, and psychiatry. Over and over again have I heard some of them say with considerable conviction that the longer they work with plants and animals, or especially with human beings, the more sure they become that there are realities and depths in the animate world that have not yet been touched, much less explored, by their sciences or any others. And many feel that the depths to be explored there are indeed unlimited.

Note, for instance, the following remarks by an eminent psychologist, Prof. David Bakan:

The self-definitional activity of man, in substance and in concept, is his most abiding characteristic beyond any specific definition of him; and both the scientific and the religious enterprises are expressions of this self-definitional activity. *This impulse presupposes that the manifest is but the barest hint of reality, that beyond the manifest there exist the major portions of reality, and that the function of the impulse is to reach out toward the unmanifest. . . .* No matter how far our explorations go, and no matter how much we manage to uncover, there is always the infinite world of the unmanifest.[6]

Returning now to the sense of mystery in nature, we can recognize in the writings of scientists at least three aspects of it related to infinity and openness. First, there is the sense of the wonder of *the infinite, unfathomable unknown.* As Victor Weisskopf, distinguished physicist, puts it in his charming book *Knowledge & Wonder,*[7] "Our knowledge is an island in the infinite ocean of the unknown." We have already referred to science's eternal ignorance of what lies beyond its horizon. Now we extend this notion to a definite sense of the infinity of that beyond, to what Bakan calls the infinite unmanifest.

But what right does Weisskopf have to speak of an "infinite ocean?" Why not simply a *vast* one? Perhaps at least a partial answer can be discerned from the context of his assertion: "Every great scientific discovery creates new problems when it solves old ones. When we know more, we have more questions to ask. Our knowledge is an island in the infinite ocean of the unknown."

I still remember how shocked I was when I heard Harlow Shapley assert, about twenty years ago, that as science adds to what *is* known about nature it does not subtract from the total of what *is not* known. This sounded like utter nonsense. When he was asked how this could possibly be, he answered, as I remember it, that it is not a question of how it *can* be but of how it *is*, a question not of metaphysical presupposition but of fact and evidence. And then he gave the evidence, namely, that in the history of scientific discovery every answer to a question about nature gives rise to more questions, and the answer to each of these to still others, and so on in a diverging series of more and more questions. If the world were a closed finite system, one would expect convergence in the long run, and science would eventually run out of anything to ask. But nothing whatsoever in the experience of science indicates that there is such convergence. Many scientists agree with Shapley, though they may say it differently.

Kenneth Boulding goes further in saying, "As our knowledge grows so does our ignorance."[8] Henry Margenau suggests the same general thought by the title, and contents, of his book *Open Vistas*. Often this sentiment is expressed much more casually. For example, at the very end of a technical paper entitled "Meson Factories," Louis Rosen of Los Alamos remarks that "if a facility can resolve present problems in a unique way, one can confidently expect that new ones will arise at least as fast as the present ones are resolved."[9]

In all probability the intent of these men is to say that the number of mystery-problems facing science, the amount of the as-yet-unknown, is unlimited, and that science will never be without significant problems to solve. In this sense the unknown awaiting investigation is infinite and unfathomable. It is not asserted, however, that any particular problems are insoluble, or that any phenomenon is inherently unknowable or unexplainable. Surely science must assume that any observable event that presents itself can in time be explained to a significant extent. And yet the thought that science's as yet unsolved problems are innumerable, and that its research will in a sense never reduce the amount of the unknown, certainly points to—even though it does not "prove" the existence of—genuine *mystery*, that *of the infinity of the unknown in nature*.

The second aspect of mystery we encounter among scientists in this connection is that of *the infinity and unfathomability of the known*, as discerned in the limitless internal depths and content of physical reality. Having looked at the boundless unknown beyond the horizon, we now look inside the circle at Weisskopf's island of the known. A statement like Shapley's, or the first part of Weisskopf's, is often interpreted as applying also to the known, that any phenomenon or bit of matter already well known will upon further investigation turn out to be inexhaustible in the profusion of structures, relationships, and processes it displays, both internally and externally. The substance wood, for example, has been known rather well for a long time, yet, as we have seen, every bit of it, cell or molecule or atom, seems inexhaustible and unfathomable.

I was delighted to discover, soon after the third volume of Tillich's *Systematic Theology* appeared, that he was fully aware of this mystery-aspect of nature; for he had this to say, in a perfectly wonderful discussion of the "greatness of the physical universe": " 'Mystery' here means the infinity of questions with which every answer confronts the human mind. Reality, every bit of reality, is inexhaustible and points to . . . mystery . . . which transcends the endless series of scientific questions and answers." In that context he points out that, while the phrase "greatness of the physical universe" usually refers to the "quantitative vastness of the universe in time and space," it refers also to the "qualitative mystery of the structures of every particle of the physical universe as well as to the structure of the whole."[10]

It seems obvious that Tillich is thinking of what Bohm called the *"infinite qualitative variety of nature"* that is apparent especially *in its depths*. This, I should say, is the third aspect of mystery to be noted here.

VII. The Depths of Time;
the Developmental Character of Reality

TIME'S RELATIONAL CHARACTER

Temporality is so fundamental and obvious an aspect of human existence that the concept of time seems quite indispensable to any satisfactory description or interpretation of the world. There is, however, something so tantalizing, elusive, and baffling—and truly mysterious— about it that it has been the subject of much philosophic debate for ages, during which time no unanimity of opinion has been achieved as to its fundamental nature or its basic significance for the cosmos. In some cultures it is regarded as essentially cyclical, in others as linear; in some as bounded, in others as unbounded—without beginning or end.

There are, of course, various kinds of time, e.g., psychological, historical, physical time. Physical scientists deal with the kind they can measure with clocks, i.e., in terms of the uniformities of motion of, say, the earth or pendulums or atomic oscillators. This temporality is especially significant for our purposes, because it refers to that dimension of the actual world without which it seems impossible adequately to conceive or describe the phenomena of motion, change, and becoming. This is physical time.

One of its features disclosed by post-modern science is that it is rather different from the way Newton conceived it to be, as set forth in his *Principia*: "Absolute, true, and mathematical time, of itself, and from its own nature, flows equably and without regard to anything external, and by another name is called duration." As discerned today it is not absolute but relational. Moreover, it has a unique relationship to space, which is also relational; and together they constitute an indissectable continuum, space-time, of which each is a component complementary to the other.

To say, from the viewpoint of physical science, that there is no separate or independent space or time but only the reality space-time is not to make a primarily philosophical assertion but rather a strictly scientific one, since it refers fundamentally not to metaphysical abstractions but to concrete things and events. What it says is that in general the timing of events calls for the use not only of clocks to measure time but also of rods to measure distance. One reason for this is that observed physical events always occur at a distance, near or far, from an observer. Since signals are transmitted not instantaneously but with finite velocities (e.g., with the speed of sound or light), the distances from the observed events and the observer must be taken into account. For example, to measure the time when a space ship is lost sight of behind the moon, one cannot simply tick off its disappearance and reappearance with some sort of stop watch but must allow for the time it takes the signals to traverse the distances from the moon to the observer. Thus space measurements become integrally a part of the measurement of time intervals, and vice versa.

Unfortunately—or fortunately—when such situations are analyzed rigorously they are found to be much more complex than these simple considerations suggest. Thus if several observers were to measure a given time interval between two events they would in general get different results, depending upon their various positions and motions relative to the events. It turns out that the simplest way of resolving such perplexing complexities is that of Einstein's relativity theory, in which time and space are regarded as constituting one integrated reality, space-time. From this point of view the only way different observers can get the same result is for them to measure the combined "space-time interval" between the events, rather than only the supposedly separate time and distance intervals. And that "space-time interval" can be computed by a formula combining those separated intervals.[1]

To have learned this about time is to have seen it in some

depth, rather than only superficially. Again we note that to see anything in depth means seeing it not in isolation but in its relational involvement with other realities, and to learn that its basic character derives in large part from that involvement.

Again we ask why so fundamental a relationship as "space-time" was not discovered until so recently. One reason is that modern science dealt only with what was essentially local rather than extended time, i.e., with events that were so close to the observer[2] that the space factors were negligible—both because they actually were small and because light signals seemed to be transmitted instantaneously. For post-modern science, however, the world has become very large and the speed of light far from infinite. Many happenings that science must consider are so far away that the space factors actually force themselves upon our attention as being not only important in themselves but in principle inseparable from the time factors.

THE PHYSICAL
CONTENT OF TIME

Not only, however, have our post-modern instruments and ideas opened our eyes to the world of extended time but to the internal depths of local or momentary time. Moments of time once regarded as negligible in duration, and empty of content, are now seen to be temporal worlds of vast depth and dynamism. Certainly not long ago a second seemed to be a very small bit of time. Now it seems very large indeed, and we know it to be packed with huge amounts of activity (temporal reality), for instance in electronic computers that achieve in one second what large teams of human computers could achieve formerly only in months or years. Consider also the incredibly many natural micro-events that normally occur within atoms in a small part of a second. Talk about millionths and even billionths of seconds is now commonplace, and we have a feeling of familiarity for the vast content that may be found within such short moments. The following graphic description by Max Born illustrates this strikingly:

The electrons in the inner shells of a light atom like lithium vibrate about 10^{17} times per second—a colossal number! Let us compare it with long intervals of time and ask ourselves the question, what happened 10^{17}* seconds ago? In one year there are $60 \times 60 \times 24 \times 365 = 3 \times 10^7$ seconds, so that 10^{17} seconds come to about 3×10^9 or 3000 million years. This is a longer time than that which has elapsed since the formation of the first solid crust on the earth. With the heavier atoms, the number of times the inner electrons vibrate in a single second is many times greater than the number of seconds since the "creation of the world"![3]

Surely a second of time containing so huge a number of vibrations of a physical electron-wave must be said to be far from empty. In view of Professor Wheeler's suggestions, noted in the preceding chapter, it is not unlikely that in the not too distant future we shall be employing very much larger numbers, and even stranger ideas, to talk about the depths of local or momentary time—of a "now."

It has been said that in science the present—now—is no more than a dimensionless, mathematical point between the past and future and that therefore it has lost virtually all concrete meaning. I suggest that this is not actually the case, and that scientists employ the term *now* in two ways, with an abstract and a concrete meaning. The one does indeed denote only a mathematical point, with no extension or content, a pure abstraction, which can be given, I suspect, little operational meaning. It does, however, have great theoretical significance, as a delineator between two periods of time or as a point on a time scale. The second scientific usage of *now* connotes a time interval, short or long, that is far from empty. Thus scientists often make statements like these: "Some time ago this object was cold; *now* it is hot." "This equipment was out of order; *now* it is again operating properly." "The cell is dividing *now*." "Crystalization is taking place *now*." "We once thought of light as waves exclusively, but *now* we know it has particle properties also." In each of these cases, the

---

* For those not acquainted with the mathematical notation used above, the number 10^{17} means 10 multiplied by itself seventeen times and is equal to the number 100,000,000,000,000,000.

now is an extended now. Were this usage not available to scientists they would be greatly handicapped in the reporting of their work, for in their professional experience the *present* is in fact often taken to be a period of time that endures "for a while," and is characterized by a degree of uniformity of happenings that clearly distinguishes that extended moment from the past or future, and is not merely a point of time separating the latter. Even the briefest of experienced moments, or concrete *nows*, are sensed as durations in which much *is* happening (not did or will happen). And I suspect that some day we shall come to sense that they are actually unbounded in depth and that therefore time as a whole—as well as space-time—is unfathomable and genuinely mysterious. Many men are conscious of this even now.

Returning to extended, rather than local, time there is another sense in which post-modern science has given us a feeling for its depth, and this is related to the spatial immensity of the stellar universe. The fact that many stars are now known to be as far away as billions of light years has great significance for our consciousness of time. Were an informed latter-day (post-modern) psalmist to look at the nocturnal heavens, he would be aware of much more than were his ancient Hebrew predecessors. Not only would he see, as did they, the grandeur, beauty, and radiance of the celestial spectacle, its stately, uniform march across the sky, and its repetitive features from day to day and year to year, but he would be aware of seeing spread out before him a tremendous panorama of time and change —in a momentary view of much of cosmic history in its physical aspects. Of course, in his reflections upon the sight he would call upon the knowledge that has come to him by means of his remarkable instruments. What this would tell him is that when he looks *now* at the stars he sees them not as they are *now* but as they were when long ago they emitted the light that enters his eyes or instruments *now*. Seeing a star ten light-years away is seeing it as of ten years ago; seeing one a billion light-years distant is seeing it as of a billion years ago. Whether or not these stars are still there *now* the observer does not know, but he does know that they were there respectively ten and a billion years ago. What he sees for the most part, therefore, is exceedingly ancient history. This is indeed seeing time in depth—in this case, the depth of its long-range extension. Here is direct evidence, and direct consciousness, of the immensity of the temporal extent of cosmic existence in its physical aspects. Here in one present *now* we become aware of the reality of a long sequence of myriads of *nows* scattered over the vast expanse of the past.

For the post-modern "seer" a momentary now-look means even more, aside from the implications of vast stellar distances. His ancient forebears knew, of course, that the stars were not all alike—some were brighter than others, and they differed in color—but not why. He, however, knows also that they differ in other respects, for instance, in mass, size, density, internal pressure and temperature, as well as in "age," and that these correlate with "color." And to a large extent he knows why this is so. The informed stargazer of today realizes also that the mere fact of a star's visibility has great significance, for it means that at some time in the past it emitted light and was therefore losing energy (typically millions of tons of mass-energy per second) and undergoing change. Moreover, he can account for the output of energy by stars in terms of a continual "nuclear cooking" in their interiors, a process in which nuclear reactions occur spontaneously and a synthesis of atomic nuclei is achieved on a very large scale.

Thus there is among the stars a variety of sequential changes, of different stages of change, and a variety of "types" of stars—all of which suggest that there must be stellar development or evolution. This insight adds another dimension to our understanding of, and feel for, the physical content of time intervals. In one glance we see in action, so to speak, countless different stages of stellar evolution. Looking at one star we see stellar evolution in an early stage. Another shows what a later stage is like. Others typify other developmental stages. One senses in this way that evolutionary development is a universal phenomenon or process; it takes in all of existence, animate and inanimate; and it is both trans-biological and trans-terrestrial.

SPACE-TIME AS THE LOCUS
OF INNOVATIVE CHANGE

This remarkable vision of long-range *time-and-evolutionary-change*, with its truly cosmic perspective, did not come to man until the post-modern period. However, the foundation for it was laid earlier, especially by the Darwinian discovery that there reigns in nature not only order and lawfulness (in the Newtonian billiard-ball sense) but disorder and randomness and thus "pure chance," and that out of this combination of lawfulness-and-randomness there emerges a developmental process or "struggle" which, given sufficient time, would bring about basic change through the emergence of genuine novelty. From the viewpoint of the notions of static perfection and complete determinateness of the world that had prevailed earlier, this was a strange and unorthodox conceptual development but a truly epoch-making one, for it introduced to scientific thought, and made scientifically orthodox, the idea of the chanciness and unpredictability of nature.

Add to this the notion of the universality of this evolutionary process, and time has been given a new meaning: that of the carrier or locus of innovative change. Prior to this development the "equable flowing of time" was thought to leave the world itself, as distinguished from human history occurring on it, quite unchanged in its essentials. To be sure, the mechanistically conceived world-machine moved with time in many ways, but it did not itself change. The thought of Darwin and his age changed all this. Not much longer thereafter could the ideas survive that the world is a machine and that time can pass without inexorably bringing change with it—in the natural world itself. In this sense extended, and especially very long-range, time began to take on dynamic significance—not that it became a direct cause of change but that fundamental change came to be seen as an inevitable concomitant of it.

It seems, however, that in the Darwinian century this vision had a predominently terrestrial perspective, rather than a truly cosmic one, and that its evolutionary thought derived more from biological than from physical evidence. Even the geological evolutionary conceptions of the time seem to have rested more upon paleontological (and hence biological) considerations than upon physical geology. And, so far as I am aware, there was no thought then that there might have been an evolutionary development of inanimate matter itself.

In retrospect this incompleteness of conception is quite understandable. Certainly the exploration of the universe had not gone far enough in either space or time to provide a sufficiently extensive outlook, or one deep enough to raise evolutionary questions about matter itself. The nebular hypotheses of Kant and Laplace[4] were ingenious, and in important respects sound in principle as judged by today's standards for cosmogonic investigation. They were, however, constructed without benefit of knowledge of the hierarchical organization of the physical universe and, more specifically, of the existence of the micro- or meta-hierarchies as we know them now. They envisaged little more than the region we have been calling the macro-world, our planetary system and the rather shallow neighboring region of stars and nebulae which was all that was actually known then. And the primordial substance of the nebulae was apparently conceived atomistically, in the Newtonian billiard-ball sense.

Post-modern science has then done two things for our consciousness of time: first, it has made us aware of its vast "internal" and "external" depths, with their tremendous dynamic contents respectively of very short-range or micro-events and processes and of very long-range or meta-ones; and, second, it has shown that time is coupled with, as an inseparable concomitant of its long-range passage, the universal phenomenon of perpetual basic evolutionary change. We speak of it as universal because we sense that it takes place throughout all of space-time-and-depth and at all levels of physical reality, animate and inanimate. Matter itself has been coming into being with time, gradually, step by step, increasing its content and complexity of structure and happening. As we see it now, not all its hierarchical levels were always in existence.

There are, of course, different contemporary cosmogonic theories of the development of the cosmos, or of patches of it here and there, such as the region of our sun and its retinue of planets. Readers would do well at this point to renew acquaintance with the writings along these lines of Gamow, Hoyle, Weizsäcker, Shapley, Teilhard de Chardin,* and others, since we should not take time out to review their theories in detail here. While their conceptions differ in many respects, most of them assume, it seems to me, that there was a time long ago when in our region of the universe there were only elementary particles, or at most only hydrogen atoms, and that in time ever larger combinations of these came into being.

As noted earlier, the particles found at the various levels of physical reality have the capacity for combination or aggregation to produce the structures of the next higher levels. We must now note explicitly that this process of aggregation has the dimension of time and is developmental in character. Because of this there has been an evolutionary development of matter-energy by a succession of epochal aggregations, each of which constituted the emergence of something new. Long-range time has thus had as its concomitant not only *change of what is* but a gradual stepwise *coming into being of what was not*—an actual emergence of genuine novelty. Thus we recognize that *with time there occurs becoming.*

This "innovative becoming" refers, however, not only to the emergence of material objects, for it brought forth also the vast profusion of qualities that, as we have seen, characterize matter in bulk. Thus the emergence of molecules and their subsequent aggregation yielded under some circumstances liquids and therefore the remarkable quality of liquidity; and under other circumstances solids and the quality of solidity; and under still others the qualities of gases; and yet others plasmas. With some there emerged metals and metalicity; with others plastics and plasticity. *And*, as we shall consider more fully in the next chapter, with the appearance of certain long-chain molecules there

---

* Their pertinent writings have all been mentioned earlier herein.

emerged the remarkable ability of self-reproduction, in other words the quality-reality of "being alive." Much later many such molecules joined with still others to produce organisms, plants and animals, with the qualities of sensitivity and responsiveness to stimuli—and more complex life. After many additional emergences, very much later, man came on the scene with the quality-realities of mind and spirit developed to a quite unprecedented degree, so much so that he became consciously creative. What he produced was a new environment characterized by civilization and cultures, and thus there emerged into space-time a new kind of evolutionary causal entity, namely, cultural evolution, which has in turn introduced into the total scheme of things novel forces, energies, and controls of unprecedented potency.

What a remarkable story this is! And what a remarkable reservoir of possibilities, and consequent actualities, has somehow been associated with time and been unveiled by its passage! And what a tremendous span of time must be wrapped up in this development! But we can now say more than that, for post-modern science has developed a variety of powerful methods for measuring extended time, so that we now know a great deal about how much time is involved and about the age of, say, the earth. Estimates based on these measurements, and on cross-checks among them, propose for the earth's age from two to five billion years.

TERRESTRIAL AND COSMIC HISTORY

To give us a sense of the timing of various developments in the history of the planet earth and of the cosmos, Prof. G. M. McKinley, of the University of Pittsburgh, has suggested the following enlightening time scale. Taking the figure of two billion years as the age of the earth, let it be represented by one calendar year, with January 1 as the beginning of terrestrial history and December 31 as the present. On this scale one day represents approximately 5,500,000 years of terrestrial history, one hour about 200,000 years, one minute about 4,000 years, and one second 65 years. According to current evolutionary thought, life, represented by the self-replicating molecules, appeared in February, unicellular organisms in April, and the primitive invertebrates late in May. Land plants emerged in the summer, and the large reptiles, brainy mammals, and birds in the fall. Then on December 31, four hours before midnight, man appeared, equipped with sensitive hands. "An hour or so later he makes tentative efforts at social life, but it is not until the last minute of the year that his first civilization is organized." The axial period occurred little more than half a cosmic minute ago, and post-modern science less than one second ago.[5]

Thus far we have touched only on terrestrial (or near-terrestrial) developments. Clearly, however, the history of our solar system is but a small fraction of cosmic history, which latter, according to present estimates, extends over at least twenty to thirty billions of years—ten to fifteen times the age of our earth. About what has been, or is now, happening in the far reaches of space-time in the evolution of matter, life, mind, and spirit we know virtually nothing. There are, however, some possibilities or even probabilities that may be of considerable significance. According to some scientists it is highly probable that there are scattered among the stars myriads of planets suitable for habitation by beings somewhat like us. Harlow Shapley goes so far as to assert that "*millions of planetary systems must exist, and billions is the better word,*" and that "we are not alone."[6] If this is so, human history, which is an exceedingly small part of terrestrial history, is an even smaller part of cosmic history, and humanity is only one of many "humanlike" races of beings in the universe. Some of these may have developed much farther than we have, physically, mentally, and socially, and some may have *come and gone*, in some sense, before our planet was born. No doubt others, like ours, are still becoming.

Other scientists will have nothing to do with this idea. They argue from the statistics of genetics that the chances of the appearance of humanlike beings elsewhere in the universe are so small as to "prove" that it is impossible. It will be interesting to see what future studies will reveal. In the meantime the fact that such possibilities are regarded as probabilities by a respected segment of the science community has for many men intensified their sensitivity to things cosmic and added to the power of the creative imagination with which they conceive and reflect upon them.

It has often been said that one of the most distinctive features of man is his awareness of himself and his world as a product of evolution, and that this was the gift of modern science. If this be so, it is post-modern science that must be credited with making this awareness truly cosmic in its outreach. This has made possible for him a more meaningful understanding of his position and role in the whole scheme of things. It means, of course, that—fortunately—he can no longer suppose himself to be the unique center of the universe, either in location or in significance. Indeed, he now realizes that he is far from the center of the stellar expanse explored thus far. As for his cosmic significance, in view of the possibility that there may well be other intelligent races of beings aside from his own, he is much less likely to make a claim to cosmic uniqueness, and especially the kind that in a self-arrogating sense he is "the crown of creation." If this be a loss, however, it is amply compensated for by the gain in cosmic dignity that comes through the recognition of his possible status as one of many humanlike beings in the universe, and even more through his understanding himself to be integrally a part of the cosmic process in more than a mere spectator's role. In this way, I believe, man is being freed from excessive preoccupation with, and anxiety about, himself and his alleged "aloneness" and is being given a more healthy sense of "belonging" and of "being at home in the universe"—at home with a sense both of responsibility toward it and of the availability to him of considerable power for discharging such responsibility.

MYSTERY IN THE REALM OF TIME

Now let us reflect briefly upon the mystery of time. Early in this chapter I said that there was something not only tantalizingly baffling but genuinely mysterious about time. For one thing there is so much we do not know or understand about it: what its ultimate nature is; whether it should be thought of as bounded or unbounded in depth and extent; whether it may also be evolving fundamentally, with the realities to which it is related or which it relates; whether causal dynamism and the evolutionary drive are only concomitants of its passage, or actual aspects of time or space-time itself. There is the question of how sure we dare be of the "truth" or "reality" of the long ranges we attribute to time and to cosmic history. Our ideas about them are, as we have seen earlier, in part discoveries of what is actually the case and in part the inventions of our minds; how much of this empirico-theoretical "mix" may need to be changed in the future to enable us more adequately to conceive time and time-space or space-time? Probably most such questions are not of the kind that can ever be answered finally and are not therefore simply temporary, as-yet-unsolved puzzle mysteries. Rather they may be intimations of genuine, unfathomable mystery—*mystery conceived as the quantity of the unknown.*

On the other hand, there is also very much we do know about time. Science's long experience with it has shown it to be such that the farther its depths are penetrated, both internally and externally, and the more is learned about its various aspects, the more questions it makes possible and the more wondrously mysterious it shows itself to be—in the sense of *mystery as a quality of the known.* Like the mystery of matter, it is forever beckoning to the investigator and unceasingly yielding more knowledge and insight —without seeming any the less unfathomable ultimately.

And this can be said also about the evolutionary process of change and becoming that seems so inextricably entwined with time. Even though there is obviously very much we do not know about it, we have come to know so much that it too appears as a most gloriously mysterious aspect of the universe—and apparently of everything in it.

One feature of evolutionary change that needs more consideration in this connection is that it is both a creative and a destructive process, and that because of it physical reality must be regarded as itself both creative and destructive or degenerative. This is the subject of the next chapter.

VIII. Nature's Unity and Disunity, Creativity and Destructiveness

THE CONTINUUM:
MATTER-ENERGY-LIFE-MIND-SPIRIT

The following two propositions are basic to the thesis of this and the next two chapters. First: all entities, events, and relationships observed by science, such as nucleons and molecules, crystals and mountains, plants and animals, men and their communities, planets and galaxies, and all quality-realities, such as hotness and coldness, liquidity and solidity, plasticity and metalicity, vitality and mentality, are manifestations of but one single integrated reality, which I have been calling "physical reality," the singleness and unity of which I now symbolize by the hyphenated term *matter-energy-life-mind-spirit*. Second: this "physical reality" is remarkably versatile and has the capacity for unlimited creativity, which down through the ages has revealed itself in the long sequence of evolutionary emergences by which the world has come into being. This view denies that any other substance or agency is needed for the scientific understanding of any physically observable entities or phenomena, or of their genesis. As science has come to know such fundamental realities of nature as matter, energy, electricity, life, and mind, they are seen to be not independent, primary substances or essences but simply contingent states of the one physical reality. How they may be regarded by philosophy or theology is another matter and is not under consideration at this point.

From older, conventional viewpoints these propositions seem very strange or even downright nonsensical, for it certainly was orthodox for a long time, both philosophically and scientifically, to espouse pluralisms and to assume the existence of many primal coexistent, coeternal, self-sufficient, and unchanging substances, fluids, or essences. Thus presumably a cold piece of iron was thought to become hot only when and because a weightless heat-fluid (caloric) flowed into it; and it became cold when that fluid departed. Similarly a chunk of glass could presumably be electrified only by inducing a hypothetical electric fluid to enter it, perhaps by transfer from another object, say by friction. Inanimate bodies became animate, supposedly, when an essence called life entered into them, and death ensued when that life departed. Similarly a living body could reason only when it was inhabited by a primordial essence called mind. Such thinking made much sense in its day, for its concepts accorded with the facts then known. Today, however, the new knowledge demands more unitary and holistic thinking.

To begin with, what do some of our key words mean, for instance the term *physical*? In scientific circles it often refers simply to physics, e.g., the American Physical Society, or the *Physical Review*. This is not my meaning here. Another usage makes it synonymous with *material* or *bodily*. This is not mine either. A third meaning is: "of nature" or "the natural." This *is* my intent, in a broad sense. I take not only matter, energy, and life but also mind and spirit to be realities that are encountered in nature and become known, at least in part, through scientific investigation. Therefore, they are at least in part "of nature" and "physical." *Nature*, in turn, means for me,[1] as I believe it does for most scientists, *the whole economy or system of observable phenomena and things, including man and his social institutions, having space-time relations and held together in a field or web of cause-and-effect relationships.* According to my usage, all the individual realities of nature, including those mentioned above, are *physical in so far as they are manifest to science.* And it is asserted here that they are all manifestations of one grand, comprehensive reality I have been calling *physical reality*.

Now just what does it mean to say that the scientifically discernible realities of nature are actually only different manifestations or aspects of that one physical reality? Perhaps we can clarify this by analogy to similar language about the familiar substance, H_2O. At low temperatures it manifests itself as solid, ice; at somewhat higher temperatures as liquid. Under still different conditions it may be a gaseous vapor, or even a plasma. To explain then what H_2O is, it is not enough simply to say that it is water in its usual sense. Actually we must refer to four entities with radically different properties and say that they are not independent realities but four interrelated states of the substance we are talking about, water-substance. No one of the four states is any more basic than the others, in the sense that it is the ground to which they are "reducible." They all have equal status as contingent forms of the elemental stuff that is H_2O and may be symbolized by the hyphenated term ice-water-vapor-plasma. Thus water-substance is a multiple reality that has the internal resources enabling it to take on amazingly different forms, with radically different qualities, as it interacts dynamically with its environment under various physical circumstances.

Clearly, then, if it makes its appearance as a solid, this is not because an independent essence called solidity has entered into it. And if it then sublimates, i.e., turns into vapor by direct evaporation from the solid state without first melting to a liquid, this does not mean that an essence, that might be called vaporousness (or vapor-essence) has invaded it and displaced the solidity (or solid-essence). To explain these different forms (and still others, e.g., the critical transitions between the stable states), we need appeal to no hypothetical substances or essences; the actual properties of the water-substance itself suffice, when correlated with the physical conditions surrounding it.

We have become so completely habituated, in this type of unifying thinking about such substances as water, that its value as a general method, and the potency of the conceptions it has brought forth, now seem obvious. It is but natural therefore that we increasingly think this way also about physical reality as a whole, beginning with the elimination of needless hypothetical substances. Caloric was banished in the nineteenth century, and the luminiferous aether early in the twentieth. Electricity, conceived as a fluid, has met the same fate. Hand in hand with this elimination of the now useless "imponderables" there has been an elimination also of the conceptually related dualisms. One of those that bit the dust early was that of space and time, which, as we have seen, was then replaced by the continuum concept of *space-time*. Perhaps the next to lose status in scientific thought was the dualism of matter and energy, displaced by *matter-energy*. In this way matter and energy became but different states of *matter-energy*, and what is called the transmutation of matter into energy (or vice versa) is no more than a change from one state of matter-energy into another.

From this point of view it is incorrect to say, as it often has been recently, that matter has been "reduced" to energy by contemporary physics and that the latter is therefore the ground component of physical reality. This reductionist position is often taken by idealists of the kind who claim that matter has thus been reduced to mind or spirit. It seems equally illegitimate to say that energy has been reduced to matter, a position taken by some materialists. Such reductions are, of course, made in the name of philosophy. There is nothing in physics itself, as I see it, that justifies declaring either matter or energy to be the more fundamental reality—any more than this could be said about water-ice with respect to water-liquid.

Today the same kind of thinking is being applied increasingly to "life." Matter-energy is believed to have the capacity for "becoming alive" simply as a sort of change of state, not by the imbuing of the inanimate with an essence called life. What we have come to see, then, is that life is simply a condition of physical reality, and that the latter is more than matter-energy alone and is at least matter-energy-life. The acceptance of this simplifying and unifying conception has become imperative because of considerable evidence that life has actually appeared in nature in this way, by the spontaneous appearance by "aggregation" of self-replicating molecules; and because in the opinion of many scientists this will probably occur soon in the laboratory also under control conditions.[2] Indeed, some assert that this has already happened there.

We should keep in mind, of course, that likening life and the process of becoming alive to a change in state of substances like water is sheer analogy. Probably the first scientist to suggest this was Teilhard.[3] While, like all analogies, it must not be taken literally or applied uncritically, it is a most useful and powerful metaphoric conception, with many important implications. In chapter IX we shall see how it can be applied also to mind and spirit, thus still further enlarging our conception of physical reality, from matter-energy-life to matter-energy-life-mind-spirit.

NATURE'S CREATIVITY;
ITS ABUNDANCE AND UPWARD PRESSURE

Now what does it mean to ascribe to this multiple reality the quality and power of creativity, as in the second introductory proposition of this chapter? Basically, of course, its meaning derives from coupling the concept of a unified physical reality with that of evolution regarded as a creative, not merely a modifying process.[4] To be "creative" means to bring forth genuine novelty, that which did not exist previously.

I reject the view that ascribes creativity to the deity alone, and restricts the meaning of creation to the origination of the primordial substance of the world, and then regards every subsequent activity as mere arrangement or rearrangement of the already-created. Indeed I would insist that to bring into being new relationships, patterns, events, and materials—as artists, poets, scientists, technologists, and politicians do—is as truly creative as is the creation of the elemental stuff of the world. As we have seen, interrelationships, interactions and events, have come to seem more fundamental than substance, even in the conceiving of matter itself. Man, then, is truly a creator, even though his creativity is of a lower order than God's; and so is physical reality, of which man is a part.

Another analogy may be helpful here, that of effluence, referred to in the Appendix in connection with the fifth meaning of mystery: the figure of a bountifully effluent fountain, characterized by what has thus far been an unceasing outflowing or outpouring, a persistent sending forth into existence, a bodying forth into ever more novel actuality of what was formerly only potentiality. As we have seen, once there were no men, and before that no birds, and still earlier no flowers, and long, long ago not even any molecules, but only elementary particles; no colors, no sounds, no smells. And then one after another they poured forth to join in an ever-growing, living stream of reality. This is what it means to say that physical reality is effluent.

Nature is still in process of becoming. Indeed it seems to be a process more than a "thing" or system of "things." That which exists is forever pregnant with possibilities for more complex existence. At any stage of its development physical reality is like a rose bud I once dreamed about, ready to unfold into a flower; then each petal somehow unfolded as though it were itself a bud becoming a new flower, and the first flower in this way became a multiple flower, and so on and on. What we have here is a vision of effluence, not of external sameness but of ever-increasing variety: from the simple to the complex and luxuriant, and from the inanimate to the animate to the organism that is self-conscious. This is why it is *creative* effluence.

For many men this vision of nature's remarkably innovating and ever-enriching effluence has led to a sense of a preferred direction, or even "purpose" in the universe. Though science itself must eschew ideas of conscious purpose in subhuman nature, it nevertheless seems clear to numerous scientists that there *is* something systematic in the flow of its major events, a definite trend in the long-range sequence of emergences; namely, from a few levels of depths to many, from relatively undifferentiated uniformity to great qualitative variety and diversity, from the inert to the dynamically self-replicating, from insensitivity to high degrees of responsiveness to environment, from atomistic individualism to social existence and community. This trend would seem to be precisely the kind that would prevail if deliberate benevolent purpose were operative, for it follows an evident pattern of development, toward a richer, more unified, and more meaningful existence. In this sense, and in terms of the "highest" values we cherish today, the evolutionary trend must be regarded as "upward"; and it has persisted long enough—several billions of years—to justify the tentative conclusion that it is a permanent, basic feature of the universe. The many transient, short-range departures from it, that have often been "downward," impoverishing or even destructive, have not canceled out the unmistakable long-range "gains."

Without a truly cosmic perspective we are likely to get a distorted understanding of history. For there is a certain amount of tyranny in very short ranges of history, such as human history, which, as we have seen, is extremely short relative to cosmic history. It imposes foreshortened temporal perspectives that are debilitating and distorting in their effect upon human consciousness. A very short time view confines the imagination, dulls the sensitivities to, and inhibits the discernment of, long-range patterns of historical change. In the exceedingly restricted field of view that human history provides, major catastrophes, such as wars with their Hiroshimas and Buchenwalds, always *seem* utterly devastating, seemingly negating any advances that may have preceded them and destroying any hope of genuine permanent advancement in the future. Worse than that, short-term history provides no way of checking on the accuracy of the "momentary" impression of the state of affairs; and, of course, from a cosmic perspective human history can of itself provide no more than momentary impressions. To use an analogy from photography, short-range history yields only exceedingly short-exposure snapshots of the human scene, and these can tell us almost nothing of the direction of its movements. From a genuine "snapshot" of a train one cannot tell whether it is standing still or moving forward or backward, whatever it may actually be doing at the time. Only a time exposure or a series of successive snapshots (as in moving pictures) allows one to conclude anything about the motion of the train. Only extended time, not local time, allows us to discern genuine trends and to distinguish between temporary losses or gains and long-range ones.

The more one thinks about this, the more conscious one becomes of a rather formidable mystery in the overall scheme of things, the *mystery of the "upward" pressure of nature's creative effluence*. Again there occur to us fundamental limiting questions. Why is the pressure of the effluence "upward" rather than "downward," i.e., from the simple to the complex, and so on, rather than the reverse? Is this only an as-yet-unsolved problem, or is it genuine mystery? How can we tell? There seems to be no clear-cut evidence that its upward direction has been "predetermined" causally in the sense that it could in principle have been predicted in advance. Indeed, many scientists insist that, as far as science can see, it is a matter of pure chance, even though they may grant that evolution is a creative process.

There is another tantalizing question. Granting that physical reality and nature have been creatively effluent thus far, will they continue to be so? There have been many major emergences in the past; will there be still others in the future, major ones yielding realities that do not now exist, with new levels and hierarchies of structure and events, or has the process come to a halt? Is it limited in time, or can it go on indefinitely? Again, *we do not know*. We noted earlier the *mystery of the existing-but-not-yet-encountered reality*. We have now gone one step further and contemplated the *mystery of the reality that does not yet exist but may in the future*. There may come to the cosmos and life utterly new dimensions it does not now possess. This has happened before.

Evolution is still going on. Why should one not suppose that it may continue indefinitely, perhaps forever? What is sensed here is the *mystery of the future, and a possibly open one without a temporal end*. I am not saying that such an open future is or can be asserted *by* science itself, but I am suggesting that it can reasonably be implied by what science has taught us about the world in our time.

The same may be said about an open past, i.e., one that may have no beginning. Science has no way of knowing whether or not there was a "first moment" of time, before which there were no physical entities, events or relationships. If the ladder of levels of depth in matter-energy is not only descriptive of the present but indicative of past evolutionary history, and if there turns out to be no ground level, may this not imply that there was no first emergence? What we encounter here is the *mystery of origins, or of an absolute beginning or no beginning.*

NATURE'S DESTRUCTIVENESS AND AMBIGUITY; MISFORTUNE AND EVIL

Thus far we have considered for the most part the admirable, wondrous aspects of physical reality and especially its creativity. There are, however, also far less admirable ones, for nature not only builds up but tears down. It wounds and heals, conserves and wastes. It terrorizes ruthlessly. Without doubt one of its most perplexing aspects is its apparently boundless depths of destructiveness and inconsistency. We now turn to these devastating and negative features.

Its *destructiveness* is evident in conflagration and flood, earthquake and tidal wave, hurricane and tornado, drought and famine, disease and epidemic; also in the prodigality of death that characterizes the so-called sabertooth-and-claw competition for survival. For many species the birth and violent death of offspring are virtually simultaneous. Millions of eggs are laid but few hatch out, and often the chances of survival thereafter are small indeed. Then too there are the myriads of false starts and blind alleys in evolution, as well as actual reversals and eliminations after long-time growth and development; witness, for example, the fate of the dinosaurs. While there can be no doubt of the long-range "upward" trend of evolution noted earlier, there can likewise be none about many shorter-range "downward" ones. The overall rising curve of development has superimposed upon it many large and small "ups-and-downs."

Nature's *inconsistency* here means its working against itself much of the time. It has developed marvelously ingenious ways of qualitatively improving the species and life in general and at the same time others equally potent for deterioration. Thus it exhibits helpful symbiosis, i.e., a relationship of mutual support or dependence, between, say, two species of animals, yet ironically also parasitism, in which one species lives on another, often causing it much pain and suffering or even premature death. As an example of a less lethal yet terribly agonizing kind of parasitism, Julian Huxley cites the case of fly maggots that live in the noses of various animals.

Another inconsistency of nature is that it does not always live up to legitimate expectations derived from known cause-and-effect relationships. The perfectly designed and constructed bridge may fail, and so may the steering device or the explosive or the medication that meets all established standards for safety. A young man and woman, both perfectly normal and healthy, may marry with the legitimate expectation of a long life of happiness, and yet within a few months or weeks one of them may suddenly become a mere mass of protoplasm, a vegetable without any genuine human characteristics. Or if they remain healthy there may yet be born to them heart-breaking monstrosities as offspring. As noted earlier, abnormal chance and usual cause do often combine to produce the unexpected mutation that is wondrous and propels individual or species toward improved existence; much more often, however, the reverse happens—apparently without reason and with tragic consequences.

Such tragic happenings are often spoken of as "irrationalities of nature." The question is, however, whether this usage is legitimate. Nature *is*, as it *is*, in its own right. From what level of understanding is it legitimate to regard low rates of survival, evolutionary cul-de-sacs, and ravishing epidemics as truly undesirable and nonsensical? Would nature as a whole, including humanity, actually be better off without them?

Now one thing post-modern natural and social science has done is to make us uncomfortable with too restricted a point of view about this. Science's cosmic perspective, its insight that man is not separate from but deeply imbedded in nature, and the premium it puts upon the concept of the *individual-in-community* rather than upon isolated independence no longer allow us to think of nature as "belonging to" or "existing for" man himself. Therefore what may seem unfortunate for him may after all not be unfortunate as far as the common cosmic good is concerned. From an overall point of view it may actually be beneficent.

To illustrate, it has been widely held that the one unmitigated tragedy of existence and undoubted enemy of man, the final threat to meaning, is death—biological death. Today we know, however, that physical death is an integral part of life. When very long ago the life of complex organisms appeared on this planet, death appeared also as a component of it, without which the stream of life could not flow on. If a larger organism is to live, there must be a continual dying of its constituent cells. Individual members of a species must die if the species is to survive. Certainly, if men did not die mankind soon would. The earth would become overpopulated, the quality of life eroded, and truly *human* existence made impossible; and in its essentials this observation applies to plant and animal life as well. A place where there would be no physical death would not be an Edenic paradise but hell. From the point of view of the overall ecology of the world, and the cosmos, death is clearly not necessarily an irrationality—be it the death of a cell, or a human being, or the human race—for we can see from an overall point of view that there might be good reason for it. This may be true also of other aspects of life that men have perennially labeled as nonsensical incongruities.

Probably then these perplexing features of nature should be called *ambiguities* (following Paul Tillich and others)[5] rather than irrationalities. This is a less presumptuous term that recognizes how complex nature's web of cause-and-effect relations is and how little we know of the many factors and values that need to be taken into account before a situation or phenomenon can justifiably be declared irrational. Also it signifies acceptance of uncertainty, randomness, and at least some inexplicability as inevitable *givens* of both human and nonhuman existence. From this point of view death may be seen as a mystery not only of a dreaded unknown but of a known discerned to have great value in the general scheme of things—even though it still remains perplexing. It is a *mystery of large perspectives and relationships, of multiple causality, and of tangled realities.*[6] The recognition of this represents a significant expansion of human consciousness. Instead of leading to excessive anxiety and preoccupation with one's self, it tends to focus concern upon broader values and needs and upon long-range local and cosmic trends or "purposes." And it demands that nonhuman beings of nature, e.g., the sparrow, the daisy, the brook, and the wind, be accepted by man with understanding and genuine fellow feeling (*Mitgefühl*) as full-fledged co-members of the community we call nature.

Another unfortunate usage is to designate the catastrophes visited upon man by nature—e.g., earthquakes and epidemics—as *evils* because they cause much suffering. While "evil" does mean injurious, it connotes more often, I believe, the immoral and wicked. In this sense evils are attitudes and actions with destructive intent which are impoverishing or debasing, rather than elevating, enriching, and ennobling, and are thus counter to, rather than in harmony with, the long-range trends of evolution. Thus conceived a tornado or deluge or epidemic is clearly not evil—even though tragically unfortunate. Animal or plant parasitism too may have terribly painful or lethal consequences; but since it is essentially instinct-bound, allowing virtually no choice, it is not evil in this sense. In the same way natural human death, say by disease or by unavoidable failure of a bridge, is not taken to be evil; whereas unnatural death, e.g., by deliberate murder or by criminal negligence or malfeasance, is. From this point of view I shall hereafter distinguish between misfortunes and evils and not classify the latter among the former.

THE NATURAL AND THE UNNATURAL

Two words need clarification, *natural* and *unnatural*. The former means normal, usual, consistent with itself, true to its kind, produced by the processes of nature; not abnormal, or degenerate, or pathological, or man-made. According to its most basic meaning today it relates to nature, conceived as a lawful, deterministic system (as in the first part of this chapter).

For a long time this conception of nature did not exist.

The world seemed for the most part inexplicable, except for its more evident regularities, and such "obvious causes" as wind, water, fire; sun, moon, stars (astrologically); and the motive power of beast and man. Moreover, much of what happened was attributed to direct action by God or the gods. Thereafter gradually "the world became natural," to quote Loren Eiseley.[7] It came to be seen as in large measure understandable, predictable, and controllable through lawfulness—Newton's laws. For a while, however, this naturalness was incomplete, because Newton felt that certain anomalies in planetary motion could not be resolved except by postulating divine intervention. Later Laplace showed that after all Newtonian mechanics did suffice and thus removed any further need for God as one of nature's physical causes. In this way all physical, geological, and astronomical phenomena "became natural." In other respects it remained even then "unnatural," since life, death, mind, and spirit were regarded as extramundane, i.e., independent of natural law, and unexplainable without appeal to the supernatural. In our time, however, these too have become natural.

Now consider the *unnatural*. What, for instance, might it mean to speak of natural and unnatural death, and to designate misfortune as natural but evil as unnatural? If *natural* means lawful and within the system of nature, can any observable happening be anything but natural? The reply must now be, I think: No, all scientifically observable events, including both misfortune and evils, accidental death and murder, are determined (in terms of probabilities, of course) by natural causes and are therefore natural—in that sense. There is, however, another meaning —as it is implied by Eiseley's profound questions: "How natural is natural?" and "How human is man?"[8] There is much evidence—from psychology, psychiatry, anthropology, and sociology—that with the evolutionary emergence of mankind there appeared in nature utterly unprecedented causal factors out of which there came quite unprecedented manifestations of goodness and evil. And in particular, post-modern science has greatly increased man's sensitivity to the abysmal depths of evil in man and therefore in nature—of which novelists, playwrights, artists, and prophets have been keenly aware for a long time.

The fact is that human beings perpetrate evils so unspeakable and damnable[9] that no amount of relativizing of ethics can prevent the shock that comes universally from witnessing them, e.g., the retaliatory slaughter of innocent men, women, and children in total war, the calculated savagery of the Buchenwalds, and the inhumane customs of slavery and racial discrimination. Many men now realize that though such phenomena may someday be explainable in terms of natural law and chance variation, perhaps as pathological states, they are nevertheless "unnatural" in that they violate men's highest sensitivities, are degrading, impoverishing, and destructive, as well as counter to the long-range creative, upward thrust of the universe. There is then one sense in which both good and evil are natural, and another in which evil is unnatural.

The *mystery of misfortune* and the *mystery of evil* are both profoundly perplexing and agonizing, but it is the latter that haunts us most today. One reason for this is that, while for quite some time science-and-technology has been teaching us how to alleviate and even control much misfortune, such a prospect with respect to evil seems very much less likely. The evidence is mounting that man's capacity and predilection for demonic savagery surpasses by far anything observable elsewhere in nature, say among the animals.[10] Another reason is that indubitably terrestrial nature is in grave danger of having its entire economy disrupted, or even destroyed, by man with his seemingly all-powerful engines of destruction. Finally, it is clear that man's wisdom has not yet evolved to great heights of profundity, certainly not so far as to assure a utopian future for him with certainty.

On the other hand, the situation is by no means utterly hopeless. The fact that evil is natural in its most basic sense means that in principle it is not only explicable but also to a considerable extent manageable, and even controllable, and need not therefore be regarded as an intractable, irremediable given of nature. It *may* be eradicable in time.

Indeed, as we shall see, it is evident even now that evil can be alleviated to an extent that would but recently have been considered quite impossible. Herein lies scientifically supported hope for the future. The question is, of course, whether man will be willing, or able, to use his newfound power wisely. What is in principle a possibility may not in practice become an actuality. Nature in no way guarantees any particular outcome—even though its long-range trend *has* been upward in direction. The *mystery* of evil is indeed genuine mystery.

Parenthetically, let it be noted that there has been no mention here of *sin*. This is because sin is a purely religious term, referring ultimately to man's relationship to God, and as such has no meaning in science itself and no place in a strictly secular discussion such as this part of the book purports to present. One can be utterly devoid of religious sensibilities and understanding and yet know beyond doubt that there is evil, even demonic evil; but not so in the case of sin. There is, then, a difference between the *mystery of evil* and the *mystery of sin*, though they are not unrelated. We shall touch on this in Part Three.

IX. The Flowering
of Mind and Spirit

THE NATURE OF MIND AND SPIRIT

We have seen that human history is only a minuscule part of terrestrial history, spanning according to McKinley's scale only the last four hours of the full evolutionary year. And man has been literate only a few minutes of that time. Yet this has been a most remarkable period, for apparently never before did radical changes and emergences occur so rapidly. "Preparing" for man took a long time, but when he arrived evolutionary activity took on a new character. His extraordinary powers enabled him quickly to bring forth a great variety of utterly new realities: tools and processes, abstractions and symbols, languages and logics, rational analyses and syntheses, measurement and experimentation, and many others equally unprecedented. In this way social rather than biological evolution came to dominate change. The arts and literatures emerged, and the religions, and philosophies, laws, the sciences and technologies—and thus man's cultures and civilizations, with new orders of good and evil, beauty and ugliness, truth and deception. Moreover, there came to this new being the capacity for self-analysis, which was quite unprecedented. He learned to investigate himself, as well as his world, with both critical objectivity and discriminating introspection —and *in depth.* He discovered that his "self," his so-called "nature," and his tremendously varied potentialities are not "possessions" or innate attributes of his own but in large part the gift-consequences of his relationships with other entities and processes and with nature as a whole. Through his knowledge and understanding he has achieved a remarkable degree of self-determination. To a large extent he is now in a position to be both the architect and builder of his own future, which could certainly not be said about any of his evolutionary forebears.

One way to summarize and interpret all this is to say that the human period of nature's history has been a time of luxuriant flowering of mind and spirit, which, according to the post-modern vision, existed in nature long before man appeared and are therefore not exclusively his possessions. With his arrival, however, those levels and hierarchies of physical reality that make for mind and spirit, above those of matter-energy-life, came to be filled out or expanded by an amazing variety of new emergences, many of which were the creations of man himself. This means, of course, that man shares mind and spirit with other living beings, and this not only illumines further the essential unity of physical reality and nature but adds greatly to our understanding of the character and role of mind and spirit in the cosmos.

Mind and spirit, as "seen through the eyes of science," are, of course, dependent upon, and continuous with, life and matter-energy, with which they together constitute the individual psychosomatic beings we call animals and men. This dependence, unity, and continuity obtain also historically in the evolution of the biological species. In our introductory discussion of these relations (chapters I and III), one of our key concepts was *aggregation*. We must now modify and supplement this notion. While its use is apt with respect to the evolution of inanimate matter, it is much less so with regard to living things. It is not too misleading to think of atoms as aggregating to form molecules, and of these as aggregating to produce matter in bulk, and of stars aggregating to make galaxies. But to think of cells or plants and animals as aggregations in the same sense seems inadequate. As the late Prof. Edmund W. Sinnott, a botanist, insisted:

A living thing is not a collection of parts and traits but an *organized system*, well called an *organism*. In this no part or process is an independent event but each is related to the others. All vital activities, in development, physiology and behavior, are so well regulated that a unified condition tends to be reached and then to be maintained. Plants and animals are interrelated wholes which tend to be preserved, or to be restored if changed, and which develop under precise control. They are not aggregates but *integrates*. This process of *biological organization* is the unique feature of living things.[1]

Doubtless some theorists of the molecular state, certainly those of the Mulliken school of thought,[2] would want to make some of these assertions about inanimate molecules also. For as exponents of the so-called "molecular-orbital theory," which is very different from the earlier "valence-bond theory," they conceive of the molecule as an integrated structure in which, so to speak, the individual atoms lose their identity, and their valence electrons are distributed, as wave functions or "orbitals," over the molecule as a whole. From this point of view all molecules are integrates rather than aggregates, and no sharp dividing line can be drawn between living and nonliving molecules. This conclusion is supported also by the views of many virologists, who find it extremely difficult to say whether viruses are living things or not. Nevertheless Sinnott is making an important distinction, one that he points up cogently by saying further in the same context:

I can best define life as *the process by which matter is brought together in organized and integrated systems capable of self-perpetuation and of change.*

L. J. Henderson believes that organization is a major category in nature, standing beside matter and energy.[3]

And Sinnott seems to agree with Henderson. What this says is that the emergence of life was made possible first by aggregation, which produced the hierarchy of inanimate physical and chemical structures, and then by integration-and-organization, which produced the next level, that of live organisms. Thus the appearance of life on earth did not depend upon a bit of it being carried to earth on, say, a meteorite from some other world (as was once proposed), or upon the direct creation on earth of a new substance-essence, "life," and its injection into an inanimate body. Rather what emerged was a new state of physical reality, or a process by which a nonliving corpus was transformed into a living, self-perpetuating, and self-changing (growing) one. And ever since this happened the first time, being born and dying have meant respectively that the operation of this same process is initiated and terminated in individual bodies.

Some living things display also phenomena of a still higher hierarchical level, that of mind. While post-modern science has learned a great deal about these phenomena, it has not produced unanimity with regard to either the use or the meaning of the term mind. Many scientists, notably psychologists, reject it completely, feeling that it merely perpetuates an error because it seems almost inevitably to connote a sort of "ghost in the machine" concept of mind, as Gilbert Ryle calls it.[4] They object, and rightly so, to the old Cartesian assumption that a human being has both a body and a mind, conceived as two distinctly different kinds of reality. Others, while also rejecting that dualism, feel that the term mind is nevertheless most useful and indeed indispensable.

After all, statements such as "he had a keen mind but has lost it," and "he has degenerated into a mere vegetable," do assert something observable. What is meant by common consent is at least this much, that he can no longer cope with problems, or even recognize that there are any, much less formulate them meaningfully. He can no longer set or achieve goals or standards for his behavior. Learning, remembering, and reasoning have become impossible for him. He may still live biologically, in the sense of vegetating. The metabolic and circulatory and other such primal biological functions may continue, but something beyond them has stopped, namely, that functioning that is denoted by the terms *mind* and *mental*—even though we may not be able to define them precisely. We can say then that losing one's mind, like losing one's life, represents a change of state, not the departure of any*thing* other than a function or process—the process of "minding."[5]

Now if there is disagreement about the use of the term mind, there is even more in regard to spirit. And yet there is a great deal being said about "the human spirit." Sometimes, to be sure, it is taken to be essentially synonymous with mind, but much common usage as well as sophisticated writing does make significant distinctions between them.

One obvious and important distinction shows up in statements like the following: Something has gone out of him. He no longer cares. There is no will to live. Somehow his spirit has been crushed. He lies there utterly dispirited. His intellect still works brilliantly—after the manner of a computer or thinking machine—*but* there is no exuberance or zest, verve, radiance, or vitality; he displays no passion; he doesn't fight back. Clearly these are utterly meaningful assertions of observable fact that point to another level of reality, above that of mind. They do not refer to "a spirit," a ghostly, disembodied entity, but to a function that has ceased, an ability that has been lost, and therefore to a change of state in one's being.

It is obvious, of course, by this time that the higher levels of reality are much more difficult to define clearly than the lower ones. Thus the state of being alive is much more complex and therefore much harder to define than the state of nonliving. That of the mind is still more so, and this is why I presented no definition of it. Of the many definitions to be found in the literature none seems truly adequate, and none has captured universal acceptance. I felt able to say more by simply calling attention to some of the human capacities that virtually everybody feels familiar with and ascribes to mind. The devising and selling of mental tests of various sorts has become big business and has done much to make us aware of many aspects of mind. In the case of spirit, however, we feel ourselves to be in rather strange territory. There seems to be nothing measurable here, nothing "objective" to put one's finger on with genuine familiarity—even though the term spirit is a standard item in our vocabulary. My negative approach, calling attention to some of the characteristics of a dispirited person, does seem helpful to not a few people, apparently because it recalls recognizable experience and phenomena. On the other hand it is also disappointing, because it fails to communicate positively the sense of the vast depth, awesomeness, and power of spirit as numerous persons have experienced it. After all man's spirit is often declared to be his most unique human quality—even more so than his mind. To say of Abraham Lincoln and Albert Einstein and Martin Luther King that they were great spirits means for many people that they were very much more than great minds, and that they were truly human. Surely in this sense spirit is the crowning glory of creation (as it has developed thus far).

SUBHUMAN AND HUMAN LEVELS OF MIND AND SPIRIT

To speak at all adequately about spirit one must refer to experience in which reality is perceived holistically and intuitively, as much as analytically and logically, and must employ poetic-artistic, as well as scientific, language. This is illustrated beautifully in Loren Eiseley's great prose-poem, *The Immense Journey.* On its dust cover appeared the caption: "An imaginative naturalist explores the mysteries of man and nature." Let it be understood, however, that this "naturalist" is also a distinguished, disciplined, tough-minded scientist. It is significant that he chose to communicate his message not through a monograph presenting data and conclusions in the usual manner of science but through a series of story-essays, accounts of experiences he had in direct contact with nature. I should like to quote from the one entitled "The Bird and the Machine."

It relates an incident that occurred in his youth, when he was on an expedition to capture live specimens for zoos. It is about a pair of little sparrow hawks, one of which, the male, he was able to capture, while the other escaped. He had found them in a deserted mountain cabin with a hole in the roof. The capture was not easy, and he had paid the price for it with a badly chewed thumb and lacerated, profusely bleeding hand. The next morning, the story goes:

I was up early and brought the box in which the little hawk was imprisoned out onto the grass where I was building a cage. A wind as cool as a mountain spring ran over the grass and stirred my hair. It was a fine day to be alive. I looked up and all around and at the hole in the cabin roof out of which the other little hawk had fled. There was no sign of her anywhere that I could see.

"Probably in the next county by now," I thought cynically, but before beginning work I decided I'd have a look at my last night's capture.

Secretively, I looked again all around the camp and up and down and opened the box. I got him right out in my hand with his wings folded properly and I was careful not to startle him. He lay limp in my grasp and I could feel his heart pound under the feathers but he only looked beyond me and up.

I saw him look that last look away beyond me into a sky so full of light that I could not follow his gaze. The little breeze flowed over me again, and nearby a mountain aspen shook all its tiny leaves. I suppose I must have had an idea then of what I was going to do, but I never let it come up into consciousness. I just reached over and laid the hawk on the grass.

He lay there a long minute without hope, unmoving, his eyes still fixed on that blue vault above him. It must have been that he was already so far away in heart that he never felt the release from my hand. He never even stood. He just lay with breast against the grass.

In the next second after that long minute he was gone. Like a flicker of light, he had vanished with my eyes full on him, but without actually seeing even a premonitory wing beat. He was gone straight into that towering emptiness of light and crystal that my eyes could scarcely bear to penetrate. For another long moment there was silence. I could not see him. The light was too intense. Then from far up somewhere a cry came ringing down.

I was young then and had seen a little of the world, but when I heard that cry my heart turned over. It was not the cry of the hawk I had captured; for by shifting my position against the sun, I was now seeing further up. Straight out of the sun's eye, where she must have been soaring restlessly above us for untold hours, hurtled his mate. And from far up, ringing from peak to peak of the summits over us, came a cry of such unutterable and ecstatic joy that it sounds down across the years and tingles among the cups of my quiet breakfast table.

I saw them both now. He was rising fast to meet her. They met in a great soaring gyre that turned to a whirling circle and a dance of wings. Once more, just once, their two voices, joined in a harsh wild medley of question and response, struck and echoed against the pinnacles of the valley. Then they were gone forever somewhere into those upper regions beyond the eyes of men.[6]

To enlarge on this story would, of course, be anticlimactic. And yet as we ponder it, the following meditation by another perceptive poet, Joseph Leonard Grucci, may serve to remind us that for many a sensitive person—scientist,

artist, poet, anchorite, or unsophisticated common man—
a bird in swift, roiling flight has magnificently ineffable
qualities that blur the precision of the kind of purely rational thinking that regards the bird as nothing more than
matter, or no more than matter, life, and mind. This poem
is entitled "Time of Hawks."

> Now autumn burned
> To coolness, dour,
> The wind upturned
> No leaf is sure.
>
> Menace of snow
> Hardens the ground;
> High a hawk goes
> Swifter than sound.
>
> *Once Leonardo*
> *(Also in the fall)*
> *Watched a bird go,*
> *I now recall;*
>
> *And Saint Francis with his birds*
> *Dreamed of brother flight*
> *Surer than words*
> *Of anchorite.*
>
> Consummate bird
> Roiling the sky,
> Your flight has blurred
> Man's rational day:
>
> His heart bereft,
> He hides belief
> And cannot grieve
> The single death.[7]

There are several things the Eiseley story tells me convincingly, even though they are not asserted by it explicitly.
Animals also have spirit. Certainly these hawks did. Surely
the female's ringing cry of "unutterable and ecstatic joy"
and the answering cry of the male, their powerful, whirling
gyre, and their "two voices, joined in a harsh, wild medley
of question and response," were very much more than only
a mental act, namely, a tremendous, exuberant, dynamic

outpouring of spirit. To be sure, there were sudden chemical reactions, complex mechanical and electrical phenomena in brain, heart, and wings, as well as quick mental decisions in flight, but there must also have been more than these. It is this "more" process that constitutes spirit. After a night in a tiny cage the male had lost hope so completely that when he was taken from it and placed on the grass, chest down, he lay there a full minute, inert, dispirited, without the will really to *live*, before in a flash the process started, the will returned, and the barely living organism became again truly a bird, powerfully alive and overflowing with proud, joyous spirit. That which makes a bird a bird had reasserted itself in full.

Spirit is, however, more than ebullience and vitality. It is also sensitivity and responsiveness, empathy and concern, a sensing of relationship and of need for mutuality and helpfulness. Animals have this too. The female hawk did not flee to "the next county." She stayed right there, above the spot where her mate was held captive, and "must have been soaring restlessly . . . for untold hours." She was watching when he was released and placed on the ground; and when he finally came to life and bolted into the blue there burst forth her ecstatic cry, as she hurtled toward the earth to meet him. There is in animal lore much evidence of this aspect of animal spirit: sensitivity to one another, to man, and to their environment with which they establish rapport.

There is much talk these days about dolphins and their great intelligence. The following story is but one of many that illustrate how they can communicate "linguistically" and solve problems. In this case, however, there is evidence also of remarkable spirit, manifested by the will of one dolphin to fight off death and by the keen concern and strong determination of its fellows that went to its rescue and remained there until he was out of danger.

The episode involved a dolphin that, during an experiment, apparently had become so chilled that it was unable to swim. Placed back in the main tank with two other dolphins, it sank to the bottom, where it was bound to suffocate unless it could reach the surface to breathe. However, it gave the distress call and the other two immediately lifted its head until the blowhole was out of the water, so that it could take a deep breath. It then sank and a great deal of whistling and twittering took place among the three animals. The two active ones then began swimming past the other so that their dorsal fins swept over its ano-genital region in a manner that caused a reflex contraction of the fluke muscles, much as one can make a dog scratch itself by rubbing the right spot on its flank. The resultant action of the flukes lifted the animal to the surface and the procedure was repeated for several hours until the ailing dolphin had recovered.[8]

SPIRIT AND FREEDOM

Something else that Eiseley's story says is that spirit can thrive only in freedom and hope. To rob it of its natural habitat and future is to crush it. To be sure, spirit fights back in spite of loss of freedom, but once freedom seems hopelessly beyond reach the spirited life cannot be sustained indefinitely. On the other hand spirit is often reborn swiftly and powerfully when freedom is restored. This is one of its most impressive attributes. More about this presently.

An important aspect of Eiseley's story is that it is not only about hawks but about *hawks and a man,* and the mountains, the breeze, the sun, and the open spaces they shared, and about deep understanding and empathy on the part of the man, and about a vivid, still tingling memory of his. It is a story about spirit of a much higher order than that of the hawks, namely, the spirit of this man, which made him sensitive to beings not of his own kind, and understanding of, and responsive to, their plight. He was truly human in knowing, though perhaps not consciously or through rational analysis, that a hawk can be a hawk only in its proper environment, and with hawkly freedom.* He felt the hawk's anguish and sensed that its spirit was being crushed. His own spirit responded mightily —with his own anguish, and by releasing the captive, and then sharing so fully in the great outpouring of joy that

---

* This is the point also of the delightful film "Born Free," about a lioness that became truly a lion only after she was freed from the well-meaning and loving but misguided, distorting, and actually enslaving care of her human keepers.

the memory of it never left him. Both such a happening itself, and the fact that its meaning and emotional content can to a large extent be shared with other human beings by means of linguistic symbols (in a story) after the event, indicates that man's spirit has developed far beyond any observable among the animals. This I take to be the most momentous evolutionary advance in terrestrial history.

Here is a being for whom the will to live and the drive toward satisfying self-fulfillment are directed toward life conceived very broadly and inclusively. For him to live means, of course, to have and enjoy food, shelter, health, mate, and other such primal biological necessities; but it means, even more, to enjoy the needs of mind and spirit, such as knowledge, beauty, truth, understanding, work, play, goodness, fellowship, responsibility, and the opportunity to be creative. These come to him not only through his genetic heritage and birth but quite as much through his relationships to the other beings with whom he shares existence. Considering the nature of these values attainable by man, and the variety of ways each of them can find concrete expression, it is apparent that for man life is a vast array of possibilities and degrees of freedom. True, for any one person their number is restricted by circumstances beyond his control; nevertheless, compared to those available to any animal* they are almost incredibly numerous.

There are several reasons why man has so much more freedom. First, he is able to change many restricting circumstances once thought to be beyond his control. He has actually achieved an amazing amount of control over nature, has been able to transform much of it, including himself, and has thus been freed from much of its inhibiting domination. To illustrate, a man is not free to fly as a hawk can, just as a hawk is not free to write a story as a man can; but man can now fly in other ways, faster and

---

* Many scientists would insist on saying "to any *other* animal." Undeniably there is continuity historically and genetically from animal to man. This does not, however, make it mandatory to speak of man as an animal without qualification. While he does share many of his qualities with the animals, there are many others, including qualities of mind and spirit, that are his uniquely.

higher and farther, while a hawk cannot write a story at all. Second, man is very much less bound by instinct, in the sense that his behavior is determined much more by his own conscious decisions. Since these may be based on what he can learn—both from his own past or from other persons and cultures through symbolic (linguistic) communication with them—this confers upon him quite unprecedented freedom. Thus in principle each new generation of humans can begin life and thought at a higher point of development, so that the range of viable possibilities for future action open to the human infant at birth, as well as to the child or adult later at times of decision, is exceedingly large. I take the term "human freedom" to refer to this tremendous range of possibilities. There is a sort of circular situation here: because of man's considerable freedom from instinct he has been able to develop novel abilities and sensitivities which led him to creative achievement, and through these have come other capacities and attainments that have added to his freedom.

TWO CONTRASTING OUTCOMES
OF HUMAN SPIRIT AND FREEDOM

Out of this situation there have come two developments that have special significance with reference to the human spirit. The first is the rise of the religions of mankind. These constitute a genuine evolutionary emergence, just as do the sciences and arts. Fundamentally they came into being because men had come to feel, consciously or unconsciously, that there is, to quote Whitehead again, "something which stands beyond, behind, and within, the passing flux of immediate things; . . . that gives meaning to all that passes, and yet eludes apprehension; . . . the final good . . . the ultimate ideal,"[9] and because, having sensed that presence, they also felt a compulsion to worship it. In reporting and interpreting this aspect of their experience men have spoken of it rather consistently in terms of spirit—their own spirit becoming aware of other spirit, Spirit of an order higher than their own, an order of sensitivity, goodness, and creativity not altogether unlike their own, yet transcending it.

I do not say, as part of this secular-scientific study, that men actually have encountered a higher, transcendent level of reality, and more particularly of spirit. This would be asserting more than can be observed or substantiated by present scientific methods. I do assert that in fact countless numbers of men of all cultures and high religions have agreed in making that claim, even though they have disagreed widely in conceptualizing that reality. It is not without significance that man, the being with matchless capacities for both critical analysis and intuitive perception, has made this claim so unanimously, even though he realizes he cannot substantiate it "scientifically." Clearly the genesis of religions is a most striking phenomenon in cosmic evolution, and one that became possible only after the emergence of a very keen sensitivity and great freedom—and spirit.

The second outcome of man's unprecedented freedom that we should note is the appearance of unprecedented manifestations of good and evil such as were mentioned in the preceding chapter. Perhaps some good and evil are perpetrated by animals. Since, however, they have little freedom of choice, by far most good and evil is the product of the human will. Thinking first about evil, without doubt man's capacity for it is tremendous and unique. Loren Eiseley, careful observer that he is, has noted this and said that in man there came upon the terrestrial scene "the lethal factor"[10] that has disfigured much of nature, made it unnatural, destroyed its equilibrium, depleted its resources, polluted its atmosphere and waters, and desecrated it with the horrors of selfishness, hatred, and premeditated death. He speaks of these in the aggregate as a "vast black whirlpool" that is threatening to engulf both man and his world:

It is with the coming of man that a vast hole seems to open in nature, a vast black whirlpool spinning faster and faster, consuming flesh, stones, soil, minerals, sucking down the lightning, wrenching power from the atom, until the ancient sounds of nature are drowned in the cacophony of something which is no longer nature, something instead which is loose and knocking at the world's heart, something demonic and no longer planned—escaped, it may be— spewed out of nature, contending in a final giant's game against its master.[11]

The science community is much more concerned about this tragic happening, and its implications for the future, than it used to be. It realizes that once atomic energy was unlocked its immediate use in war was far from reassuring as to man's good sense. Nor is it at all certain that cybernetics, another powerful resource for the transformation of the world, will in the long run be beneficent for either man or nature as a whole. Scientists and humanists alike fear that the new technology made possible by atomic energy and cybernetics may lead to the dominance of man by his machines. Moreover, man may commit racial suicide; even if he doesn't the quality of his life may degenerate until it is quite worthless. Many scientists have a sense of urgency about this, as did Norbert Wiener, the late pioneer, genius, and prophet of the "age of cyberculture," when he said, "The hour is very late, and the choice of good and evil knocks at our door."

Not the least disturbing trait of this upstart, man, is his tendency to "play God." Having achieved almost godlike power over nature, he acts altogether too often as though it exists for him exclusively and he is entitled to do with it whatever he wishes, regardless of the consequences for other beings. Thus Eiseley quotes a fellow scientist who wrote not long ago:

"Balance of nature? An outmoded biological concept. There is no room for sentiment in modern science. We shall learn to get along without birds if necessary. After all, the dinosaurs disappeared. Man merely makes the process go faster. Everything changes in time."

To this Eiseley remarks, as would many another scientist today:

And so it does. But let us be as realistic as the gentleman would wish. It may be we who go. I am just primitive enough to hope that somehow, somewhere, a cardinal may still be whistling on a green bush when the last man goes blind before his man-made sun. If it should turn out that we have mishandled our lives as several civilizations before us have done, it seems a pity that we should involve the violet and the tree frog in our departure.

To perpetrate this final act of malice seems somehow disproportionate beyond endurance. It is like tampering with the secret purposes of the universe itself and involving not just man but life in the final holocaust—an act of petulant, deliberate blasphemy.[12]

Can there be any doubt that something utterly "unnatural" has emerged in nature during the human period, something diabolical that just doesn't fit into the age-old scheme of things symbolized by the long-range upward curve of evolutionary development? Surely this malignity is truly evil and unnatural, because it is destructively and lethally against the main thrust of nature with its creative drive toward integration, organization, unification, and community. During the extremely short career of man the curve that has been upward for several billions of years has been wrenched sharply downward and is now in grave danger of "hitting bottom." So powerful is this lethal factor that it is now threatening in one brief, terrible flash to destroy much or all of what it has taken evolution long ages to produce. The question is, of course, whether this is but a short-range drop in the curve, a momentary oscillation, after which the normal upward rise of the curve will be resumed. We do not know and cannot know. The old predictors of the future are no longer adequate in view of the presence in the situation of the new and unpredictable lethal factor. Certainly the old comforting notion of assured, inevitable progress[13] is no longer tenable.

COUNTERVAILING REMEDIALITY

On the other hand, this supposedly factual account would not be accurate or complete if it did not point out also that man is by no means completely and incorrigibly lethal and that his evil tendencies are not the only utterly new factors in the situation. Man *is* capable also of quite unprecedented altruism and goodness. Thus he has inserted calculated benevolence into nature-history, and observably strong countervailing remedial forces, designed to reduce now, and eventually to control, both calamitous misfortune and evil*—and possibly even to eliminate the latter. That he

---

* Notice that here again there is no mention of "sin." Nor is it claimed that a scientific remedy for "sin" has been or can be devised.

may not be able actually to achieve this goal, or even want to, does not change the fact that there are now in the system of nature potent new processes that are by design remedial with regard to misfortune and evil.

One of the agents of man for accomplishing this has been science-and-technology. Science has sought to discover the causes of misfortune and evil, and technology (including those of its components that are based on the social sciences) has been providing techniques for their control. In this dual endeavor they have for some time been signally successful with respect to the nonhuman aspects of nature. For a long time, however, they were thought to be impotent with regard to the remedial transformation of man himself, since he, especially his so-called spiritual nature, was considered to be "outside of nature" and its causal system. It was believed almost universally that an "evil person," say, one with compulsive homicidal or kleptomaniac tendencies, could not be changed into a "good" useful one except through so-called religious conversion. For a "crazy" person even that possibility seemed closed off, and he was "put away" in an "insane asylum," usually for life, without any thought of a possible cure. Now we know a great deal about mental illness, including criminality and insanity, and can in many cases effect cures predictably by means of surgery, drugs, electric shock, and psychological or psychiatric treatment. This has brought about a much more humane attitude toward the mentally ill and the problem of evil. Today if a man kills a number of people, deliberately or otherwise, we ask first of all— before taking punitive action—whether or not he was mentally ill. Indeed, following the lead of the distinguished psychiatrist Karl Menninger, we wonder whether punishment as conventionally conceived is not itself inhumane and criminal.[14]

The situation is, then, that potent techniques do exist for the benevolent, predictable transformation and control of persons and societal evils and that these are accompanied widely by humane attitudes and understandings in regard to their proper use. There seems to be no reason why their efficiency should not improve further until it is possible in large measure to control deliberate or pathological evil. This development of remedial processes directed against both the misfortunes and evils evident in nature-history is one of the most remarkable emergences in the human period. And this fact is not negated by the evident possibilities for further evil that this development itself brings with it.

Moreover, this development has for many people, scientists and others, become the basis for hope for a better world in the future. They think the curve of evolutionary advance that has been bent sharply downward in the human period *can* be turned upward again. It seems undeniable that there is this possibility, and this could not have been asserted on any basis of substantial evidence until recently. In the perspective of this hope, the present time, the twentieth century, is seen as a period of transition in terrestrial evolution, another change of state. It is a time of the incipient emergence of new realities that will in the future be regarded as further flowerings of mind and spirit, consistent with the creative upward thrust of the long-range development of the past. The major emergence expected is that of *humanity as an organic whole,* as distinguished from humanity as simply an aggregation of many individuals. Thus to the series of past major emergences—elementary particles, atoms, molecules, plants, animals, men—there would be added still another, the new social communal organism: humanity. And this would presumably come about by the same creative process of aggregation-organization-and-integration that has been operating throughout terrestrial history.

THE NEXT GREAT EMERGENCE? INTEGRATED HUMANITY?

The language used here is again obviously analogical, similar to that of Teilhard in *The Phenomenon of Man.* An integrated mankind is visualized as being achieved by individual human beings coming together to constitute a new entity, much as molecules join to constitute a crystal, or as they are aggregated, organized, and integrated into a living organism. Thus the entity, humanity, will bear a relationship to its constituent men and women similar to that of the biological cell or of a physical crystal to its constituent molecules. This analogy is helpful in several ways. First, it helps us to get a feel for the process by which a unified humanity can be brought into being as an *integrate,* to use Sinnott's instructive term. What it will take is a bringing together of individuals and subgroups and then their organization and articulation into one integrated, systemic whole. Second, it may allay some of our fears, by helping us to see that, far from requiring the enslavement or dehumanization of the individual, this process may multiply his degrees of freedom and the possibilities for richer and more human creative existence.

The process of unification and organization, and thus integration, is not necessarily an unmitigated evil when applied to individual free men in the formation of an integrated humanity. Hasn't the frontier history of our country shown clearly that when the lone mountain man or isolated settler accepted absorption into families and communities, and these further united into organized counties and states and so on, he thereby gained, not lost, his true freedom— freedom conceived as the totality of avenues or possibilities for significant creative thought and action, rather than as mere release from constraints? To be sure, the isolated mountain man had almost complete liberty in the sense that there were very few social restraints upon his mobility and behavior. He did not have to be a gentleman; he could "do as he pleased" with virtually no law to say yea or nay. But he was not free to achieve much of anything except to satisfy a minimum of biological needs. When he married and became a settler he had to give up some of his freedom *from* constraint but thereby gained much more freedom *for* a fuller biological existence, for creating family and community, for engaging in the arts and crafts, in commerce and politics, or in the building of systems of thought, all of which become possible only through communally integrated living.

One is reminded here—returning to the analogy of a change of state—of what happens to a molecule of water vapor (very far away from others and virtually free to move in any direction and with any speed) when it congregates with others to produce, say, a drop of water or a snow crystal. It does lose its freedom to move at random and becomes bound by and to others in definite structural interrelationships, but it thereby acquires the freedom, i.e., range of possibilities, to participate in the creation of many phenomena and realities which would have been completely beyond its capacity in its isolated state. It can now contribute to the reflection and refraction of light and thus to the painting of the rainbow, the iridescence of the butterfly wing, or the sparkle of the waterfall or the snow-clad mountainside. Molecules integrated into the structures of crystalline solids, such as metals, help to generate and transport electric power. In the nervous systems of men they participate in the transmission of decision-making messages by means of electric impulses. In plants they are involved in the production of mutations and thus in the emergence of new varieties and species.

Nor should it be thought that within these physical or social integrates the single individual loses its identity or function and becomes an inert, static, helpless, do-nothing entity. Far from it; for, as we have seen, investigation of the depths of a water drop or snow crystal or living cell has disclosed that any molecule in it is a tremendously dynamic system of systems which together contribute positively to what Donald Andrews calls the symphony of the world and of life. Moreover, because of its interactions with other entities of the integrate, and with the integrate as a whole, the molecule's contribution to the symphony is richer than it would be otherwise.

Similarly, an individual person in a community, or in the overall new humanity, need not lose his own identity or significance. It is much more likely that, the more relationships he enters into there, the more unique a person he will be and the more significant a function he will be able to perform therein. Therefore, though the expected "new humanity" may possibly turn out to be a monstrous totalitarian dehumanizing machine, it is at least as probable that it will be a remarkably democratic, humane, and profoundly fulfilling societal organism in which all its individual constituents can be *themselves in the most meaningful and satisfying way possible.*

THE POWER
OF SELF-TRANSCENDENCE AND LOVE

Potent support for this hopeful vision comes most convincingly from the fact that persons, unlike inanimate molecules, display qualities of spirit, particularly those that make for self-transcendence by the individual and for self-conscious communal attitudes and relationships. The first of these qualities is love, of a kind and to a degree not found at subhuman levels of existence. We now know on scientific grounds what the great seers of our race have known for a long time, namely, that to be loved and to love are basic necessities of human life, not luxuries. Without love, children and adolescents cannot feel secure or mature normally. Old age needs it quite as much, though for other reasons. For the intervening years of adulthood, there is much evidence that even though a person is surrounded with the most perfect of goods and comforts, and the most expert of professional services, if none of these is accompanied by love his life will be tragically empty or even distorted.

Next we know that all people need at least two kinds of love. One is that of the so-called I-Thou relationship: conjugal or filial love, or, say, the affection of deep friendship or of the master-disciple relationship. This love is accompanied by one or more of the manifestations we speak of as deep feeling: stirring emotion, profound understanding, sense of unity, desire for mutual helpfulness, erotic passion, and still others. The other kind is a more distant love and is directed toward casual acquaintances or passers-by who need recognition, one's neighbor, or the stranger who is in need.

While these two varieties of love differ in the depth of personal involvement, and usually of emotion, they both have what seem to be the most fundamental ingredients of love: an awareness of the presence and value of the other person as a fellow human being, rather than an inconsequential object; sensitivity and responsiveness to his mood and need; openness and receptivity that make for mutuality and understanding; and a desire to be helpful—without thought of advantage to oneself.

Another feature of human love that we are becoming increasingly aware of scientifically (through the social sciences) is its tremendous transformative and creative power. It functions not simply to make life more pleasant but to transform it and make it creative. Man is a promise- or prophecy-fulfilling being, especially if the prophecy comes out of unselfish love. When a boy is told, by someone he respects and believes, that he has the makings of an artist or a scientist, this is likely to do something to him, create a new possibility for him, and release energy and drives within him that may turn that possibility into reality. The physician who says you'll get better, the nurse who says you already look better, the teacher, the classmate, or the employer who says that you'll make good in your job, may all release such transforming, prophecy-fulfilling energy.

It must surely be clear that in these manifestations of love man is truly self-transcending, reaching beyond himself and his own immediate concerns and needs, giving of himself as creative, transforming power and influence in the lives of other beings. Moreover, it must be obvious that it is precisely this kind of manifestation of spirit that makes for genuine mutuality, and devotion to the common good, and therefore for the establishment of community. This is why Teilhard has designated love as *the* cohesive force that makes genuine community possible—without the coercion of tyrannical brute force and enslavement. Says he:

Love alone is capable of uniting beings in such a way as to complete and fulfill them, for it alone takes them and joins them by what is deepest in themselves.

Mankind, the spirit of the earth, the synthesis of individuals and peoples, the paradoxical conciliation of the element with the whole, and unity with multitude—[for these] to be incarnate in the world all we may well need is to imagine our power of loving developing until it embraces the total of men and of the earth.[15]

I take this statement to be thoroughly in accord with post-modern scientific insights in regard to the nature of man, and community, and love. Indeed it is a scientific, not primarily religious, statement that expresses an observable aspect of the world and therefore part of the post-modern scientific vision.

A profound analysis of love as a causal factor in the future evolution of man has been provided also by Edwin A. Burtt, who suggests that one aspect of love is to be open and responsive to the experience of others—both human and nonhuman others—and to share such experience, and thus to make it part of one's own experience. This, he suggests further, is the only way true knowledge and understanding of both persons and things are achievable. It means transcending what is often called "pure objectivity." Since genuine community is inconceivable without true mutual knowledge and understanding, Burtt concludes that

ultimately, growth in each individual and in the human race is growth in unobstructed sensitivity and alert responsiveness—that is, in love. The essense of cosmic evolution at the human level would seem to be unending progress from the greatest love yet realized toward the greater love that always lies ahead.[16]

If the human spirit were not capable of such growth in love, the hope for a restoration of the upwardness of the curve of evolution, and for continued development in that direction, would be futile. Burtt feels, however, that "already we have seen persuasive evidence" that it does have that capacity.

THE GROWING SENSE
OF COMMUNAL MORAL RESPONSIBILITY

Still another spirit-quality of *men* that undergirds hope for the emergence of an integrated *Man* is their growing sense of moral responsibility for the common good. Morality* is life lived respondingly, and therefore responsibly. It is not a particular part or area of life in which there are particular kinds of problems that may be designated as

---

* Morality is not herein taken to be synonymous with religion. Morality may be enhanced or impoverished by religion, depending on the religion; but it is not religion.

moral ones. Wherever and whenever men make decisions, there morality enters the picture as a sense of obligation to decide responsibly, with an awareness of consequences for all beings, human and nonhuman, that might be affected by the decisions made, and with a desire to be held responsible for those consequences.

One of the advances in morality that has come to men in the post-modern period is an increasing awareness that so-called moral principles for responsible decision-making must not be taken as absolutes or as rigid laws to be applied indiscriminately or uncritically in all situations. It is an extremely important part of contemporary insight— in recognition of the primacy of relationship and event as determinants of reality, and of their dynamic and changing character—that the moral problem is always relative to its context, and that moral principles must therefore be conceived and applied adaptively, not absolutely.

Moral principles are thus taken as properly flexible guidelines rather than as rigid laws, and this confers upon them much dynamic power and usefulness, more than any rigid law can possibly possess. It is like the well-known difference between the elastic, compliant strength of tempered steel and that of unyielding, rigid, untempered iron.

Now I suggest that it is precisely this quality of dynamic, yielding strength, rather than that of unyielding fixity, that makes for the kind of moral fiber that is needed for the global communal moral fabric of the future. For it is of the very nature of community that its members and subgroups adapt responsibly to one another for the common good, rather than holding uncompromisingly to individual conviction and independent rights. It is the tree (and community) whose parts can individually bend with it under the onslaughts of wind and storm that survives and grows stronger, while the one whose parts do not yield is uprooted and dies. It is also this kind of internal mutual adapting, yielding, and strengthening by its individual constituent entities that one might expect to see in a community undergirded by love, and a sense of interdependence, and responsible concern for the good of one another and of the whole.

part three

**Insights of the
New Religious
Consciousness**

X. The Mystery of Transcendence-Immanence

NATURE'S INEFFABILITY

Sooner or later any study of physical reality leads to the subject of ineffability, for it seems that not only is reality unfathomable in the far reaches of its depths, but, insofar as it can be fathomed, the experience and knowledge it yields is not completely or adequately expressible linguistically—not even in the "languages" of the arts. In the modern period it was thought that nature could in principle be described and presented completely by scientific theories that supposedly pictured reality in one-to-one correspondence between concept and physical entity. Light "really" was waves, and there "really" was an aether through which such waves could be propagated. Scientific method seemed supremely potent, not only in logical inference and genuine knowledge but in description. Eventually everything would not only be known but be told—completely and with precision. To speak at that time of an ineffability of scientifically observable nature would have been regarded as meaningless. To be sure, the raptures of love and the beauty of the raindrop were ineffable, but these were not recognized as real from a scientific point of view, whereas the chemical reactions of love acts and the dispersion of light by raindrops were. Today, however, if my appraisal of the post-modern situation is correct, scientists are keenly aware that there is probably no aspect of nature that is not ineffable to some degree.

The human mind has not evolved equally in all directions, and in many respects it is still disappointingly weak. Our languages, for example, are much more potent for saying some things than for others. Thus in our own culture

it has been for quite some time much easier to talk meaningfully about quantities than about qualities, to describe
an automobile rather than the taste of apple pie or the
fragrance of hyacinths. One can say without difficulty how
large a car is, how much it weighs, how many windows and
doors it has, and what its geometric shape is, and specify
the number of cylinders of its engine, the safety devices,
and so on. Provide enough of such information and you
have said most of what seems important about a car. Many
words are available for such purposes.

In the case of apple pie, however, what is one to say?
Just how *does* it taste? Like apples? Well, yes, but only
approximately so, for certainly apple pie and apples are
distinguishable in taste. And, anyway, how do apples taste?
One can say: not like strawberries or onions, perhaps more
like pears. But how specifically do *they* taste? Such adjec-
tives as bitter or sweet, tart or bland, and the like are helpful but singularly vague. The fact is that we simply haven't
produced enough words and ideas with which to tell adequately how things taste or smell or feel tactually, or to
describe accurately the different pains that may plague us,
or the joys that delight us, or the variety of nuances of
tonal combinations encountered in Mozart's or Bartok's
music, or the impact of different personalities upon, say,
our emotions.

Admittedly in regard to qualities the poet's language of
symbol, metaphor, analogy, and myth is superior to that of
the sciences, whereas the latter excels in regard to quantity, logic, and precision. And yet they are not altogether
different. One is reminded of Robert Frost's perceptive
observation:

There are many other things I have found myself saying about
poetry, but the chiefest of these is that it is metaphor, saying one
thing and meaning another, the pleasure of ulteriority. Poetry is
simply made of metaphor. So also is philosophy—and science, too,
for that matter, if it will take soft impeachment from a friend.[1]

Surely it is not at all an impeachment when Frost thinks of
science in this way; witness, for instance, what the late
physicist, Philipp Frank, went so far as to say:

The main activity of science . . . consists in the invention of symbols and in the building of a symbolic system from which our experience can logically be derived. . . . The work of the scientist is probably not fundamentally different from the work of the poet.[2]

The reason for this, he said, is that "reality in its fulness can only be experienced, never presented. . . . Every presentation, scientific or poetic, proceeds by creating symbols."[2]

As philosopher Frederick Ferré observes, an "element of mystery . . . must always veil the relation between conceptual synthesis—however intelligible—and reality,"[3] and this is why, as we have seen repeatedly herein, scientific discourse also finds it necessary to employ symbolic language to a considerable extent. The symbolic systems Frank referred to are the theories and models of science, which, as interpreted by critical realism, inform us a great deal about nature while yet not functioning as pictorial representations of it—thus leaving much of it undescribed.

A theologian who is aware of this contemporary understanding of science and its methodology is Ian Ramsey, who points out:

Models, whether in theology or science, are not descriptive miniatures, they are not picture enlargements; in each case they point to mystery, to the need to live as best we can with theological and scientific uncertainties.

It is in these ways and for these reasons that we may say that theorizing by models is the understanding of a mystery whose depths are never sounded by man's plumblines, however long and however diverse these lines may be, however far developed.[4]

What theologian, philosopher, and scientist seem to agree on here is that science's contemporary use and understanding of theories and models, as intentionally symbolic rather than pictorial in function, is an indication that it has found nature to be only partially knowable *and*, more than that, only partially expressible. Thus post-modern science has contributed to man's awareness of the *mystery of nature's ineffability.*

Incidentally I reject the view—too often a cynical one— that it is nonsense to *speak* of anything as being ineffable (for instance, divinity and divine presence) since, if to be ineffable means that it cannot be put into words, it is but good grace to remain silent and not make claims (or theologize) about it. But this is not the idea at all. There is probably nothing about which it is impossible or inappropriate to say anything at all. Furthermore, *the connotation of "nature's ineffability" is not that we cannot say anything about it but that we cannot say nearly enough.* Man's experience of it, including science's experience, always exceeds man's ability to conceptualize it adequately; hence his perpetual wonderment about *what-is-known-but-cannot-be-said* quite satisfactorily.

There seem to be two aspects of the ineffability of nature as "seen through the eyes of science," one somewhat specific and the other more general. As to the former, the sense of our not ever being able to say enough comes in part from the new consciousness of nature's immensity, or possibly even its boundlessness in space-time-depth; from its tremendous complexity, along with its evident simplifiability; and from its vast qualitative variety in structure and process. Then there are also those features of it that Ramsey speaks of as scientific uncertainties: its indeterminacy and unpredictability that block any effort to be completely precise in specifying what happens to individual entities, rather than to great numbers of them, and especially its overall positive spontaneity and creativity that bring forth utter novelty.

Regarding the more general aspect of nature's ineffability, the encounter with natural phenomena often evokes a consciousness of dimensions or manifestations of reality that lie beyond the purview of science. Not infrequently this brings with it a sensing that mystery surrounds not only the scientifically known or unknown but also that which can be—and is—experienced in other ways. This is the point of the observation by Whitehead quoted in chapter I, "When you understand all about the sun and all about the atmosphere and all about the rotation of the earth, you may still miss the radiance of the sunset."[5]

This radiance is sensed as being or extending beyond the scientifically known or knowable. It is the point also, I think, of a remark by physicist Henry Margenau: "I would be tempted to say that the ratio of what we know scientifically to what we do not understand in scientific terms has been, is and will forever be zero. This is the reason why I believe that science will never do away with politics, poetry and religion."[6]

I suspect that it was this feature of nature, its including what lies beyond scientific perception, that Philipp Frank had in mind, at least in part, when he suggested that "reality in its fulness can only be experienced, never presented."

HUMAN THRESHOLD EXPERIENCE

At this point let us consider the remarkable characteristic of mankind, referred to in Robert Frost's remark quoted a while ago: man is the being who enjoys *the pleasure of ulteriority.* What a wonderfully suggestive expression this is! According to Webster *ulterior* refers to the other side, the beyond, "over the horizon." Man is truly human when he feels a compelling urge to wonder about the ulterior, the unmanifest, beyond what is at the time known and expressible—and takes pleasure in it. Philip Wheelwright speaks of this by means of another suggestive expression: Man is the being with *threshold experience.*

> Man always lives on the verge, always on the borderland of something more. He is the animal, apparently, who has built restlessness into a metaphysical principle. . . . Indeed the intimation of something more, beyond the horizon, belongs to the very nature of consciousness. To be conscious is not just to be; it is to mean, to intend, to point beyond oneself, to testify that some kind of beyond exists and to be ever on the verge of entering it.[7]

Still other writers speak of this as the *limiting experience* of man, experience at the limiting boundary between the known and unknown, where so-called "limiting queries" arise, where wonderment—more than the analytic, critical question—takes over. In elaborating his theme Wheelwright speaks of the thresholds of *time*, of the *world*, and of the *unseen*.

As I see things, it is at the threshold of the unseen that one wonders and reflects upon just what Whitehead could have meant by the radiance of the sunset, for it is here that many men come to feel rather compellingly that human seeing is not confined to physical perception and that there is very much about the world that is real and would be missed if this were not so. Isn't much of what is most precious and meaningful to us, and of what we are most sure, known to us by means that transcend our senses? Is it not for the compelling reality of its radiance that we most prize the sunset? Doesn't the haunting bitter-sweet of Beethoven's last string quartets require for its actual hearing very much more than acoustic listening? The love shining from the eyes of a bride, the pride of a mother in her son, the fascinations of numbers, and the compulsions of reason: are these not all *realities* treasured by the human spirit? And yet our being sure of them surely does not rest only on physiological perception.

For the most part the questions that are asked in threshold experience differ significantly from those asked otherwise. For one thing, of course, they pertain to what is beyond the verge or brink, to the ulterior that is not obvious, to what is not clearly perceived or conceived. For another, they seem to be evoked by rather indistinct intimations more than by clear-cut perceptions. It is important, however, in this connection, to distinguish between so-called proximate thresholds and the ultimate threshold. There are many beyonds and therefore many thresholds: the beyond science, yet within nature (e.g., the radiance of the sunset); the beyond the arts, beyond the rational, beyond the conceptualizable; the threshold between the inanimate and life, between life and mind, mind and spirit. These are all proximate, nearby gateways. Finally there is the threshold of the ultimate, beyond all proximates and immediates. At this threshold especially one experiences "intimations" or "feelings" or "sensings" of a different kind of a beyond, signaled by what Peter Berger has in a recent delightful book called rumors[8] rather than by reports in the usual sense. Moreover, the questions and reflections that present themselves in *this* threshold encounter seem to be born less of intellectual curiosity than of personal existential concern, brought forth by a sense of what transcends the world of physical reality, and the world of immediate concerns, and is discerned to be of ultimate worth and meaning—that which matters most. It is in this way that men and women become conscious of *ultimacy* and its unfathomable and ineffable mystery.

As we shall see presently, while science itself does not lead to or reveal the ultimate, it does provide a mode of access to its threshold—not so much through compelling logical deduction as through intuitive insight that may be even more compelling. And it does this by "pointing" toward ultimacy; as Tillich put it, "Reality, every bit of reality, is inexhaustible and points to the ultimate mystery of being itself which transcends the endless series of scientific questions and answers."[9]

"POINTINGS" TOWARD THE "ULTIMATE"

In what sense can known reality, and especially scientifically known reality, be said to "point" toward anything that transcends scientific inquiry or to "the ultimate mystery of being itself?" First, one senses that anything truly mysterious comprises far more than it is sensually perceived to be, that much of it is hidden in the unseen or not-yet-understood beyond, or that what is seen is a breakthrough from that beyond. Thus the manifest points to, or intimates that there is, an unmanifest beyond and evokes wonderment about it. Certainly the mystery aspects of physical reality which we have been studying herein, and which seem inexhaustible and unfathomable, do point in this sense to a "more" or a "beyond," beyond what has come to be known thus far.

Second, a pointing beyond itself may be in either a horizontal or vertical direction, analogically speaking, toward what is at the same hierarchical level or may be at a different one above or below it. When we designate a "beyond it" as "transcendent" we mean that it is sensed to be in a vertical direction and at a higher level. From this point of view the mysteries of a bit of inanimate matter, such as a water drop, are regarded as pointing to what is *for it* transcendent mystery when they point upward toward the levels of life, but not when they point sidewise toward other mysteries of essentially the same kind, i.e., to other species of inanimate matter. Similarly life points upward to mind, which transcends it, and mind to spirit transcendent above it. And finally we may say that all of the mystery-reality we have called matter-energy-life-mind-spirit, with which science is concerned, points beyond itself, intimating the existence of levels of Being above it and of an ultimately Transcendent one, "beyond the endless series of scientific questions and answers." There are involved here, I suspect, both rational and nonrational pointings, reasoned and intuitive ones, and probably always some of both. The discussion of the ineffable in nature, in the preceding chapter, presents a variety of pointings (though not all of them toward the transcendent), some of which come for the most part from formal analysis and others from informal reflection or intuitive perception.

A third and more specific case of pointing from scientific considerations toward a possibly ultimate Transcendent may be found in the perennial question of the ultimate *Why?* of things. I doubt that there has ever been a scientist who has not at one time or another asked that haunting question. Why *is* physical reality this way rather than another? And why *is* it at all? Does it have any eternal significance?

As has been said interminably, science cannot and does not even try to answer ultimate *why?* questions. It simply "explains" *how* things known to exist do in fact interact to produce phenomena and happenings. This information is, of course, of immense importance, but it does not explain ultimately *why* things interact as they do rather than in another way. The *why?* of that remains utter mystery.

The fact is, however, that science is such that its quest for *how?* seems part of a larger quest for *why?* While science does not answer the limiting question of *why?*, it certainly does evoke it powerfully. This is because actually the scientist seeks not only knowledge but understanding[10] —even though he realizes that complete understanding is not to be had through science alone. No wonder, then, that his search for answers to successive preliminary whys (hows) leads him sooner or later to ponder the final limiting question of *Why?* This is one way that science points to ultimate mystery, or even leads to the threshold of it, though it does not in itself reveal it.

In part this unquenchable longing for a final explanation, from above the level of *How?*, comes out of modern and post-modern man's keen sense of the *givenness* of things. Here is another, the fourth, pointing toward a transcendent beyond, toward some sort of a "giver"—however this may be conceived. There are two aspects of this.

To begin with, we sense that the fundamental nature of things, the overall scheme of things, the matrix or context within which we operate, is something to which we *must* submit, and which calls for discipline on our part if we would succeed in understanding it. Thus the artist and engineer must certainly reckon with and adapt to the materials with which he would work. Similarly the scientist must adjust to the matrix of natural law. His awareness in the laboratory of what is often called the "cussedness of nature"* is but the discovery of the stubborn, unyielding ways of nature from which there is simply no escape. They are there to be accepted as they are. Here "given" refers to the inescapable "is-ness" of things.

Also, out of this sense of their is-ness comes the further feeling that these so-called "givens" are really "given" to man, i.e., are not of his own doing. Post-modern science has made us deeply conscious that the universe is a great creative process in which, to be sure, man has an active part, but which has levels, hierarchical structures, and operations that extend far beyond him and are quite beyond his control. Some theologians have interpreted this awareness correctly, it seems to me, as a sense of our creaturehood, as, for instance, Bernard Meland has in the following remark:

The context of human existence . . . presents to each of us a sense of something given, to which we are related in elemental ways. However far we develop and use our human powers, we do not slough off this elemental condition of being creatures of a Creative Process that is not made by us. . . . It is given as a primordial fact of our existence.[11]

---

* A term made famous by James B. Conant a few years ago, and immediately understood and accepted by the science community.

Elsewhere he speaks of the restoration to us of a "vivid sense of creaturehood" as one of those significant developments of our time that have alerted us to the "distinctions between our thoughts and reality," and between "that which we understand or is available to understanding, and that which is beyond our comprehension."[12] This is a pointing—to a genuinely mysterious, transcendent creativity dimly discernible as the Ultimate Source of the givens themselves and of the matrix of their observable *how* relationships; and therein is intimated the answer to the ultimate *Why?* of existence. Here in this haunting *Why?* we *may* encounter Ultimate Mystery, according to the seventh meaning of mystery considered in the Appendix, namely, *the mystery of radical questionableness.*

There are still other pointings, at least for some people, intimations concerning the character and existential significance of the transcendent creative mystery-reality. Most of these I shall discuss later with reference specifically to the subject of religion and "God." At this point, however, I would like to illustrate such pointing by reference to Spirit (not spirit) as the ultimate quality-reality.

INTIMATIONS OF ULTIMATE SPIRIT

The pointings considered thus far seem rather general in character, intimating little more than that reality extends beyond the manifest into the realm of the unmanifest; that in that mysterious beyond, and beyond all proximates, there is something called "ultimacy"; and finally that it is the reality of ultimacy that perennially evokes man's haunting radical query of the ultimate *Why?* But this seems terribly abstract and vague and leaves one with the impression that the ultimate is simply an undifferentiated, characterless, empty "something." There are, however, other pointings also, powerful and much more revealing ones, with more definite and specific intimations. Some of these arise from man's experience with the manifestations of spirit in human and nonhuman existence.

Unfortunately, however, the term *spirit* has widely been regarded in our time as an embarrassment to serious thought, because of connotations regarding ghosts, good and evil "spirits," disembodied immortal souls, and so on. Many persons have felt, therefore, that it is one of the categories that should be discarded by contemporary thought, especially religious thought, which has perhaps employed it most frequently. On the other hand some distinguished thinkers, notably Tillich and Meland, have felt that it must by all means be retained, because properly interpreted it can have rich meaning for post-modern man. They seem to be suggesting also that terms can be maximally meaningful for religion today only if they have deep roots in the realities of secular existence—and that the concept of spirit is so rooted and is therefore not expendable.

Now this secular foundation for the understanding of spirit I have tried to provide at least in part in preceding chapters, and it seems to me to be consistent in its essentials with Tillich's point of view. He speaks of life having the commonly recognized dimensions of the inorganic and organic, plus that of spirit. He distinguishes this from the psychological dimension of inner awareness and sets forth its meaning as follows: "As the power of life, spirit is not identical with the inorganic substratum which is animated by it; rather spirit is the power of animation itself and not a part added to the organic system." He then designates "man as that organism in which the dimension of spirit is dominant."[13] His approach, like mine, denies the legitimacy of any reductionism that would establish either a materialistic monism or a dualism of matter and spirit. He rules out such reductions by what he calls the principle of multidimensional unity, which in terms of the symbolism of my approach might be called the principle of the hierarchical unity of levels and/or states. For some purposes the symbol of *dimensions* is more helpful than that of *levels*; but for others the latter may be, as for example for the next consideration.

It is because man is aware of the reality of animating spirit at his own level that there can come to him intimations of an animating reality at levels above his own. Seeing spirit as the creative and unifying power in animal and man opens his consciousness to Spirit (using Tillich's upper-case symbol) as the creative and unifying reality in all realms of Being. This is why it makes sense to so many people to speak of God in terms of the symbolism of spirit and Spirit. Here, then, is an important case of a particular mystery-reality of nature (spirit) pointing to an analogous transcendent reality beyond (Spirit).

We have studied two aspects of spirit that Meland regards as especially significant for religious thought. The first is that spirit manifests itself not only in animation but in sensitivity and love, out of which its creative power derives; and the second, that spirit achieves its maximum power and meaning in community. For Meland, therefore, ultimate Spirit is a communal reality of sensitivity and gentle, loving might.[14]

So conceived the ultimate spirit—or Spirit—is far from being only a nondescript, characterless "something" in the beyond. It is an awesome reality that displays the qualities of spirit to a transcendent degree. Consider also the remediality of nature and man. The remarkable emergence of remedial processes set into motion by the human spirit against evil—after man had himself introduced most of it into the world—has for many sensitive people pointed to a higher reality of Spirit. They sense that here there is at work in life much more than only the spirit of man, and that man's remedial action is actually a participation in the remedial action of transcendent Spirit. While science cannot, of course, itself observe any ultimate process of that sort, such remedial action as it can observe provides intimations of it. There can be little doubt that the curve of evolutionary advance *was* bent down ominously with the coming of the lethal factor in nature-and-history; it is equally evident, however, at least to him who can perceive things in depth, that there is another causal factor that must be reckoned with: man's ability to change things remedially in response to, and in participation with, ultimate remediality—which we shall later designate as divine.

"ANGELS"? "SIGNALS OF TRANSCENDENCE"?

There is yet another kind of pointing toward ultimacy which contributes specific intimations regarding the character of the ultimate. It comes out of anthropological studies by Peter Berger, as presented in his book, *A Rumor of Angels*. He points out that basically the term *angels* means "God's messengers" and need not be equated with medieval imagery portraying them as "personal beings" with "spiritual" nonmaterial bodies, including wings. Therefore, he suggests, its fundamental intent would not be violated if it were taken to mean "signals of transcendence" encountered "within the empirically given situation." He says:

> By signals of transcendence I mean phenomena that are to be found within the domain of our "natural" reality, but that appear to point beyond that reality . . . prototypical human gestures that may constitute such signals . . . certain reiterated acts and experiences that appear to express essential aspects of man's being, . . . not what Jung called "archetypes"—potent symbols buried deep in the unconscious mind that are common to all men. The phenomena . . . are not "unconscious" and do not have to be excavated from the "depths" of the mind; they belong to ordinary everyday awareness.[15]

Among man's prototypical gestures that are germane here are those arising out of his propensity for order, for play, for hope oriented toward the future, for damnation, for humor, and for worship.

To illustrate Berger's reasoning, let us consider the first of these in some detail.* Man's propensity for ordering and systematizing things, his ideas, his natural environment, his social structures and processes, is one of his most obvious traits. Without it there would be no art, or science, or religion; no education, politics, commerce, or technology. Moreover, Berger feels, men have a

> compelling faith in order as such, a faith closely related to man's fundamental trust in reality. . . . Man's propensity for order is grounded in a faith or trust that, ultimately, reality is "in order," "all right," "as it should be." Needless to say, there is no empirical method by which this faith can be tested. To assert it is itself an act of faith. But it is possible to proceed from the faith that is rooted in experience to the act of faith that transcends the empirical sphere, a procedure that could be called the *argument from ordering*.
> In this sense, every ordering gesture is a signal of transcendence.

---

* Supposing that the reader will want to study the others in detail in Berger's book.

Also in generalizing on this, Peter Berger continues:

In the observable human propensity to order reality there is an intrinsic impulse to give cosmic scope to this order, an impulse that implies not only that human order in some way corresponds to an order that transcends it, but that this transcendent order is of a character that man can trust himself and his destiny to it.

Similarly the gestures of joyful, liberating play transcend by their prototypical intent the ordinary world of experience in time and space and create a universe of their own, one that points to a world of eternity. "In joyful play it appears as if one were stepping not only from one chronology into another, but from time into eternity."[16]

The other gestures Berger refers to—those expressing man's unquenchable hope for a new and better world, those damning hellish evil as inconsistent with the primordial goodness of things, and those of religious ritual and worship—can also be interpreted in this way as signals, or intimations, of ultimate mystery and transcendence. While the reality thus intimated cannot be "proved" to exist "beyond doubt," it does seem powerfully to evoke man's response to it in these gestures. To understand man—and the cosmos—fully it is necessary to recognize these propensities and gestures as primal traits of the truly human being. And it is not unscientific to regard such gestures as responses to the *actual* evocative promptings and presence of an *actual* "transcendent," rather than as mere "psychological projections" of the needs or wishes of the human ego.

To the list of gestures that Berger has identified as prototypical, and that are significant for our present subject, I would add at least three more taken from our earlier discussion of intimations: those arising from man's propensity for loving, for creating, and for remedial action against evil. An anthropological analysis of these, similar to Berger's, would show, I think, that they too may be regarded as signals of transcendence, in this case pointing to a reality that is transcendently loving, creative, and remedial.

Another such gesturing is man's myth-making. Now a myth is not an untrue story but a profoundly true one, symbolically speaking. It is a literary form that has to do with the momentous threshold questions of the essential nature of reality, of life and death, and of the origin and destiny of good and evil; it communicates by means of metaphoric narrative what is intuited or known about these with ultimate concern; and in so doing it constitutes a gesture toward the transcendent.

TRANSCENDENT AND *IMMANENT*

Now let us turn from the subject of transcendence to that of immanence. My thesis is that nature, including human experience, provides strong intimations also of ultimate immanence. In other words, it points toward ultimate mystery, which in accordance with, say, biblical belief is not only transcendent to the world but immanent in it—God who dwells in us and we in him. Using Whitehead's language, it points toward the mystery that he sensed "beyond, behind, *and within* the passing flux of immediate things" (italics mine). According to common usage, it is the "beyond" that connotes transcendence and the "within" that suggests immanence.

Too often, these ideas are taken to be mutually exclusive, as though God *must* be conceived as either transcendent or immanent, one or the other, but not both. Thus much of conventional theism has been transcendental, insisting that God is "wholly" above and beyond the natural world; and so also has neo-orthodox thought, with its doctrine of divine revelation vertically from above (*senkrecht von oben*). Bishop John Robinson, on the other hand, has insisted that God is not in any sense "out there," in the "beyond," but "within" us, thus conceiving him as essentially immanent. As Meland points out:

Formulations of the Christian understanding of the nature of God have swung between conceptions which have lifted the reality of God above and beyond the wretched affairs of men, . . . and conceptions which have immersed God's reality wholly in the affairs and feelings of men.

Then he suggests that from "this rhythmic alternation . . . one should distill the obvious insight that both transcendence and immanence are essential even to a limited and tentative formulation of the character of the living God."[17]

Tillich came to the same conclusion about the biblical symbol "Kingdom of God": "In order to be both a positive and adequate answer to the question of the meaning of history, [it] must be immanent and transcendent at the same time. Any one-sided interpretation deprives the symbol of its power."

He pointed out that this unitary conception is thoroughly biblical, as evidenced by the Pauline expression "God being all in all," and reminded us that "the Kingdom of God is . . . a kingdom not only of men; it involves the fulfillment of life under all dimensions. This agrees with the multidimensional unity of life: fulfillment under one dimension implies fulfillment in all dimensions."[18]

This last remark is very much to the point for our subject. God's Kingdom takes in all reality in all of its dimensions or levels. To be sure, it is within us, but *not only* within. It extends beyond us, but *not only* beyond. In terms of this inclusive understanding, divine transcendence and immanence are complementary, rather than mutually exclusive, conceptions; and this insight helps us see how nature provides intimations and signals of ultimacy in both transcendence and immanence.

Thus if we may speak by analogy of a higher level of the hierarchy as transcendent to lower ones, then we may also speak of a lower one as immanent to the upper ones. If the many known levels in the vertical dimension of physical reality point upward to the possibility of still others not yet known, or still to emerge, and finally to ultimate transcendence beyond those, then the same may be said about immanence, with respect to the opposite vertical direction: downward toward the interior depths of reality.

For many persons, then, physical reality's many levels and seeming unboundedness in depth point toward ultimate divine immanence within it. A second, and more powerful, intimation of it comes from physical reality's apparently unlimited creative effluence, that hints of ultimate creativity at work *there*—within. Man's compulsive search for a physical ground level may be viewed (as in Berger's thought) as a prototypical gesturing signal of divine immanence, as this is implied in the concept of the ground of being.

This, then, brings us finally to the thought that the concept of divine immanence may after all refer simply to an aspect of divine transcendence. Perhaps it is man's proclivity for spatial, higher-or-lower, inner-or-outer analogies that is responsible at least in part for a tendency to differentiate rather sharply between transcendence and immanence—as though they were separate realms or entities of reality, or radically different relationships that God sustains toward the world.

I suggest that in its fundamental meaning the term *transcendent* actually does not refer directly to spatial or temporal relationships, or to a dichotomy of the external and internal—even though the term *immanent* does refer specifically to the within. What "the transcendent" refers to is the supreme and ultimate in the mystery of goodness, tenderness, sensitivity, love, creativity, and remediality—all conceived as existing and operating everywhere, and at all levels of the world. Its first syllable, "trans-," refers not to a spatial beyond but to the "infinitely more than" anything observable directly in us or the cosmos. If the term *transcendent* is given this meaning, then immanence is indeed but one important aspect of it, not something different from it.

Since in our post-modern era there is so strong a drive toward unification and integration, intellectually and otherwise, this way of thinking of the transcendent and immanent is surely more fruitful than others. Perhaps in order to emphasize this I may be permitted another hyphenation: ultimate mystery, God, is transcendent-immanent, not one or the other. I believe this mode of thought is consistent also with man's actual experience of mystery and intimations such as we have considered, for in this experience one is not directly aware of any polarity or separation with regard to the within or without of things.

I especially like the way in which Albert Outler puts it:

> This Mystery is immanent in every finite process at the same time that it also transcends all finites. Here, then, is the provident ground of the entire creation, with all its primordial possibilities; here is *the ambience of all its events and occasions;* here is the Good.[19]

It is the phrase I have italicized that appeals to me especially. An ambience of *all* its events and occasions is necessarily ambient at all levels of existence, that of the elementary particles, of the molecules, of the biological organisms, of the galaxies, as well as in all of history. Recalling the quotation (chapter II) from *A New Catechism,* this all-pervading ambience, whence come the myriads of intimations of the Ultimate, "is in our own home. The beings around me—men, plants and even objects—are a mystery which grows as I penetrate their nature."

Clearly this experience of the omnipresence of mystery and intimation does not itself differentiate between transcendence and immanence; hence my feeling that the latter is simply an aspect of the former.

XI. Today's Biblical Religious Consciousness

THE MEANING OF "BELIEVING IN GOD"
The term "God" has appeared several times in the preceding chapter. Since the subject there was *ultimacy* and *nature's intimations of it,* how did "God" get into it? Is it self-evident that ultimate mystery must be "God"? Suppose a transcendent-immanent reality does exist, and does signal its presence and character at least in part through nature's mystery, why should it be called "God"? The question is, then, what such terms as "God" and "believing in God" mean.

There are, of course, many different views about this. The one I expound here emerges from the biblical tradition. Unfortunately, although biblical insight has been one of the most potent determinants of Western thought, it is not widely understood today. In fact it has become so distorted in the common mind—both outside and inside of church and synagogue—that its conception of God no longer seems worthy of attention by thoughtful people. Indeed, for many persons it constricts or impoverishes human consciousness, rather than expanding and enriching it. This is most unfortunate, because properly understood it is not at all the nonsense it is alleged to be. It is not inconsistent with either contemporary man's understanding of the world or what he hopes for and values most for the future.

There have been in the West two kinds of conceptions of God, those relating to *the God of the philosophers* and those to *the God of the Bible.* The former emerge primarily from philosophic reflection and the latter from man's faith experience. To put it this way is to oversimplify somewhat, for these modes of thought are neither utterly different nor completely separable. It does, however, call attention to an important distinction.

It cannot be emphasized too much that biblical religion is not primarily a religious philosophy, or a system of beliefs, but a life of faith; and that this faith is definitely not credulity or submission to religious authority but an attitude of serenity and trust toward life and the world. It is the acceptance and affirmation of "the way things are" as being good and making sense. It is awareness and certitude of the worthwhileness and dependability of the universe, and its God concept derives empirically from that faith.

A most remarkable expression of this faith is the following amazing assertion by Paul (Romans 8:28, PHILLIPS), that "To those who love God ... everything that happens fits into a pattern for good." Elsewhere (Ephesians 5:21, PHILLIPS) he underscores this with the admonition to "give thanks for everything." Surely to do this would be to accept the way things are and thus to have faith in God as the ultimate provident ground of "everything."

As the theologian Roger Shinn puts it, "To believe in God means to testify that life is not 'a bad joke' or 'a dirty trick.' ... It is to say that we live in a world where words like reverence, fidelity, and love are not nonsense."[1]

The late H. Richard Niebuhr expressed it thus:

Radical monotheism . . . is a form of confidence and fidelity. . . . When the confidence is . . . put into words, the resultant assertion is not that there is a God, but that being is God, or better that the principle of being, the source of all things and the power by which they exist is good. . . . What otherwise, in distrust and suspicion, is regarded as fate . . . or blind . . . chance is now trusted. It is God.[2]

It is in this way that the biblical idea of God derives more from faith than from philosophical speculation and construction.

A well-known remark by Martin Luther may help to clarify this: "Whatever then thy heart clings to and relies upon, that is properly thy god." This is a truly profound insight, and it points straight to the heart of biblical thought about deity. It is evident, of course, that men's hearts cling to and rely for support upon a large variety of life-entities and that there are therefore many faiths and many gods—gods of men's own choosing, such as one's own self, or humanity, nature, one's country, race, party, sex, money, business, science, religion. Any of these may be taken as one's god—or gods. Such a god, however, turns out to be disappointingly inadequate as the object of faith or as the foundation upon which to build a life. Sooner or later it fails to deliver, in courage and hope, unselfish love, and moral stamina. Now it is a remarkable fact that in times when such faiths and gods do fail, men may be given another faith, the faith in the ultimate *God*, above, beyond, and against the proximate gods. This is to say that they come to see, in a revealing experience of reorientation and reconception, that no *partial* reality or principle can possibly provide adequate, permanent support or meaning for life in all its contingencies and uncertainties, but that reality as a whole, or its ground, *can*.

Two things happen at such times of reorientation. First, men come to realize what was formerly beyond their apprehension and comprehension, namely, that reality in its entirety, with its overall pattern of relationships, events, and processes—the way things are—is an abiding, unshakable actuality that does not pass or fail, and that its character is such that their lives can be built upon it with complete confidence. Second, there is born for them faith in the primordial source and end of that actuality, its creative principle and molding power—God—once hidden but now revealed through the pattern of the world's "flux of immediate things."

Though this way to faith, and thus to God, is undeniably biblical, and should therefore not be too unfamiliar to us, it is in fact very strange to many people and therefore difficult to understand. For further clarification, therefore, let us turn again to the thought of H. Richard Niebuhr, with reference particularly to the passing of the gods and the coming of faith in God.

We arrive . . . at the problem of deity by setting out from the universal human experience of faith, of reliance or trust in something.

. . . Now if this be true . . . it is evident that men have many gods. . . .

Yet . . . none of these . . . exists universally, or . . . can guarantee meaning to our life . . . save for a time. They are all doomed to pass.

What is it that is responsible for this passing . . .? We may call it the nature of things . . . fate . . . reality. But whatever name we call it, this law of things, this reality, this way things are . . . the *"void"* out of which everything comes and to which everything returns . . . this . . . abides when all else passes. It is the supreme reality with which we must reckon.

Now a strange thing has happened . . . our faith has been attached to that great void, to that enemy of all our causes, to that opponent of all our gods. . . . And insofar as our faith, our reliance for meaning and worth, has been attached to this source and enemy of all gods, we have been enabled to call this reality God.[3]

Clearly to find this yielding, trusting, all-encompassing faith means to find not a god but ultimate God. For to "believe in God" and trustingly to accept "the way things are" are one and the same thing.

SENSING THE ULTIMATE
QUALITY OF EXISTENCE

To many people such faith seems utterly ludicrous. Much of contemporary art, literature, and philosophy sees life as ugly and terrifying, meaningless or even absurd. Sartre's reaction to life is one of disgust and nausea. Simone de Beauvoir has a character in one of her novels speak of "the utter rottenness hidden in the womb of all human destiny." Many lesser folk also feel life to be dark and inimical. Let a person live in a rat-infested, overcrowded, cold tenement, or feel the indignities and terrors of racial discrimination, or remember the bestiality of an extermination camp, and his view of life is not likely to be rosy and optimistic. Understandably, then, if this is all he can see of life and its overall complexion, faith in God, and the very idea of God, must inevitably seem empty of meaning.

Many other people, however, who are no less discerning and have experienced the same indignities and terrors, feel that this view of things is far too restricted. They do not deny the existence and power of utterly devilish evil and nauseating rottenness in human existence; but they see also that there are operative in it other realities that are even more powerful, namely, sensitivity and tenderness, patience and long suffering, sharing and giving, love and understanding, remorse and forgiving, as well as curative and remedial action against evil. To large numbers of them there have come the biblical vision and faith that, incredible though it may seem, there is a purposive pattern into which somehow all happenings do fit—for good. It is this faith that gives rise to the Western monotheistic idea of God.

Plainly this way of conceiving deity, in terms of the faith and hope it generates, differs radically from the more popular one that stresses the philosophically postulated attributes God must presumably possess in order to be intelligible or rationally explicable. Almost always, it seems, when people are asked what they mean by "God," they start with: God is the absolute, the infinite, perfect, omnipotent, omniscient, omnipresent, the eternal, and the like; the prime mover, the ground of being, or even Being itself—all highly abstract notions. Only rarely does their reply focus upon the concrete faith experience through which the idea of the gods or of God attains meaning, when the existential need for God is felt and the choice is made as to what or who shall be one's deity. The fact seems to be that most persons speak about the divine almost exclusively in terms of metaphysical abstractions. And yet in biblical thought such abstractions are conspicuous largely through their absence. This, then, is how the two approaches to God differ basically in attitude and method. While we shall see later that metaphysical speculations and abstractions are extremely important when *in theology* biblical "faith seeks reason," the recognition of the primacy of the faith experience is essential to a proper understanding of the biblical religion and of its conception of "God."

There is a most significant parallel here to the "way of science" in its attempt to understand nature. In science too there have been two approaches, one through a priori concepts of what an orderly nature "must be" like, supposedly the only way it can make sense; the other through a posteriori concepts derived more directly through experience with nature itself. These have been called respectively the deductive and the inductive approach. It was the former that dominated most thought about nature prior to the days of Galileo, and to which most of Galileo's adversaries appealed in challenging his unconventional claims, which were based squarely on observational experience, e.g., that heavier objects do not always fall faster than lighter-weight ones and that the moon, admittedly a celestial object, is far from "perfect" just as terrestrial ones are.

What was so unconventional about his method, and that of the science that followed, was his insistence that what really matters is not how nature "must be," as deduced from "first principles," but how it "actually is," as it reveals itself to be through human experience. I submit that biblical thought has a similar concern and that its path to the "knowledge of God" is parallel and similar in kind to that of science that leads to the "knowledge of nature."[4] In both, one must distinguish carefully between experienced reality and one's mental images of it. In both, experiential findings take priority over metaphysical presuppositions. And in both, the most fundamental, elemental experience is one of faith: the one faith in nature, the other faith in God. Finally, in both, such knowledge and understanding as are attained are far from being either complete or final. Always there remains a vast unknown that has not been touched and much of the known whose mystery has not been plumbed. Anyone well acquainted with the scientific way should have little difficulty understanding and appreciating the biblical one, and vice versa. It is mainly because biblical religion has this basically empirical orientation that I feel that it should appeal strongly, as indeed it does in not a few cases, to postmodern men, whose thought is molded to so large an extent by the similar orientation of science.

It has frequently been asserted that the God of the Bible is no more than a mental construct of men and has therefore no objective existence. This charge of nonobjectivity may indeed apply to the "God" of many varieties of speculative thought, but certainly not to all of them. Moreover the assertion misses the point in the first place in regard to what is meant by the biblical "faith in God," and it indicates a misapprehension of the nature of man's approach to God *and* God's approach to man—as this remarkable, reciprocal, dual revelatory process is understood biblically. According to this latter mode of thought *the fundamental question in this connection is not whether a God exists but whether, among the many realities that are known to exist, there is one which, by virtue of its goodness, power, dependability, and the force and depth of its concerns and demands, is worthy of man's trust and whole-commitment —and worthy therefore of being his God.* Putting it another way, the biblically oriented religious quest is a search among existing realities for one with the quality of deity, i.e., with the power to generate faith and all its concomitants. What goes on here is not that man creates his god or gods, but that he chooses, designates, and commits himself to God.

THE "SOURCE, GUIDE,
AND GOAL OF ALL THAT IS"

Different people, of course, make different choices. Some see the quality of deity in one or more of the many partial realities of power they encounter in life and therefore designate these as their gods. Probably all men do this consciously or unconsciously, at some time in their lives, perhaps even repeatedly. Some, however, come to see that genuine and wholly sufficient deity resides in or characterizes *only* that which has no given name but has variously been called "the void," "the abyss," "the enemy," "fate," "the All," "the Ultimate," "the way things are." They see that this strange and mysterious reality "abides when all else passes" and is "the supreme reality with which men must reckon." It is this unique divine reality or its ground, which Paul has called the "Source, Guide, and Goal of all that is," that has generated and then captured men's faith and has become for them God. Let us recognize, then, that in this way a unique, actual reality has been selected, accepted, and installed by men as their God, but that it was not created by them in this process. Nor does that reality cease to exist (or die) if thereafter its God-status is repudiated or disregarded by man.

From this point of view the process called "divine revelation" is basically the disclosure not of the existence of a supreme reality called God but of the God-character of supreme reality. It is not so much that in the revelatory experience one encounters something utterly new as that the old, and to some extent already encountered, is seen in an utterly new light and that one enters into a new relationship with it. One's eyes are opened to see that the reality-matrix of the cosmos and of our lives is creative and remedial, "for good," and has faith-generating aspects —and is therefore to be accepted as God. One's gods are shattered, but God abides and is allowed to take over. One then perceives, conceives, and relates differently to all of life and the world. Not only are men's eyes opened but their minds and hearts also. So radical a change of consciousness is experienced in this disclosure event that it is commonly called "conversion," and so unpredictable and unmanageable is its happening that it is interpreted as being a gift that has come only by God's grace and not at all through one's own efforts.

Sometimes this occasion of revelation and reorientation comes in a brief moment of sudden unprecedented illumination and transformation, and sometimes it extends over a long period of time. It may or may not involve extensive study or travail of mind and heart. But never, apparently, is it brought about through the coercive pressure of deductive logic which allows no other outcome. There is no way to "prove" that the basic pattern of life is or is not "for good" or, for that matter, that there is an overall pattern at all. Indisputably, different persons or communities can look at life as a whole and, without violating any of the rules of reasoning, evaluate it very differently, some regarding it as "utterly rotten" and others as clearly "for good" and indicative of deity. And yet despite this lack of irrefutable logical rigor in the coming of faith in God, the existential certitude the new consciousness and relationship confer is in its potency quite without a parallel in any other experience of life.

There are, of course, cogent reasons for the lack of logical rigor just mentioned. For one thing, faith is not a purely intellectual matter. It is an orientation of the whole person, not of the mind alone. It has to do with much more than "knowledge," in the usual sense, and is therefore very different from a mere epistemological problem. As we have noted, it pertains to the goodness-character of the universe, and "seeing" this and reasoning about it is done with the "heart" as well as the "head." Inevitably, therefore, there are trans-logical and nonrational elements in both the disclosure process that calls forth faith and in that faith itself.

For another thing, the object of faith, i.e., "the void," "the abyss," "the way things are," the "Source, Guide, and Goal of all that is," God, can obviously not be precisely conceptualized as ordinary objects are. As the Niebuhr quotations plainly indicate, it is reality at its most intractably real, "the supreme reality with which we must reckon" and which no experience can avoid or thought disregard—and yet is elusive and mysterious and beyond adequate linguistic depiction or formal logical treatment. It includes all of the reality our experience discloses and our words denote, but also very much more that is hidden in the tremendous reaches of its unfathomable mystery. No set of premises can completely represent or enclose it conceptually, and no conclusion derived deductively from these premises can apply to it with complete rigor. There is simply too much there that the underlying assumptions or postulates do not touch and the deductive process cannot handle. Purely logical reasoning is therefore never completely adequate in regard to both faith in God and a conception of God. The coming of faith is much more like the phenomenon of falling in love and the burgeoning of faith in a person, or in one's country, or in an all-demanding cause, than like the inexorable forcing of a conclusion by the process of formal deduction. It is not illogical, in the sense of being nonsense, but neither is it fully logical, in the sense of representing exclusively rigorous reasoning.

The scientifically minded especially should be able to appreciate this, because, as we saw in Part One, the most profound and cherished understandings of science have also come about through a partially nonlogical process, including the gradual dawning of insight; the slow coming to see and feel the content and significance of general principles (such as the causality and conservation principles) that are not obvious at first glance but eventually become the very foundation upon which a whole science rests; the becoming aware of primordial realities and interrelationships that make possible grand overarching understandings (such as the physicochemical nature of life); the intuitive grasping of broad perspectives in nature-history (such as evolution)—all with relatively little pinpointed, formal analysis or rigorous syllogistic reasoning. Surely this is the way scientific *faith in nature,* as well as the scientific *concept of nature,* came about. In both science and biblical religion there is a "coming to see," and a growing confidence, that the way things are (relative to their respective concerns) makes sense. In both there is a compelling sense of the fitness and rationality of things—though without unimpeachable proof of it.

Even though the faith experience is not characterized by completely rigorous logic, it does not follow that there is no logic in it at all. I, for one, do not share the derogatory view that the basic biblical beliefs are insufficiently critical and discriminating, in the sense that they cannot be validated by the process called falsification.[5] The charge is that the belief that all happenings fit into a pattern for good is held in spite of much evidence to the contrary; and, similarly, that God is held to be love no matter how much unlove or actual hatred or diabolical evil there is in the world. How bad, it is asked, would the situation have to be before such beliefs would be relinquished? If they were retained under any and all conceivable circumstances, and if no conceivable conditions whatsoever would cause their denial, could they possibly be genuine truth-claims? Surely a claim that something is true, that does not thereby also declare its opposite to be untrue, has no genuine truth-value.

Now for me this charge of the unfalsifiability of theological assertions is not convincing. In the first place, it is simply not true that biblical beliefs are maintained despite all evidence to the contrary. In the second place, in their more mature stages of growth they rest not only on direct experience but also on careful analysis and critical reflection. Their central insight—namely, that the universe is fundamentally good, and its Source therefore God, and that God is love—would not be espoused under all conceivable circumstances.

After all, the world is recognized to be contingent. It need not have been as it is. "The way things are" *could* conceivably have been otherwise, exhibiting a radically different matrix of given entities and causal relationships— or with no causality at all. There *might* have been no love in it, or loving *might* normally have resulted in hatred or misunderstanding or confusion; in which case, according to the methodology of biblical thought, its "Source, Guide, and Goal" would have had to be designated as *Diabolus* rather than *Deus*. The world *could* conceivably have been such that brotherhood and community, mutuality and sharing, sensitivity and redemptive suffering could not have emerged in it. Natural beauty *might* have been an impossibility; and the physical act of looking at the sunrise or waterfall, or of listening to the songs of birds or the sighing of the wind, *might* have been intolerably painful rather than pleasurable and beneficial. So could the act of touching anything, say, one's mate. Events *might* have been utterly unpredictable and unmanageable, the naturalness of "nature" inconceivable, and rationality nonexistent. There *might* have been no possibility of human creativity, and therefore of the arts, sciences, and religions, and of business and politics. Evil *might* have been not only present but completely irremediable and ineradicable. Life *might* have been unmitigated boredom or hell. Surely in such a world it would have made no sense to claim that God is love. And referring to the quote from Roger Shinn, life would indeed have been "a bad joke" or "dirty trick." The fact is, then, that it is not at all difficult to state what some of the conditions might be—within a cosmic scheme different from ours—which would make faith as we know it impossible and our present basic beliefs or truth-claims unacceptable, or even unimaginable. It is not the case, therefore, that biblical beliefs are inevitably unfalsifiable.

To be sure, given the present cosmos with its general scheme of things *as it is*, the believer cannot point to any event that could possibly occur therein that would itself invalidate his fundamental belief that all happenings fit into a scheme for good. This does not mean, however, that he is gullible or willing blindly to believe anything whatsoever, regardless of the pros and cons. Rather it means that he is simply being consistent in his conviction that the world is not self-contradictory, and that it would not therefore bring forth anything that would not "fit," or would in this sense be an anachronism in violation of its fundamental, constitutive matrix. The scheme could conceivably have been different, but *as it is* it is consistently purposive for good. Had the scheme been radically different, self-contradicting and "for evil," so also would have been the character of the creative ground of its being—and it would not have generated faith and qualified as God.

THE MEANING OF "FOR GOOD"— AND THE "PROBLEM OF EVIL"

Paul did not, of course, declare all particular happenings in the world to be good. He knew all too well that many of them are tragically unfortunate or even demonically evil. He believed not that the character of individual events is invariably good but that the pattern or matrix of their occurrence *is*. He admonished us to "give thanks for everything"—as a whole—not for every single thing. It is the *way* things are and their fitting together that is for good, not necessarily all *things* themselves.

At this point we should look more closely at the expression "for good" and make more explicit what until now has been only implicit in this study, namely, that "for good" is not synonymous with simply "good." In our context the former has the flavor of expectancy, of development, of resolution of difficulty and tragedy in the future, and of sensing benevolent purpose; whereas the latter seems to connote only approval of, or contentment with, an existing state of affairs. "For good" implies that there is in any given situation, as well as in the general scheme of things, a pressure toward more good and less misfortune and evil. It is in this sense a transformative pressure in life "for good," and Paul saw it as resulting from the unceasing creative and transformative action of God.

How such action for good may be understood in terms of natural causes is suggested in the following remarks by Robert L. Calhoun:

> The consequences of sin cannot be annulled, but they can be worked into new life patterns, in the midst of the complex interworking of natural, social, and divers other factors that make up man and his total environment, in such fashion that the outcome is positively though never perfectly good. And one who becomes acutely aware that this is so not by merit nor prowess of his own, but by grace of powers beyond his own, may find himself irresistibly persuaded of the living presence of God.[6]
> . . . out of wreckage again and again has come new life.[7]

Note carefully what is suggested here. Misfortune, catastrophe, evil, and sin are realities of life and thus causal factors in the world. Once they occur, their consequences follow inevitably and cannot be undone. However, the consequences themselves become causal factors with which still others become entwined so that together they transform the situation. The world can therefore be said to be so constituted that the effects of evil "can be worked into new life patterns . . . in such fashion that the outcome is positively though never perfectly good." This is the meaning of its *remediality for good.*

To illustrate, out of the death of Socrates, and Jesus, and Abraham Lincoln new life did come to the world. The destruction of the Roman Empire and the Pax Romana by the barbarian hordes from the north was at the time a tragic disaster; during the French Revolution terrible evils were perpetrated; the American Civil War was stark tragedy fraught with much injustice and terror. Yet out of these terrible events there did come more abundant life and new manifestations of the good. This sort of salvaging and transforming action that brings forth future good out of past evil can be seen not only in the world at large but also in the lives of individuals; witness the innumerable stories to that effect not only in the Bible but throughout the great literatures of the world; and it is to such action, I take it, that the biblical concept of redemption and deliverance—in its truly fundamental meaning—refers.

This process has an important two-fold aspect which Professor Calhoun did not mention explicitly. First, such a redemptive working out of eventual new life patterns usually requires considerable time. Second, it results from the interweaving of the consequences of evil acts not only with other causal factors that co-exist with them at the time but often also with newly emerging ones that change the situation by radically altering the balance of power and dynamic thrusts innovatively and transformatively for good. Naturally, for biblical faith every such appearance of a major new reality, and of the train of transformations that follow in its wake, constitutes a momentous event seen as a mighty creative and redemptive act of God. For the Old Testament writers the covenantal call of Abraham, the deliverance of Israel from Egyptian bondage, and the giving of the law at Sinai were such events. Each of them injected into the causal network of the world a new reality—a new insight, or new motivational relationship, or new structure of power—that produced an additional increment of pressure "for good." For Christians the supreme example of such "mighty redemptive acts of God" has been, and still is, that of the "Christ event," when a new reality entered the world that was quite unprecedented in its faith-generating power and when a tremendous effluence of remedial power occurred that brought forth a "new creation," a new community (the church), and a new way of life dominated by faith, hope, love, and loyalty to Jesus Christ. The world has never been the same since then. For Christian faith there was no longer the slightest doubt that the world's processes are *for good*, and its creator and maintainer, its Source, Guide, and Goal, is God.

Looking at things in this way makes for a more truly biblical attitude toward the so-called *problem of evil*. Popularly, and according to the "way of the philosophers," the problem seems usually to be stated somewhat like this: How can the existence of evil be reconciled with the concept of a perfect, all-powerful God of love? Biblical thought, however, has rather consistently gone about it differently. Like the Bible itself, it accepts the fact of existence of evil without argument and then concentrates almost exclusively upon the question of what its tragic presence in life means to God and man and nature. Thus biblical faith's basic concern is not so much ontological, pertaining to evil's origin, as it is existential, relating to its remedial modification or elimination. To put it another way, *biblically the problem of evil is the problem of the liberation of the world and of individual men from its dominance and power* and eventually even from its very existence.

Biblical faith, with its positive acceptance and affirmation of the value of human existence and the world, has been a desirable option as a way of life largely because the way things are, and therefore its Source, Guide, and Goal, are seen to be remedial and redemptive for good. In the historical development of this faith the concept of God as healer, reclaimer, deliverer, redeemer from misfortune, evil, and sin came to the Hebrew people long before the idea of God as creator. While the present form of the Old Testament, which begins with the creation story of Genesis, suggests that for biblical thought the theme of creation has first priority, actually other and much older books of the Old Testament are almost completely silent about it and, instead, abound in stories indicating lively awareness of God as deliverer. It seems almost as though a community of faith comes to realize that its God is the creator of the universe only after, and because, it has known him as redeemer. Seemingly, in a sense the latter insight is a prerequisite to the former one.

Thus the biblical faith does not regard evil as a fixed absolute of existence. It discerns in the world processes through which evils are transformed for good. Moreover it recognizes that while new evils do put in their appearance from time to time, there emerge also new resources for dealing with them redemptively—as in our time, when we do have agonizingly difficult problems but also, as noted in chapter IX, remarkable ways of ameliorating and perhaps even solving them.

"THE LIVING GOD"

Now let us note that to talk this way about the biblical faith and its God, and particularly about creation and redemption, is to introduce into religion the conceptuality, language, and imagery of contemporary science. More specifically, it is to opt for the momentous idea that the world is incomplete and still becoming, and its contents and characteristics changing—in such a way that misfortune and evil can and do contribute in the long run to eventual outcomes for good. For faith this is to declare that it is the Source, Guide, and Goal of this creative-transformative world and process that is its God.

In affirming this, biblical faith employs a most suggestive symbol: not only does it speak of "God" but of "living God." Thus it provides a profound religious interpretation of the scientific insight that physical reality, and indeed the entire cosmos, is creatively effluent in the sense developed earlier. Also it employs another biblical conception, that of "continuous creation." Just as a person who is truly "living" is continually active and productive, so God is envisioned as living and engaged in continuous creation —and always present in all situations as the unceasingly transformative-creative factor for good.

The emphasis upon *for good* coupled with *living God* and *continuous creation* is of supreme importance for biblical religion. For it conceives the supreme quality and significance of divinity to lie not so much in its infinity and omnipotence, or irresistible might, as in its boundless goodness and unabating grace and love, with which it incessantly generates faith, hope, and love among men and women and acts upon the world remedially *for good*. Returning to the opening question of this chapter, *it is not at all self-evident that nature's intimations of ultimate mystery point specifically to God.* A being or Being might conceivably be the absolute and ultimate One, and even be the transcendent-immanent and overwhelmingly numinous mysterious creator, and yet not be God—if it were not above all else *good and for good*. It might in that case be Devil, creator and maintainer of a universe dominated by evil and terror, and the destroyer of goodness and serenity. Biblical faith is confident that the intimations of ultimacy do point to God, because it discerns ample empirical evidence that the character and developmental thrust of life and the universe are indeed for good.

THE GOD OF TENDERNESS

As the living God is experienced and conceived by biblical faith he does not, however, operate only upon the universe as a whole, or at the levels of its overall structures and processes, but within the hearts and lives of individual human beings—witness, for example, the following deeply moving affirmation found in the book of Job: "God my Maker, who gives songs in the night (Job 35:10)." Another translator puts it more specifically: "who gives songs of gladness in the night."* The night is not always a time of gladness; but when it is, and songs come to our lips, their source is God—as sensed by the biblical consciousness.

What a remarkable conception of God this is: God, the giver of songs of gladness! And especially songs that come in solitude! Let us consider just a few of its implications. First, however, an observation: Many persons, even habitual readers of the Bible, are utterly surprised when they learn that this is a verse—and conception of God—from the Bible, and especially when they discover it to be from the Old Testament. Somehow most people seem to feel that despite all the obvious teachings of the Bible that God is love, and the loving Father of Jesus Christ, the God of the Bible is a hard God, one who is to be feared, who, as portrayed especially in the Old Testament, is vengeful and a God of wrath—and anything but the kind of God about whom it could be said that he gives songs in the night.

---

* This biblical passage with its rich meaning came to my attention forcibly for the first time through a sermon preached by Paul L. Lehman, of the Union Theological Seminary, in 1965 at The Pennsylvania State University. I am indebted to him for this.

And yet this verse from Job is by no means the only one of the kind, as the following ones attest: "at night his song is with me, a prayer to the God of my life (Ps. 42:8)." Notice especially also the tender feeling tone of the expression "the God of my life." Another: "The Lord is my strength and my song (Exod. 15:2)." Again: "Behold, God is my salvation; I will trust, and will not be afraid; for the LORD GOD is my strength and my song (Isa. 12:2)." Note the repeated personal emphasis on "my"! Further: "He put a new song in my mouth (Ps. 40:3)." "You shall have a song as in the night when a holy feast is kept; and gladness of heart (Isa. 30:29)."

One of the most significant events in the history of biblical consciousness in the twentieth century has been the rediscovery of the Old Testament as a book displaying keen religious sensitivity and profound insight—as is illustrated so amply by the passages just noted and by the beautiful and moving insight that for each individual you and me God is the very near giver of songs in the night. For increasing numbers of people this has contributed to a most meaningful expansion of their understanding of the entire Bible—and to a rediscovery of the reality and power of the tender elements of the universe *and of the God of tender relationships.* So much for the observation; now some implications!

Fundamentally, I suppose, it is not so much the songs themselves that are so precious as gifts of God, as are the states of mind and heart from which they flow. There are in the total range of realities very few that are as convincingly indicative of the "for good-ness" of the universe as the humming or singing of a woman while dusting or ironing or suckling her child or the whistling of a man doing his chores. For they indicate contentment, joy, peace, and, at least for a time, absence of anxiety. Therefore "God, the giver of songs" means God, the giver of such states of mind, and of the conditions underlying them. This takes in a great deal, including such diversities as beauty and truth, creativity and adventure, honesty and unselfishness, friendship and family, work and play, material and nonmaterial possessions. For the biblical consciousness it means also such realities as repentance, reconciliation, forgiveness, redemptive suffering, faith, hope, and so on.

On the other hand, songs are exceedingly precious in themselves, as celebrative outpourings of the spirit and as manifestations of the symphonic character of the universe and of its tender elements. The joyful sounds and halle-lujahs of song, poetry, instrumental music, and the dance have been an integral part of the religious response to life and its God for a very long time—certainly, as far as biblical religion is concerned, ever since the early dawning of the first axial period of human history, when the first writings of the Old Testament came into being. It would not be misrepresenting that religion if it were asserted that its God is the ultimate reality whose presence evokes not only awe and holy fear (*Ehrfurcht*) but the spontaneous making of joyful sounds.

In terms of physical power the sounds of song are, of course, exceedingly weak and must be counted among the tender or at least feeble elements of the cosmos. A full-sized orchestra or band doing its utmost rarely puts out more than a fraction of one watt of power. The mightiest of singers would have to keep on singing for several years before the accumulated sound energy he put out equaled the small amount of energy required to heat up a single cup of coffee. Yet how powerful the sound of song can be —and is—in other ways! Its power is of a piece with the physical feebleness, yet tremendous might, of color in the hands of the artist and of rhythm executed by the dancer, as they affect human moods, emotions, thought, and will. No coercive, violent force ever equals these in their per-suasive, evocative, and transforming power, and therefore in determining the quality of human existence. Such might is of a piece also with the delicate yet authoritative orga-nizing power of life as it is discerned in the lowliest flower of the tundra as well as in the most majestic of redwoods.

It was in recognition and celebration of the gentle might and actual supremacy of these and all other tender ele-ments of human existence and the cosmos that the flower

people wore flowers and bells and the youth of Consciousness III go in for gay colors and sounds and espouse commitment to nonviolence and peace. Thus it is that they
would achieve revolution by consciousness, rather than by
coercion; and this "way of the lilies" is the way to which
genuine biblical religion also is committed.

THE CHRISTLIKE GOD
AND THE WAY OF LOVE

Perhaps the most serious criticism that has been leveled
against the so-called counter-cultural movement and the
drive toward revolution by consciousness is that they have
been too unconcerned with "practical matters" and have
not clearly conceived or articulated a basic organizational
principle for the structuring and operation of the kind of
society they desire so passionately for the world of the
future. While this charge of lack of practicality and realism is not deserved altogether or without qualification, it
does raise some extremely important questions that cannot be ignored (and will be considered in the last chapter).
At this point, however, we should note that this is precisely
the criticism often leveled at basic Christianity. The parallel
between primitive Christianity and the contemporary movement toward revolution by consciousness is in some respects rather striking—perhaps the latter can learn something from the long historical experience of the former,
and perhaps society as a whole can profit from pondering
both.

In an important sense Christianity is not a religion at
all but a reborn consciousness, an unassuming but potent
style of life, faith, and ultimate concern. He whom Christians call their Lord bequeathed or enjoined no code of
specified beliefs and ritualistic practices required of his
followers—which is what "religion" is commonly taken to
mean. What seems to have impressed the pagan world most
when it was invaded by early Christianity was not a new
religious philosophy or novel system of ritual but the way
the early Christians loved one another, their neighbors,
their enemies, and their God. And what a God! A God who
loved men and who ruled by love and self-sacrifice, rather

than by arbitrary, monarchical, and punitive power, and who was like one Jesus of Nazareth, a young Jew whom they experienced as the "Christ." This is why his followers were nicknamed CHRISTians.

What seemed especially odd was the fact that this Jesus was not a great celebrity and had no "status" socially, ecclesiastically, or politically. He had been known only in a very small spot of the Roman empire, in Palestine, and had made his impact upon his companions and contemporaries for only a very short time, being in the public eye not more than one to three years—after which he was denounced and executed as a criminal. What an unlikely and inauspicious beginning this CHRISTian movement and way of life had! And how innocent, naïve, and impractical its outlook on life was, and its "program for action"! What "action"? To love everybody, especially the unlovely and seemingly unlovable, and even one's enemies. And to choose the tender and peaceful ways of life and work—as did Jesus. Yes, the early Christian community was at least as "unrealistic" as is Consciousness III in our day! It too believed that what is *most needful* is a "new heart," a "new mind," a "new being," a new consciousness to which all else that is good may be added—but without which none else can be.

And yet, "It was this faith," remarks Roger Shinn in a remarkably perceptive study, "that went on to shape a culture and . . . became imbedded in the life and culture of many societies."[8] Apparently it turned out not to be so impractical after all! Its devotees did contribute to the life and work of the world. They engaged in commerce, in the vocations, and professions and entered the arena of politics, and for their guidance the community did "develop political theologies," just as the Christian church is trying to do now. True:

In so doing, it made mistakes. But the mistakes were not in seeking involvement in society. The mistakes were the familiar human mistakes of too much absolutizing of doctrine and practice, too much righteous cruelty, too much self-concern. Whether making those mistakes or correcting them—and the church did both—Christian faith became imbedded in the life and culture of many societies.[9]

214

Let us not, however, lose sight of just what faith we have been considering. It was not, and still is not, primarily a faith in, and commitment to, a remarkably charismatic personality and his ideals. This is something too many of the so-called "Jesus people" today seem to have forgotten, or in any case do not realize. This Jesus was, to be sure, truly charismatic; he spoke with authority. But his sayings, the insights he conveyed, the power he displayed in the deeds he did, and the faith he evoked were all in behalf of the God of his fathers, whom he sensed, with keen passionate awareness, to be also his own heavenly Father. In him and through him many men, women, and children came to sense the reality and character of God—in all the meanings noted in this chapter—and much more. This is why he came to be known as Jesus Christ, in a unique sense the anointed of God, and why for the CHRISTian community he came to be regarded as the supreme revelation of *God as Love*. Nothing more true or meaningful can be said or known about God than that he is love—of the kind and quality discerned in the life of Jesus. And this is why the great missionary apostle of Christianity was able to say, while enumerating the everlasting and indestructible realities of life and the universe, that "the greatest of them all is love (1 Cor. 13:13, NEB)."

This is the most basic and potent of all organizational principles that can be proposed for the structuring and operation of any society—now and in the future. I believe that many persons of the counter-cultural movement today sense this keenly, and that this is the most fundamental aspect of Consciousness III. Let no one say that this is impractical! I suggest, however, that even love can go astray—as it has so often in Christianity—unless it is and remains rooted in and responsible to ultimate Love: God.

One thing biblical religion can claim, as Shinn points out about Christianity: it has

kept some awareness of transcendence—a transcendence that prevented total engulfment by any institutions, political or ecclesiastical. Sometimes clumsily, sometimes profoundly, Christian faith expressed that transcendence, whether in mysticism or monasticism or sacramentalism or in the midst of the common life.[10]

Here is wisdom, born of long experience, which may be commended to all men as a resource for the future: forget not the ultimate and transcendent reaches and grounding of love!

XII. The Developmental Character of Biblical Religion

ALTERNATIVE DOCTRINAL VIEWPOINTS IN CHRISTIANITY

It is obvious, of course, that the biblical consciousness is not characterized by uniformity in the way it conceives of ultimate reality and formulates its doctrines. Certainly this is the case in Christianity, where such fundamental realities as "faith in God" and "God" have been interpreted in many different ways.[1] Let us consider this next, and begin by recognizing that many Christians would say that the interpretation put forward herein is quite inadequate or even erroneous. I hope a discussion will both clarify the nature of such differences and call attention to aspects of biblical faith that have not yet been noted explicitly.

To illustrate such differences, let the position taken here represent one alternative: that of Western monotheism as interpreted by such men as H. Richard Niebuhr (in his *Radical Monotheism and Western Culture*) and Robert L. Calhoun (in his *God and the Common Life*). In presenting my understanding of it I have employed contemporary idiom and insights as much as possible. Numerous Christians, however, doubt that any portrayal in this vein can possibly represent genuine biblical faith and belief. They would say more specifically, and let this be a second alternative, that my "God" is far too pale, nondescript, and nonpersonal, whereas the biblical God is not only glowingly and vitally personal but is even a triunity or trinity of three specifiably different persons. Furthermore, they would assert that God is much more the direct determiner of all that happens than I have depicted him to be, and that nothing, not even evil, can or does exist or occur without his specifically willing it, or at least consenting to it. As for natural law, it is no more than his disposable agency, and he suspends or intervenes in its operation from time to time at will, to perform miraculous deeds for his people when they are faithful to him or to chastize them when they are not. Moreover, according to this view, redemption, far from being at all explicable in terms of "natural events," is an utterly "supernatural" process by which men who turn to Christ are "saved" from sin and eternal damnation through a ransoming, propitiatory, substitutionary transaction between God the Father and God the Son.

Biblical faith, it is urged further, does not rest upon any kind of "general revelation," i.e., upon insight about the way things are in general, but upon "special revelation," i.e., upon truth that is either implanted directly in the minds of prophets by "divine inspiration" or that comes to them through unusual and specific supernatural occurrences wrought by God as he intervenes directly in the natural order. "The essentials" of biblical faith are therefore not so much general attitudes and insights as specific ones. Finally, any claim (such as I make) that "in its essentials" biblical faith is in accord with the contemporary scientific outlook is held to be patently false, since most of the "real essentials," such as the idea of an intervening God, are manifestly repugnant to the scientific mind.

Clearly there are here two substantially different ways of thinking, both claiming to be Christian. Now my thesis about them is that, while each of them does represent the convictions of a large sector of Christianity, and each does indeed differ markedly from the other, the difference is not one of basic intentionality, as though there were here two opposing faiths, one true and the other false. It is rather a matter of form: one faith, but two forms of expression. They profess the same fundamental monotheistic faith in the one God who creates and redeems, though they employ different "models" or imagery in thinking about how God may go about doing the creating and redeeming.

If this thesis turns out to be true, as we inquire further, it will signify, I suggest, that while the biblical faith which comes to men in the revelatory experience of divine disclosure is definite, firm, and confident, it does not lead to, or require, complete uniformity of doctrinal interpretation or formulation. Rather it allows, and indeed calls for, a variety of belief-formulations suited to different cultures and times, or even to different kinds of human temperament or social background. This is one of Christianity's most remarkable characteristics, one without which, I suggest, it would not be suitable for the counter-cultural future, which the new consciousness senses must be pluralistic. This important characteristic derives in large part from the fact that biblical religion is a historical phenomenon and is therefore developmental and subject to innovative change. As we have seen in Part One, an important element of the post-modern consciousness is the realization that no reality whatsoever is truly known or understood except in a long-range perspective, because inevitably it changes in time and is therefore always still becoming. Hence no concept or doctrine is adequate if it remains fixed in meaning or form while its referent undergoes developmental transformation. All this applies to the religions —just as it does to the arts and sciences. They and the ways of life and thought they generate are realities embedded in the causal system of the cosmos as participants in its development and metamorphoses. This historical and developmental aspect of Christian understanding and belief is so important that we must give considerable further thought to it.

Prior to that, however, a parenthetic remark: The proliferation of such alternatives is often regarded as scandalous. Doubtless this has all too often been excessive. What is unfortunate about it is not, however, the multiplicity itself but the despicable and tragic competitive, acrimonious, and intolerant attitudes that accompany it so frequently. Wars have been fought and much blood has been shed in defense of this or that idea opposed to another. My plea is, however, that these sad facts should not be allowed to eclipse the equally important fact that the biblical consciousness has been remarkably creative in bringing forth and being hospitable to, alternatives of novel conception and belief as the need for these has arisen. It simply is not true that Christianity has been utterly inflexible and intolerant of new ideas.

Now let us consider more fully what it means to say that the biblical consciousness is developmental.

THE MEANING
OF "DEVELOPMENTAL RELIGION"

Certainly Judaism and Christianity have developed; they did not appear on the scene full-blown. Today they are not the same as in the time of Moses and Isaiah, or of Jesus and Paul, or even of Maimonides, Aquinas, and Luther. This applies also to the individual components of religion, its institutions, practices, ideas, and beliefs. They are all dynamic realities that affect, and are affected by, life and the world in many ways. While the faith of a man or community comes in an experience of disclosure, its coming and its content are conditioned by such factors as the prevailing political or economic structures, emotional patterns, world view, ethos, and mythos. And when they change it does also.

Thinking more specifically about Christianity, one might have supposed that such fundamental concepts as love, goodness, sin, redemption, revelation, creation, man, and God have had fixed and eternal meanings. But this is definitely not the case. All of them have changed markedly with the passage of time. Take, for instance, love, than which there is no more basic a concept in all of Christian thought; Daniel Williams has shown recently that its meaning has undergone profound transformations in the past and that therefore "love has a history" and "creates its own history."[2]

John Dillenberger has come to the same general conclusion with regard to all the major aspects of Christian faith. Moreover, he has identified two styles or modes that have characterized Christian thought at different periods of the distant past, and a third that has been in the making more recently. So different are these that what was said theologically in one of them may actually seem to contradict what was or is affirmed in another. Says Dillenberger:

The redirection of world views and cultural reorientations are sometimes so drastic that they do not allow a previous understanding to be understood as it was once known. To repeat a past formulation on the assumption that it is eternal can be so deceptive that, while thinking one has said the same as the past and been faithful to it, one has in point of fact said the opposite. . . . Orientations to problems, the direction one comes to them, may so change how one sees the issues that an allegedly identical answer turns out to be a radically different one.[3]

We can no longer repeat the past, for the repetition of the past does not guarantee the continuity of intentionality articulated in previous theological statements.[4]

This is what meticulous historical analysis has shown. This *is* the way of Christian faith as a historical reality, and it is exceedingly important for the question of what are its essentials. If Dillenberger's findings are correct, what is essential, or "true to the faith once delivered to the saints," *is not and cannot be* a particular formulation of belief, or even scriptural statement, taken as fixed in meaning. For as he points out further:

As a community wrestles with the reality of its foundations, the truth which has formed it also reshapes or reforms it. New aspects of truth then become manifest. . . . Those who would arrest the light which breaks forth . . . may have a passion to keep the historic faith intact; but when the older formulations are differently understood in later ages . . . heresy may actually result in the very process of trying to prevent it.[5]

This can hardly be overemphasized. It is dangerous and futile to identify faith with its doctrinal expression at any one stage of its development, or to engage in a perpetual return to a past taken to be definitive for all time. Truth is a living entity, and to be "true to it" means to live and grow with it. It will not do to give the impression that its growth has been arrested and its doctrinal form frozen, early in its history or at any other time. *Genuine orthodoxy recognizes the value not only of truth's continuity but of its creative pressure toward change.* It discerns the essential intent of truth in both the old and the new and realizes that it is the new that reveals the intent of the old, or even amplifies it. I especially like the following remark by Dillenberger about faith-and-theology as a lively, imaginative, exploring Gestalt of the human spirit:

Theology may be described as delineating the contours of faith. Faith is the encompassing perspective from which all that is said is seen, . . . *a believing shape, a discerning apprehension, a lively thrust of imagination,* . . . deep stirrings of the human spirit . . . [that] transform and create thought.

Faith . . . creates a kind of content, but at the same times takes its shape through many other avenues of knowledge. . . . Faith . . . tenuously reaches out into, and is influenced by, all that it touches.[6] (italics mine).

Orthodox thought's concern is then with a succession of many contours which growing faith assumes in time, not with only one regarded as normative for the rest.

Now let us return to the two seemingly contradictory conceptions of redemption and related matters. Clearly they represent two styles of religious thought. The one employs primarily personalistic mythical imagery, which the other shuns. The former sees redemption being achieved by direct divine action: the Son of God assumes the burden of men's sins and through his sacrificial death pays the ransom price that releases the God Father from the necessity of punishing the sinners themselves for their sins. The other style, illustrated by Calhoun's thought, visualizes redemption as being wrought by God through natural remedial and developmental processes that transform the situation—for both individual sinner and the world—and bring forth "new patterns of life" for good. Two more contrasting styles would be difficult to conceive. Yet one senses that both express faith in the God who is dealing effectively with evil, and that therefore they are but different contours of one faith.

It is evident too, I suggest, that these shapes belong to different ages and cultural climates, the one originating in the distant past, and now waning, while the other is of the present and actually still in the making. To say that the one is old is not, however, to derogate it. It was in its time an authentic, meaningful formulation of Christian belief—and for many people it still is. While for very many people its imagery seems strange now, for a long time virtually everybody understood it, including those who did not "believe" it, because it employed language that was current. Now that conceptuality is no longer in common usage and does not accurately communicate the intent of faith. Indeed, it illustrates Dillenberger's point that repetition of an earlier doctrinal formulation may even misrepresent it; witness the typical contemporary reaction to the Apostles' Creed, with its "only begotten Son," "conceived of the Holy Ghost," "born of the Virgin," "descended into hell," and so on. These phrases simply do not say now, except to the expert, what once they did say clearly. Only rarely does one who uses them regularly in religious discourse understand them in their original meaning. This is why faith is said to be in transition, seeking a new form of creedal expression.[7]

MAN'S BECOMING NATURAL— AND ITS CONSEQUENCES

But why this great change in style? Is it that the "human condition," or elemental human experience, is changing, so that new categories and modes of thought are needed to interpret it adequately? The answer, I suggest, must be Yes! Human existence has already changed significantly, and it will continue to do so. *It has become nature-al.* I say "nature-al" at this point, rather than natural, to emphasize the in-nature aspect of humanity and its existence. Actually I do not mean anything essentially different from what was called "natural" in chapter VIII, and I shall hereafter use the latter term. Man now knows that he is not separate from nature but embedded as completely in its causal complex as are molecules and rockets. *Man's thought patterns and feelings about himself in relation to nature are different.* Also, as noted in Part Two, *his cosmic status has changed.* He has entered the self-determinative phase of his evolution, in which he has acquired immense power and can do much that was once thought to be possible only for God. He can now be, within limits, both architect and builder of his own future and that of the world. If he has needs, these are expected to be met through his own resources. If catastrophe threatens, such as flood, fire, drought, or epidemic, technological experts are called in, and if they can't help there seems to be no use looking elsewhere for relief—not even to God.

All this is so familiar now that it is almost impossible for us to imagine what the situation once was—and to realize how tremendous a revolution has taken place in our thinking and feeling about nature. The fact is, however, that nature used to be for all practical purposes a closed book. Walter Ong, a professor of English at St. Louis University who is unusually sophisticated about scientific matters, has studied this with great care and shown that most people in the Middle Ages, and well into the eighteenth century, felt themselves to be helpless pawns in a world most of which they did not understand. They lived in "what we would consider paralyzing insecurity," subject to the horrible fears resulting from "the regular loss of most of their children before adulthood, by . . . death" from utterly unknown causes.[8] For the most part it was a grim world, as far as man's relation to nature was concerned, and one great tantalizing, incomprehensible puzzle. Today this is no longer the case. We understand nature to an amazing extent. It makes sense to us in many ways, and we find it to be friendly, in the main, and trustworthy. And we do not at all feel uncomfortable about being an integral part of it.

As was to be expected, for many persons this tremendous change in their relationship to nature—their becoming natural—is profoundly affecting both their religious faith and their way of thinking and speaking about God, their beliefs, conceptions, and mythical understandings. Increasingly they find science's knowledge of nature to be a rich source of revelatory insight about the character of the universe and about God. It is this experience that has given rise to the need for such new forms of religious doctrine as were discussed in the preceding section. They find it impossible to think in terms of the old ones. And for many persons this provides additional support for their faith, and a momentous expansion of their religious consciousness. Let us consider this in some detail.

NATURE AS A SOURCE
OF INSIGHT FOR FAITH

To get down to specifics, I suggest that today the insights embodied in the following affirmations constitute powerful reasons for confidently accepting life and the world as basically meaningful and *for good*. They point to aspects of reality that are truly faith-generating for many men in our time. With these truths in their minds and hearts they can face the future, confident that the ground of being is *for* them, *not against* them. These insights are not, of course, specifically Christian, but this simply means that they are universally acknowledged aspects of the way of things. The first is that *the observable events of the world are understandable to a large extent in terms of cause-and-effect relationships (laws of nature) among its constituent entities.* Second, *much of nature*, including man and his social structures, *is not only explicable but predictable and manageable* to a large extent. It can be changed by man to improve himself and his environment for good, and thus to make life more abundant. Third, *nature itself exhibits patterns of change for good*, aside from those man imposes upon it. There are at least two of these: the universal long-range process of evolution and the shorter-range processes that bring new life out of wreckage in particular situations (as suggested by Calhoun). Fourth, *nature is creatively and innovatively effluent, so that much change is brought about through the emergence from time to time of genuine novelty.* Fifth, *the morality of nature is characterized to a remarkable degree by constructive, symbiotic cooperation and mutual aid.* It was formerly thought that evolution of the biological species was achieved mainly in blood and gore, by sabertooth and claw, i.e., by survival of the fittest in destructive competition. More recently, however, biology has been accumulating evidence that this has been greatly exaggerated. All of these propositions refer, I submit, to faith-generating aspects of reality; and today we not only *think* them but *intuit* and *feel* them as well.

These pattern-aspects of nature are widely held to signify that nature is hospitable to human inquiry and control, rather than forbidding or inimical; that it is dependable and comprehensible in large measure, not haphazard or rationally opaque; and that it is both transformable and itself dynamically creative, rather than intractable and statically sterile. To recognize and say this is to express a powerful faith, a faith that removes much of the fear and dread of nature that dominated men for so long a time. If anything is to be feared, this faith says, it is our ignorance of nature, our high-handed interventions in it, and the evil uses to which we may put our knowledge of it. As far as nature itself is concerned, the more we learn about it, the less we need fear it, and the more we can trust it and enter with joyous expectancy into its life and further development. In his relations with nature man has therefore much solid ground to stand on; he can be sure it will yield to his desire to transform it for better and will support him as he commits himself to living the good life—though he realizes that this support is by no means unequivocal or completely at his command.

This, then, is the aspect of faith that comes out of man's natural experience and the insights of science. Often this is regarded as a faith in its own right, called the "scientific" or "humanistic" faith. I can see no objection to this. It certainly is a potent faith, and it is not in principle inimical to biblical faith. It becomes so only if it claims ultimacy for itself, by denying what biblical faith affirms, that the range of reality extends beyond nature and man and that *the ultimate Source, Guide, and Goal of nature, in all its scientifically discernible levels and aspects, is creating and redeeming God. Without this latter* (sixth) *affirmation, faith remains secular* and rests, legitimately as such, only on nature and man taken as gods. With it faith becomes religious and rests upon the ultimate creative principle or reality that transcends nature and man, and is taken as God. As biblical faith sees it, this sixth interpretive affirmation, about God acting creatively in nature, does not in any way contradict the factual affirmation—embodied in the first five and made by secular faith—that nature is a self-consistent (though not self-sufficient), creatively effluent causal system, the operation of which can be understood (scientifically) in terms of the laws of nature. Indeed, biblical faith in its contemporary interpretive modes regards all six affirmations, and still others like them, to be mutually consistent and quite necessary to an adequate expression of the faith in our time. Just how that is possible rationally, and within what kind of philosophic framework, we shall consider in the next chapter.

One more such insight! For the new biblical conscious-ness the term *miracle* has taken on a much more truly reli-gious meaning, and the need for the idea of miracle in its formerly common meaning has virtually disappeared. For a long time the God of the Bible was thought of in practice, if not always in theory or sophisticated theology, as the god of miracles, i.e., the god of the gaps in, or of the sup-posed exceptions to, the general pattern of happenings, and therefore the god whose existence could be "proved" by appealing primarily to events that lay outside the realm of natural law. This was one reason why the unusual, "spe-cial," and "mighty" deeds of God in history have so often seemed more convincingly revelatory of God than have the ordinary occurrences of nature. Today's biblical sensitivity, however, finds it difficult to see why the God "of all that is" is not the God of the common and more easily understood happenings quite as truly as of the special and miraculous ones; and why for faith the former should not reveal his presence and activity as truly as the latter.

Notice that I say "as truly," not "as convincingly." Ad-mittedly, men are often impressed much more by occa-sional spectacular displays of love or power than by the more frequent ordinary ones. For Jews the mighty exodus experience seems to have been far more indicative of God's love than were his day-by-day presence and guidance. For Christians the same must be said about the unique, epoch-making Christ event. For happily married spouses the great ecstatic moments have usually seemed most memorable. All this is perfectly proper and understandable. Isn't it, however, a sign of growing maturity and strengthening faith when the simple, unspectacular, common relation-ships and occurrences of daily life are also sensed to be *truly*—even if not as momentously—revelatory of the love of God or of spouse?

It is in this sense that I suggest that biblical faith is growing more perceptive and potent as it becomes more explicitly aware of God's creative and redemptive action in nature as well as in history, and not only in the so-called "mighty acts of God" but in the lesser ones hidden in the everyday operation of nature's causal system. It is this enhanced faith, with its more inclusive nature-and-history (or nature-history) perspective, that has brought forth the more recent way of thinking about redemption and related subjects. And for this faith, knowledge and understanding of the operation of the historical-natural causal system increases, rather than diminishes, the sense of the reality, presence, and mystery of living, creative God.

Nevertheless, there are exceptional experiences, and it is when one of them is sensed to have an unusual and profoundly religious impact and significance that there may arise the need for the term miracle. Thus *miracle* may be defined informally as an event in which God is sensed to be present and working out his purposes of love and redemption in an especially wonderful, mysterious, and convincing way. A genuine miracle is therefore always a truly revelatory event, disclosing divine creative and remedial love, never a merely magical display of power and authority for the sake of authenticating itself. According to this conception, whether or not such an event can be explained scientifically has nothing whatsoever to do with the question of whether it is a genuine miracle or not.

Paul Tillich puts it more formally and argues convincingly that a miracle has at least three necessary distinguishing features: it is, first, "astonishing, unusual, shaking"; second, "it points to the mystery of being"; and it is received in "an ecstatic experience." In none of these aspects does it "contradict the rational structure of reality," and "it cannot be interpreted in terms of a supranatural interference in natural processes."[9]

Now I submit that the post-modern mind, and especially the new youth consciousness, need no longer shy away from talk about miracles, where they are so conceived. Indeed, on the positive side, I suggest that their experience of expanding awareness of the limitless range of levels and dimensions comprehended by reality, and of the boundless diversity of kinds of its personal and cosmic events and processes, calls today for the use of more rather than fewer words with the connotations of the miraculous.

For its meaning is rooted linguistically in "wonder" and "the wondrous" and especially the dynamically wondrous. The miracle is, so to speak, the active mode or voice of mystery. We are no longer inclined to deny the reality of the unexpected bursting forth of glowing health where incurable illness seemed to prevail; the revival of the seemingly completely crushed spirit; the compelling eruption of utter goodness, or beauty, or sensitivity out of the seemingly unmitigated evil, or unrelieved ugliness, or apathetic or callous insensitivity; the redemptive transformation of estrangement or even hatred into love. Indubitably these are realities—and realities that do not occur every day. But when they do happen, and are sensed as extraordinary manifestations of the power and purposes of the Ultimate in the transformation of situations for good, then the need arises for the concept of the miraculous, and others like it, if there is to be adequacy in communicating about those experiences themselves, as well as about the more common aspects of life which disclose the dynamism of ultimate mystery.

It should be noted that, in the propositions referred· to as faith-generating, there appear qualifying or hedging phrases such as "to a large extent," "to a remarkable degree," "though by no means unequivocal or completely." These are required in recognition of the ambiguity and indeterminacy aspects of reality considered in chapter VIII. Therefore, these qualifiers should not be regarded as primarily negative in intent. They derive from positive observations of what *is* the case, rather than of what *is not*, namely, that *the processes of nature are determined by both natural law and pure chance—which combination makes for a degree of flexibility in the causal scheme of things. It also brings about creative thrusts toward change, by the unpredictable emergence of permanent novel additions to reality and by the occasional occurrence of extraordinary, transient, and unrepeated phenomena*, which may or may not be interpreted by the religious consciousness as miraculous. I offer this as a seventh proposition of the faith-supporting kind. It seems, then, that if one takes the "Source, Guide, and Goal of all that is" as one's God, he should keep in mind that the "all that is" refers to both permanent and transient reality, both ordinary and extraordinary events. This is why it makes sense to affirm—and celebrate—the genuine possibility and actuality of the miraculous, and of the God of the miraculous (though this does not mean that all events that have been designated as miracles in the past have either occurred or been worthy of that designation).

NATURE AS A SOURCE OF INSIGHT FOR ETHICS—AND ABOUT "SIN"

There is another area of religious concern for which the study of nature can provide important understandings, namely, that of morality, ethical values, standards for conduct, and the human condition of sin. The views about the secular aspects of this which I share with others, and especially with the youth culture, have been indicated briefly in the last section of chapter I. Feeling that introduction to be sufficient for present purposes, I wish now only to formulate explicitly certain principles that were only implicit there—and sensed more than reasoned—and to explore their significance relative to the biblical concept of sin.

Let us begin with an assumption. Since the universe operates for good, in the sense we have discussed, *human life, both individual and communal, should be lived in harmony with the basic characteristics and mode of operation of nature.* From this premise, coupled with postmodern scientific insights about the nature of reality, there seem to follow some important propositions to be stated presently. First, however, let us consider the subject of *sin,* as distinguished from *evil.*

As mentioned briefly earlier, sin refers to a relationship between man and God, whereas evil has meaning without regard to deity and commonly denotes violation of moral principles. Sin, on the other hand, refers to more than that, namely, to a state of mind and heart that brings forth evil. Biblically speaking, it is a malady, aberration, or perversity of the human spirit, and especially an estrangement from, or even rebellion against, ultimate Spirit, God. In a

sense evil deeds are but the symptoms of deeper difficulty
—sin, and it is to this that divine redemptive action is
applied. This is why Christian thought has regarded redemption not only as punishment and propitiation but as
an act of healing and reconciliation, of God seeking through
love, self-sacrifice, and forgiveness to reestablish a broken
relationship with his wayward children.

Again we must note that most people today find this
personalistic and mythic language about sin and God to be
very strange. It fails to communicate its intended meaning.
However, for the new consciousness that has experienced
becoming natural the idea of sin can be profoundly meaningful. Thus it has been suggested that what has been
called estrangement from God may mean in the first place
estrangement from the cosmos—all of nature and its creatures, including men—and therefore from its creative
ground, its Source, Guide, and Goal. It may also mean
shaking a defiant fist at the universe, refusing to accept its
way of things, going one's own independent self-willed
way, being lethally for evil rather than creatively and
remedially *for good*. As Loren Eiseley put it so perceptively,
it is "like tampering with the secret purposes of the universe itself . . . in deliberate blasphemy."[10] So it is that
the post-modern consciousness can understand with great
clarity that sin is not-loving nature, man, and God.

By the same token, for the naturalized faith-conscious-
ness the term "to love God" has acquired profoundly enhanced meaning. It refers not only to its obvious meaning
—loyalty and devotion, when God is conceived as exclusively personal—but also to meaning that becomes possible
when God is thought of as both personal and nonpersonal
and as acting always through natural forces. Thus it means
aligning oneself *with*, rather than *against*, the creative and
remedial love processes that faith can now discern, through
the eyes of psychology and psychiatry, and other social
sciences, within the causal system of the universe. It means
to accept for oneself the divine cosmic purposes and values
revealed through those processes. And it means to be sensitive and responsive to the eternal mystery of Becoming, as
well as Being, and to be utterly open to revelatory and

redemptive-remedial realities and insights still to emerge in life and the cosmos.

That this ought to be the case is, of course, precisely what the assumption of a few moments ago asserts. The question is, however, what the basic characteristics of nature referred to there are. What are the divine cosmic purposes just mentioned as being revealed by its natural processes?

As the result of our studies in Part Two I suggest for a list of the most fundamental realities and values of the cosmos: first, its interrelationships and interdependencies, which determine the "nature" of entities and out of which come interactions and events; second, the wholeness of systems out of which alone emerge the many quality-realities without which the universe would have little if any meaning and no life, or mind, or spirit, or tenderness and love; third, the holistic drive toward the aggregation and organization of individuals, be they human or otherwise, into whole-structures or communities; fourth, its dynamism and developmental-evolutionary thrusts that bring forth in time a succession of novelties—with increased possibilities, and therefore actualities, for good; fifth, the processes of remediality, by which improved patterns of existence develop for individuals and communities out of misfortune, evil, and wreckage; and sixth, the supremacy of tenderness and love in the gamut of cosmic causal forces and efficacies.

Combining these insights about the character of reality with the assumption about what human life ought to be like yields, I believe, the following general principles which are typical of others we cannot discuss herein. *First, those values are legitimate and consistent with the cosmic scheme of things which tend to conserve or create and maximize such relationships as make for optimum mutuality, interdependence, and wholeness;* and those are undesirable and cosmically incongruous which tend toward the maximum of utter independence, self-sufficiency, isolation, and fragmentation. That is wrong which makes for the enhancement or glorification of the individual-unto-himself rather than of the individual-in-community. That is sin which shatters the life-giving relationships between men and their God, and therefore also those between man and fellowman and between man and his fellow creatures in nature.

Second, human ideals should contribute to the dynamism of life and to its developmental-evolutionary thrust toward change and the emergence of novelty—for good. That is wrong, and incongruous in our dynamic universe, which hinders or blocks such change, or insists on maintaining the status quo for its own sake, or because there are dangers involved in change. Faith must not be stopped by danger, but must face it courageously and creatively—as well as cautiously. It is sin to get in the way of God's creative and developmental purposes and pressures. In the last chapter I shall suggest that this principle demands that biblical faith be future-oriented in glad expectancy of the emergence in the not too distant future of an integrated humanity and the reign of shalom in a "new earth."

The next principle pertains to the realities of force and power, organization and structuring, which are absolute necessities in the cosmic, as well as any social, scheme of things. *Third, human life—individual and communal, national and international—should be dominated by the tender and persuasive elements of life, and most of all by the strongest of these, love.* Morality is life lived sensitively, respondingly, and responsibly, and empowered by the tender might of mutuality. That is wrong which is dominated by self-centeredness, insensitivity, and hatred, and is brought about by disruptive coercion and violence.

From this principle there follows an important corollary which has special relevance for technology: *In a truly human society the qualitative aspects and values of life should in man's strivings take priority over quantitative ones.* Its character must not be determined, or its life be controlled, by the myth of the machine, or the demand for unrestricted *affluence.* In other words, what this calls for is an economy of plenitude rather than plenty (as envisioned by Lewis Mumford), and a technology of flower power rather than of megapower—with all that is suggested by the call to consider the lilies.

It bodes well for the future that the new consciousness

is increasingly becoming aware of the primacy of these principles (and others related to them) and committing itself to them. For the biblical consciousness none of this is fundamentally new, as its perennial central motif of love attests. What is new, however, is that biblical religion has become natural and is coming to see that these insights and principles are revealed not only through the special events of history but through nature—and the whole cosmic scheme of things—as well. This in turn is bringing with it new realizations, sensitivities, emphases, conceptions, and goals. In this way biblical faith is experiencing a momentous transformation of its contours, and new manifestations of its truly developmental character. But there are serious problems of an intellectual nature which need solving during this time of transition, and we must look at these next.

XIII. Difficult Perplexities
for Today's Faith

GOD AND THE SYSTEMIC
INTEGRITY OF NATURE

We must now face the fact that a large sector of the post-
modern consciousness feels that all talk about God is undesirable, because it seems, first, to be useless and, second, to
pose insoluble problems. Even within the communities of
biblical faith there are serious misgivings about this; witness the recent "God is dead" talk. More specifically,
among Christians there is a spreading conviction that many
traditional beliefs no longer conform to what we know
about the world and therefore need drastic revision—especially beliefs about how God operates in nature, e.g., to
restore persons to health or give them their daily bread or
songs in the night.

Thus far we have portrayed the biblical understanding
of "God" largely in terms of faith's basic "sensings," and
of insights that come in disclosure experiences, and without reference to more critical considerations. Now more
than that is needed.

Consider the following affirmation, which is, I believe,
acceptable to most Christians: *It is in God's continuing
creative activity that biblical faith sees the ultimate continuing source of nature's existence and evolutionary development, and it is in his unceasing redemptive activity that it
sees the ultimate continuing cause of the transformative
and remedial processes that operate in nature and history
"for good."*

The problem for the new consciousness is how, if there
is indeed God, he may be conceived to act in all realms and
at all levels of a world which patently operates according

to natural laws, which is itself creative, and whose phenomena and happenings are thought to be explicable in terms of its own resources—without recourse to the concept of "God?" And what does the term "ultimate cause" imply in this context? Does it mean for faith that any idea of "immediate" day-to-day causal activity of God in nature is no longer tenable?

Let us be quite clear about this: The question is not how God actually acts in nature (if he does act in some sense) but how biblical faith may reasonably conceive him to act. Faith simply cannot *know* what God's essential nature and activity are. Its so-called "knowledge of God" results from a combination of experience and observation, on the one hand, and of critical reflection and mental construction, on the other—just as does science's "knowledge of nature." What we are considering, then, is how faith may conceive or "model" God's activity in nature.

Some Christians avoid such questions, feeling that they lead to undesirable speculation about God. They prefer to conceive of him simply as the redeemer-creator without whom the experienced realities would not be. For others, however, this is not enough, because for them the question of *how God does it* seems too persistent existentially, and too crucial intellectuallly, to be ignored, especially in the light of the following post-modern understanding. In so far as creative and remedial-redemptive processes are experienced by men, these must occur as changes in their bodies, and particularly in their brains. Therefore, to say that God gives men faith and reorients their thinking and behavior is to assert *at least* this much, that *somehow* God affects the cybernetic or "computer" processes of their brains, through changes in the electrical and chemical reactions among the atoms of which those brains consist. Does it make sense to suppose that God does this? If so, how? If not, what alternative is there?

Basically this is not a new problem. Ever since science has conditioned men to the idea of laws of nature, believers have been perplexed about such matters. In the modern period, however, this difficulty seemed not too serious, because, in harmony with Cartesian dualism, those laws applied to matter only, and not to mind and spirit. Even if one felt hesitant about believing that God operates directly upon atoms and molecules of the physical world, as a deus ex machina interfering in the natural system of causes, one could still believe unhesitatingly that he acts efficaciously in the realm of spirit, and therefore upon human minds and wills.

Since then, however, as we have seen, the "nonmaterial" entities, life, mind, and spirit, have turned out to be but manifestations or states of what I have called physical reality; and the entire psychosomatic organism we call man, including his mind, has been found to be integrally a part of the causal system of nature. And so in our time we do have a problem, and a rather serious one. For if there is good reason not to think of God as directly causing changes in, say, the weather, or in the motion of a car on the highway, wouldn't that reason disallow also any thought of his causing changes in the human brain, and therefore in the human mind and will? There seems to be no essential difference between these two types of phenomena—and, presumably, causal activities of God—in nature.

What is a post-modern Christian or Jew to say to this? His very instincts cry out against any deus-ex-machina or God-in-the-gap conception that depicts the deity as "intervening" as a physical cause anywhere in nature, and thus determining the behavior of atoms or electric circuits, either in general or in particular situations, in ways that would violate nature's systemic integrity. To think this way of God seems to him to be utterly undesirable. And yet his faith-instincts cry out with equal vehemence against complete conceptual banishment of God from the causal system of nature. This is a grim dilemma. His instincts rebel, however, not only against each of its horns but against any idea that life and reality are so constituted as to make such a dilemma necessary in the first place. Surely—and here is where faith about "the way things are" asserts itself, be it secular or religious—there must be a better way of thinking about these matters, and without having to relinquish any truly basic insights of either the biblical or scientific consciousness!

Certainly, equally serious difficulties have been faced in the past and been resolved by adopting different styles of thought or of belief. In our time science has undergone tremendous changes, as we have seen, and not least in the very area of our present perplexity: the reign of natural law in the cosmic scheme of things. We may expect, therefore, that biblical religion, which we have depicted as genuinely developmental, will also be able to adapt to the new situation. And indeed some very imaginative thinking is being done along these lines. One suggestion has been that traditional theism be modified drastically.

Let us see what this might mean.

MODIFYING TRADITIONAL THEISM

A suggestion by Prof. Leslie Dewart of the University of Toronto is that some of the absolutistic features of traditional theism be relinquished.[1] Its idea has been that God is an *absolute* (albeit benevolent) monarch, with *absolute* power, whose will is supreme and *absolutely* determinative, who has in his mind a detailed, fixed blueprint of the entire history (past, present, and future) of both the world and each individual entity in it. Nature is *absolutely* dependent upon him in the sense that nothing happens in it without his willing, or consenting to, it directly. God is also the *absolutely* unconditioned, unmoved mover, who moves molecules, worlds, and men but is not moved or conditioned by them. The suggestion is that much of the difficulty we are wrestling with stems from this kind of absolutism and that we should rid our thinking of it. Now that we are aware that all scientifically known reality is relational, wouldn't it be better to think of all reality, including God, as relational also, rather than as absolute?

This would not violate fundamental understandings of biblical faith, since it has actually not been absolutistic in the way the more extreme forms of theism have been. Certainly the Pauline conception of God as Source, Guide, and Goal is not. There is wise flexibility and fluidity in that language. A real guide is not an absolute determiner; he maintains a noncoercive relationship with the guided one, whose autonomy and freedom of decision he supports and protects. In the God-talk of biblical faith—both of the past and the present—one finds many other terms also that are similarly relational in their connotations of God, e.g., Spirit, father (in the nonautocratic sense), tutor, teacher, counselor, persuader, participant, companion, partner, spouse (the well-known biblical imagery of the bride and bridegroom).[2] None of these has absolutistic implications.

Similar remarks apply also to the terms Source and Goal. God as Source is where the stream of reality, existence, and life originates, and from which continue to flow all possibilities for meaning, goodness, beauty, truth, creativity, healing, and all else that is and becomes. But the implications of this figure of the Source are very different from those of a fabricator-God stamping out the forms of reality upon predesigned patterns that fix its characteristics for all time. Nor does the image of God as Goal imply a predetermined target toward which mankind and the cosmos *must* develop. A goal is not genuine if it is set *for* someone without his choice—even if that goal is in some sense God.

It must be evident that my thought owes much to the Pauline concepts of God as the "Source, Guide, and Goal of all that is" and of a "pattern of happenings for good." This is because they typify admirably an impressive style of thought that was characteristic of biblical faith in its early stages and yet turns out now to be remarkably contemporary—and clearly relational. This is evident not only in the writings of Paul but throughout the Bible and much of the postbiblical literature of faith. The phrase, "the God of Abraham, Isaac, and Jacob," has rather consistently stood for a relational conception of God, as one who was conceived primarily in terms of his concrete historical deeds and his very real nearness to his people and world— in sharp contrast to a God defined abstractly in terms simply of his own essence. Much of theism has exemplified the latter, nonrelational mode of thought. If then we accepted the Dewart suggestion we would be moving away from that kind of theism, and yet not be violating biblical insights about God, but would actually be moving closer to them in their basic meaning.

Another suggestion is that traditional theism has in its

concepts and imagery separated God too far from the world and mankind—by excessive insistence on his transcendence and wholly other-ness while minimizing, or even denying, his immanence and any likeness to other reality. When men suppose God to be so completely separate, as though dwelling in an altogether different realm, they tend to suppose also that he acts in nature only by forcible intervention from "on high." Thus the term "ultimate cause" spoken of in the affirmation we are considering actually comes to mean no more than simply a supernumerary cause injected into nature's system of natural causes, thus upsetting the natural balance of things. And so we have the conceptual spectacle of God affecting a person's thought and behavior by imposing temporary external controls upon the physical functioning of his brain and of its constituent particles and circuits. Thus God would after all not be a relational persuasive Guide, honoring human freedom, but rather an absolute ruler who forces his way into the brain from the outside and then causes it to behave without a choice in his way. Suppose, however, that "transcendent" is taken to include the "immanent" as proposed in chapter X, and thus not "wholly other and completely beyond nature," then God could be conceived as indigenous to nature, acting "from within its own depths" persuasively, as though from its very heart—without violating its systemic integrity.

Other suggestions have also been made for the modification of theism, and we need to discuss some of them. First, however, we should be reminded that, as noted in chapter II, it is the utter mystery of that which "stands beyond, behind, and within, the passing flux of immediate things" (Whitehead) to which religion, including biblical religion, is the worshipful response. Let no amount of conceptual or doctrinal thinking about God obscure this primal fact; nor the additional fact that the disclosure experience, out of which faith comes to men, yields no new knowledge in the sense of information, and no specific divinely authorized doctrine, but a new understanding, or way of looking at and responding to the world and its Source, Guide, and Goal. And what is especially remarkable about this understanding is that it increases and intensifies, rather than diminishes, one's sense of the mystery of things—and of God.

Christianity has often seemed to imply that, because of "the historic revelation of God in Jesus Christ," it can claim conceptual or doctrinal certainty and finality concerning the divine. The fact is, however, that, while because of the Christ event some things may not be said about God and others must be, this revelation has actually added to, rather than subtracted from, the Christian sense of the mystery of God. Never before was faith so fully aware of how very little it really knows about God *and* of how surpassingly wondrous is that which it has been given to know about him. As the Roman Catholic theologian, Gabriel Moran, remarked recently, "The closer God drew, the less conceptualizable he became....God did not become obvious and comprehensible in Christ. He became more confusing or at least more paradoxical; that is, we are driven to re-examine our most basic presuppositions of what God should be like."[3] Is it not absolutely necessary to say something like this if one has really grasped or been grasped by the significance of ultimate mystery for faith—as well as for its conceptions and beliefs?

Certainly the sensing of this should be reflected unmistakably in the intellectual stance of biblical thought as it engages in the formulation of doctrine. It must be humble thinking that does not claim more than it ought; that realizes that no conceptual formulation, theological or scientific, can possibly present reality completely or adequately, and especially when the reality under consideration is ultimate mystery. Also it must not claim for its formulations the status or authority of "divine revelation."

On the other hand, it would seem also that an appropriate belief-stance is not only one of humility and reticence but also one of confident expectancy and venturesomeness, looking forward, though not uncritically, to change in belief and mode of theological thought as the world changes and new reality emerges in it. This is precisely what characterizes much discussion and questing within the ranks of post-modern Christianity today. Let us not, then, hesitate in further investigating theism for its adequacy and inadequacy for our time and the future—and particularly with regard to the problem of this chapter, namely, the relation of God to nature. Theism is not sacrosanct and untouchable. As it has been for a long time, it is still subject to development and change.

What other suggestions have been made for modifying it? Here are a few more by Leslie Dewart, to whom we have referred before, taken from his challenging book, *The Future of Belief:*

The Christian theism of the future might not conceive God as *a being....*

Christian theism might in the future not conceive God as a person —or indeed as a Trinity of persons....

There is no divine manipulation of the puppet-strings of history, ... no predestination, ... no divine command to history. ... For God's "omnipotence" not only means that all history is possible, it also means that all history is *free....*

The Christian concept of Good may develop in the direction of shedding its supernatural character.[4]

These passages out of context must not be taken to indicate Dewart's specific theological leanings, present or past. They are tentative, exploratory gropings, as he explicitly states.* But they are not mere blind gropings in the dark; rather, they are sophisticated, systematic weighings of real possibilities for future thought that seem likely to grow out of ideas that are current now. It should be emphasized that what we have here is no mere passive and reluctant yielding to change feared to be inevitable, but an active desire to bring about gladly and responsibly such change as may make faith's beliefs more consistent with, and truly contributory to, what is known now and is likely to be in the foreseeable future.

This is not, of course, the place to discuss all of these; but I suggest that, as we now return to our main subject, we do consider the second: the personhood of God. Thus far we have spoken of God in various contexts as Source,

---

* Indeed, he has developed his ideas further in other books.

Guide, and Goal, as the ultimate Mystery, ultimate Spirit, the Redeemer-Creator, "my Maker, who gives songs," the transcendent-immanent One, Being, the Ground of Being, Love, and still others. The question now is whether God conceived in such a variety of ways should in our time be conceived also more particularly as "a person or trinity of persons"—which conception has had a long and fruitful history in the past. Some Christian scholars insist that it is at the very center of biblical thought and must be retained. Others urge that what is central in the biblical consciousness is the awareness of God not as a person or persons but as *personal*, which is something quite different. And still others prefer saying that God is *both personal and nonpersonal*, which is to say that God is somewhat like a person but not altogether so, and that God is in some ways not at all like a person but more like, say, force or power, or light, or truth, and love.

One is reminded of the situation discussed in chapter IV, when physics was confronted by the utter strangeness of the newly discovered micro-entities, when electrons and atoms, which had been regarded as particles, turned out to be only somewhat like particles, while also being somewhat like waves—though actually not waves. As we remember, at the time this seemed disconcertingly paradoxical, but when physics learned to adapt its ways of thinking, its models, and its language to the new findings, there resulted profound understanding and a vast expansion of scientific consciousness.

In its essentials this is just what has been happening in Christianity also. The conception of God as a trinity of persons has prevailed there for a very long time—and for good reasons. Now, however, large sectors of the new consciousness sense that this no longer suffices. For in the new natural-historical setting of human existence the connotations of "God" as the "Source, Guide, and Goal of all that is" far surpass those of "person," though "God" is also at least personal—as well as nonpersonal. I confidently believe that biblical thought will be able to adapt to this new development with novel ways of thinking, innovative models and symbols, and enriched beliefs, thus contributing to a mighty transformation of religious consciousness. And by the way, I understand that this kind of change is going on in other religions also.

Perhaps the reader is wondering why, in view of all this, I still employ personal pronouns in my God-talk. The answer is that I know of no more satisfactory practice. Quite frankly, I feel very uncomfortable using the pronoun "he" to refer to God. It seems so utterly inadequate. Yet to resort to "it" is much worse. At least a "he" or "she" has the qualities of highly developed mind and spirit, whereas an "it" manifests them in at most a rather rudimentary way, and more often than not it manifests none at all. To use the hyphenated "he-or-it" seems at the very least linguistically awkward and unaesthetic. So I shall continue to refer to God with a personal pronoun, hoping that the reader will with me impute very much more meaning to this usage than one would in other contexts. Perhaps our language will some day evolve to the point where it will have much more adequate resources for communicating about the ultimate reaches of personal and nonpersonal reality—and therefore about God. This would have tremendous value for a modified theism.

TWO LEVELS
OF REALITY AND DISCOURSE

Consider now an important aspect of our problem not noted explicitly before, namely, that it deals with basically different levels of reality, those of ultimacy and those of physical reality, or nature, and that corresponding to these there have developed two different vocabularies, or languages, neither of which suffices for adequate talk about the levels of reality of the other. Thus scientific discourse which refers to the levels of nature does not itself deal with those of ultimacy, and with such ideas as God and ultimate cause. Similarly, religious language which does speak of ultimacy does not directly deal with such ideas as the weather, the brain, and natural causes, which refer to the levels of nature. And, of course, neither language can itself handle questions that involve both levels, such as those about how nature and God relate to each other dynamically. In ordinary discourse about both levels the two languages become so badly entangled that serious semantic errors occur almost inevitably.

What we have here, then, is the kind of problem which can be solved only by means of what is called a meta-language, or a philosophic system that employs more inclusive concepts than either of the other languages does, and thus provides a way of talking about both levels with but one overall language and system of ideas. This need to think philosophically as well as religiously has characterized biblical religion for a long time, and history has shown that seemingly intractable difficulties often yield to resolution under the clarifying light of an appropriate philosophy.

This suggests, then, that to solve our particular problem at least tentatively, and if we were to adopt the proposals for doctrinal change made thus far, we should seek a system of ideas which conceives God as relational, rather than absolute, and as personal and nonpersonal, rather than as a person or persons; and which brings God and nature much closer together in thought than they have been in traditional theism—and can thus help us to imagine how God can be deeply involved in the internal operation of nature without violating its systemic integrity.

The most promising philosophy available today from this point of view is, in my opinion, process thought as represented in the writings of Whitehead, Hartshorne, Teilhard, and their followers, including Cobb, Meland, Ogden, Pittenger, Williams, and others. This thought is widely regarded as rather difficult; however, this is probably due more to its strangeness than its formidability or complexity. Thus it takes the world to be fundamentally a process, and a society of events, rather than a materialistic system—which is certainly far from conventional.

This is not, of course, the place to expound process thought extensively. We should, however, consider this much, namely, wherein its strategic value lies for the two-levels problem I shall hereafter refer to by the hyphenated term, nature-and-God. The answer is, I think, that, first, its world view is empirically derived from human experience, in all its levels and dimensions, and thus rests upon both the sensory and nonsensory perception of reality as demanded by the new consciousness. Second, both its basic conceptions and the tone of its feelings and intuitions are distinctly post-modern. Even the vocabulary commonly used to set forth the distinctive features of the contemporary scientific world view is indigenous to the discourse of process philosophy. Thus we have spoken, in Part One, of the world as a mysterious, restless, vibrant, living organism, forever in process, and pregnant with possibilities for novel emergences and developments in the future. We have spoken of it also as relational, societal and communal in character. We noted the interiority, depths, and levels of physical reality; the variety of its qualities and structures displayed at different levels; its polarities of complexity and simplicity, order and disorder, predictability and unpredictability, lawfulness and chance; its seemingly unlimited creativity and destructivity. All this fits naturally into the language of process thought, in obvious contrast to that of traditional theism. This, then, is the first evaluative point to be made about process philosophy: It has the conceptual resources for adequate reference to nature in terms of our post-modern conception of it.

This judgment applies also to its conceptual relationship to the level of ultimacy. Everything asserted in Part Three about faith's sensings of God as living, relational, loving, redemptive-creative, and transcendent-immanent seems to me to fit naturally into the conceptuality of process thought. One need not renounce faith's basic understandings of God in order to feel comfortable using this philosophy for religious thinking. Thus we may say that process thought has the conceptual resources for adequate reference to the level of ultimacy.

These two items are, however, only minimal, in that they represent only the least that must be the case if process thought is to be useful for our purposes, namely, that it enable us to converse accurately about what we know experientially about the nature and God levels *separately*. What must be the case also is that its concepts enable us to construct a model of what transpires beyond human conscious experience by way of interaction between the levels. Here, too, process thought has much to offer (and this is the third evaluative point), though it is naturally enough not yet wholly adequate in this respect. The way it seeks to achieve this is by postulating that the realities of nature and of ultimacy have certain properties beyond the purview of science and biblical faith respectively, but not in violation of their basic insights; and these postulated overtones of connotation make possible a theory of the dynamics of the inter-level relationship nature-and-God. It should be understood, of course, that these supra-components of meaning are not intended to correspond to any realities discoverable by either scientific or religious experience—and they certainly must not be taken literally.

CONSTRUCTING A MODEL
RELATING THE TWO LEVELS

Let us now note some of these strategic postulations in brief detail. The order of their presentation is admittedly not so much logical as pedagogical. First, process metaphysics eschews sharp discontinuities, dichotomies, and dualisms in favor of principles of continuity and holism. This is, of course, in harmony with post-modern scientific thought that renounces the dualisms of matter and energy (in favor of the continuum of matter-energy), of space and time (in favor of space-time); that renounces the pluralism of matter, life, and mind (in favor of matter-life-mind). Furthermore, process thought enlarges on this principle by denying the traditional duality of the natural and the supernatural, and thus the complete separation between God and the world. This makes way for the biblical idea that God is in the world, while at the same time it is in him, an idea that represents panentheism, rather than conventional theism (though apparently not all process thinkers explicitly espouse panentheism).

Next, God is taken to be the great exemplification of cosmic characteristics, rather than their great exception. In theism God is in general terms the wholly other, i.e., what other realities are not, e.g., the one reality who is not relative but absolute. Similarly, traditional theism conceives other realities as in some sense temporal and spatial, but not so God. In process thought, however, if other realities are relative (or relational, as I prefer to say), God is even more so—indeed, he is the infinitely relative (or related) one; if other realities are in process, God is supremely so; if they are "moved" by others, he is "moved" by them even more deeply. If physical reality is creative, God is more so. If other realities are to be thought of as occasions rather than substances, so is God—as the presiding occasion, the supreme exemplification of occasionness. So it comes about, for reasons to be considered presently, that God is conceived as the great co-reality: co-sufferer, co-rejoicer, co-worker, co-redeemer, co-creator, co-presence, and more. For many Christians it sounds strange at first to speak of God as, say, co-redeemer. But this expression simply recognizes that, as we saw in Part Two, nature's processes are remedial, transformative, and redemptive, in the sense that they do bring forth healing and new life out of past wounding, catastrophe, and wreckage (as suggested by Calhoun). To recognize this does not, or need not, detract from the recognition of God as the supreme redeemer —without whom there would be no redemption at all. The idea of God as co-redeemer actually adds profoundly to the meaning of both "God" and "redemption." And the other co-concepts have similarly enriching value and meaning.

Third, for process thought nature's entities are all both objects and subjects to one another. Thus even molecules and protons are subjects that experience other entities as objects, and are themselves objects experienced by the others as subjects. The verb commonly used for this "experiencing" is "to prehend," which denotes a sort of feeling, or sensing, or being aware of, or grasping, or influencing another entity; and conversely it means also a sort of being felt, or sensed, or grasped, or influenced by another. These terms are not, of course, genuine synonyms but represent suggestive analogies. A molecule is thus thought to prehend another *somewhat* as (by analogy) sensing beings sense one another, or *somewhat* as conscious beings are aware of one another. Thus inanimate things are postulated to be capable not of sensing in the psychological meaning, but of prehending—which is very different from, yet analogous to, it. The term "prehend" thus denotes an efficacious relationship at a level of the reality and activity of entities beyond the humanly experienceable levels of nature. God too prehends, and is prehended. It is in this sense that God moves and is moved by other prehending entities. And it is in this sense that God and all other entities are both objects and subjects.

Fourth, this prehension by which entities are efficaciously present to one another is postulated to be noncoercive in character. Thus God affects the behavior of other entities not by force, in a monarchical sense, but by what may by analogy be called persuasion, or a luring on, or loving guidance. This is in harmony with both the biblical theme that God is love and the insight of contemporary social science that love is indispensable to genuinely human exis-´ tence and is probably the strongest influence encountered in it.

Fifth, every entity or occasion has a "subjective aim," or purpose, or drive, which determines the general direction of its passage, or its transformations into subsequent occasions, or the range of possibilities within which its subsequent becoming must remain, and which thus delineates or establishes its abiding unique individuality. To illustrate, the subjective aim of a certain species of atom is to be a sodium atom, and not any other kind, which means that there is available to it for future becoming a particular range of possibilities, such as to join with many other sodium atoms in forming a chunk of sodium metal that acts in a certain distinctive way when in contact with water; or that can emit a particular type of bright line spectrum of light; or that can react chemically with chlorine atoms to form table salt. Similarly, the subjective aim of a certain kind of egg is to be a chicken egg and to become a chicken, rather than a turkey. To say this is not to assert that a chicken egg is conscious of its purpose. Its subjective aim is a postulated supra-reality at a level quite beyond those of physical reality where consciousness in the usual sense exists. It is that aspect of a chicken egg that effectuates its becoming a chicken rather than a snowflake, or pine tree, or volcano, or anything else.

God also is conceived to have a subjective aim, namely, to be the "Source, Guide, and Goal of all that is" and to make it possible for all concrete happenings of nature-history to fit into a pattern "for good." It is in terms of this eternal aim and purpose that God's so-called "primordial nature," or unchanging character, is conceived. It is because he is always like *this* that biblical faith is possible and men have taken him to be God rather than, say, Satan.

Sixth, it is a fact, however, that all things change in time to some extent. Animate ones grow or decay, become larger or smaller, become more or less responsive to their environment, and so on. Inanimate ones are eroded or corroded, or dry out, or absorb water, or are scoured by water or wind, or undergo changes of state, and much else. Hence process thought postulates for all actual entities not only a "primordial nature" but also a "consequent" one, that changes in response to its changing environment. All actual things are characterized by both permanence and change, preserving their identity and undergoing modification. Every cat remains during its lifetime a cat; none has ever been known to turn into a whale or a carnation. But no cat remains unchanged; nor does any other natural thing.

Accordingly, God is also conceived to have not only a primordial nature but a consequent one as well. He is always the God who in love redeems and creates, but he and his love are always changing and becoming in loving response to other entities about him. He is the great participant, with his creatures, in the affairs of nature-history, and this does not leave him unmoved or unchanged. Thus, just as the universe is becoming, so is he.

Seventh, there are for this philosophy two kinds of entities: those of abstract potentiality or possibility for actualization, designated as eternal objects; and those of concrete actuality, designated as actual occasions. Moreover, each occasion is regarded as an aggregate of both actualities and possibilities. An occasion such as a newborn child, for example, would seem rather meaningless, useless, and empty of content if it were felt to be no more than it actually *is* concretely. But it becomes profoundly meaningful when seen as a bundle of both actualities and possibilities—for future comeliness and personality, for love and care, for growth and achievement. At an advanced age the ratio of its actualities to possibilities is reversed, and eventually only one possibility remains, that of death. As long as it is a human being, however, it has both actualities and possibilities. And this is the case for all other actual objects, be they animate or inanimate.

Finally, what do such terms as cause, causation, causal efficacy, natural cause, and ultimate cause mean for process philosophy? What they refer to is the passage or transformation from abstract possibility to concrete actuality, and the process by which certain possibilities are selected for actualization while others are not. Causation is, then, the driving force or efficacy of the process by which *this*, rather than *that*, particular actual occasion comes to be, and after it the next, and so on. It is the explanatory principle for the process of concretion, of turning the abstract (possible) into the concrete.

Here again process thought employs with profound understanding the insights of post-modern science. It recognizes that the older conception of a single-stranded connection between cause and effect was inadequate. As we saw in Part Two, causal relations are always many-stranded, more like networks or systems of circuits, and all of nature's entities participate efficaciously in all of them. A "cause" is complex and includes many kinds of forces and influences—physical, psychological, and social, such as gravity, love, and public opinion—all of which are parts of the causal system of nature. To be sure, in most situations many, if not most, of the forces at play in it are for practical purposes negligible in their effect; but in principle they are there.

What is especially impressive about this vision is the all-inclusiveness and extensiveness of its conceptions of both nature as a whole and of its individual constituents. It regards every "thing" in it as coextensive with the universe, in its prehending causal reach, and therefore as an occasion in the life of the entire cosmos, rather than a mere isolated event. It considers also that all the entities of the universe contribute efficaciously to the concretizing of each such occasion (even though the effect of most of them may be negligible practically). Being so inclusive, it allows even less conceptual room for any supposed interventions by a deus ex machina than did the older and more restricted conceptions of nature's causal system. There just aren't any gaps left in which a God of the gaps might operate, especially since all creative and redemptive action that human beings experience, and *know* anything about, is seen to occur within this broadly conceived "nature," as the result of processes also broadly conceived to be natural.

This vision's inclusiveness has also a vertical dimension. It sees the reality of all entities to extend beyond the levels of observable nature to the supra-depth levels of ultimacy. Thus, while it conceptually rejects divine intervention from the "outside," it definitely provides for divine causation "within" nature, without violation of its systemic freedom and integrity. It does this through the postulates considered a while ago which enable it to talk with semantic rigor about both ultimate and natural causes, and therefore about the dynamics of the inter-level relationship of nature-and-God.* Let us see how this works.

HOW GOD MAY BE THOUGHT TO ACT FROM WITHIN NATURE

Let us now consider some helpful summarizing statements by Norman Pittenger in regard to the role process thought conceives God to play in bringing about the happenings of nature:

First, process thought would insist that it is always through the activity of God that things come to pass, although God is not the only agent in creation. On the one hand, the divine activity is the

---

* There are two books, by Birch and Overman,[5] that employ process philosophy and theology in dealing specifically with this problem and thus provide fine introductions to this thought. More general, but brief, introductions are provided by Pittenger[6] and Hamilton.[7] Barbour[8] compares it critically with other contemporary schools of thought. The general reader should have no serious difficulties with any of these. Most rewarding eventually will be, of course, the great classics by Whitehead, Hartshorne, Meland, Williams, and others referred to earlier.

ultimate grounding for events; it provides the ultimate efficient cause which turns mere possibility into sheer actuality. On the other hand, God is the final *end* of all that comes to pass, since it is the fulfillment of his purpose (or, in Whiteheadian language, for the "satisfaction" of God's "subjective aim") that the process goes on, with consistency and its new emergents. . . . His all-inclusive functioning is the *basic* ground of each and every occurrence; . . . the sufficient *ultimate* explanation of what occurs. . . . Each new event rests back upon and is an expression of . . . the originative and final purpose which is divine.[9]

This is the first claim of process thought with regard to our problem of nature-and-God, namely, that God is both the ultimate grounding (Source) and the final end (Goal) of all occurrences. I take it to be saying essentially what the theme affirmation asserts at the beginning of this chapter. It is God's continuing activity that is the source of nature's existence and evolutionary development, and the ultimate cause of the transformative processes that operate in nature and history for good.

Second, the phrase "God acts" means that

the divine causal efficacy, moving towards the fulfillment of the divine aim, is in varying degrees the dominant element in each successive occasion. . . . God is precisely that factor which provides both the "control" and the "efficacy" which brings the occasion about . . . not by arbitrary . . . overruling . . . but by the persuasive moulding of new possibilities . . . and by offering the "lure" which evokes from each occasion in the ongoing process the movement towards satisfaction of its "subjective aim." This aim, it must be remembered, is the identifying quality of each specific actual event as it goes along its own particular routing within the process as a whole. So God as the "principle of concretion" can operate without for a moment reducing the value of, or in any way negating the role played by, the freedom of the creation.[10]

What this visualizes is that God performs a persuasive, luring, molding function (as Guide) in nature, which is definitely not that of an arbitrary, overruling, intervening, absolute monarch. His influence is potent in varying degrees, but it never violates the freedom of nature, or any of its entities.

At all times the temporal succession or flow of happenings (occasions) in the world is determined by a combination of efficacies and causative drives that arise out of two subjective aims, and their interaction upon each other, that of God and that of nature. Out of this situation there arise two kinds of causes, the ultimate and the proximate or natural causes respectively, those that operate between the ultimate levels of God and the proximate ones of nature, and those operating at the levels of observable nature only. The ultimate causes come from God's prehending persuasive influence upon the constituents of nature, and from nature's prehending influence upon God. This is not to say that these reciprocal efficacies are equally potent; indeed they are not. The ultimate causes represent God's active creative and redemptive participation in the process of becoming of each occasion and of the universe as a whole, and the proximate ones represent nature's own contribution to the process. God's causative pressure is exerted through

the materials of the world as they have come to exist. He works in and through, with and by, for and on behalf of all those actual entities which at any given moment are present. Through his tenderness and by means of his "lure," he moves them towards those self-decisions which can bring about great and greater good. He offers ever more widely shared opportunities for enhancement; and throughout the process he works towards the appearance of a realm in which his own satisfaction of aim in a realm of love becomes also the satisfaction of the creaturely aim and hence a sharing of love, as the creation moves forward toward richer life.[11]

Notice that what we have here is a beautiful conceptual scheme for visualizing how all entities and happenings of nature-history may possibly come about as the result of both God's and nature's continuing creative and remedial activity, and thus making post-modern sense of the theme affirmation of this chapter. It takes the world to be, by analogy, a society (of occasions) rather than, say, a machine. It recalls that in the social domain subjective aims and self-decisions, values and ideals, as well as lures, persuasions, and love, function as genuine causes, and then takes the "ultimate causes" of the universe to be of that sort. It conceives such causes to be those that operate at the level of ultimacy, those by which the transcendent-immanent God "moves" all entities of the world "from the inside" and by which they "move" God from within their own depths—where God is present to them.

These purposive forces that make for ultimate causation are, of course, not directly observable in nature because they are superposed upon, so to speak—or perhaps better intraposed within—the observables which science describes in terms of natural laws. Thus natural causes come into play when entities make the self-decisions referred to by Pittenger, and proceed to carry them out in ways that are consistent with their own subjective aims. This, then, is the way the dilemma referred to earlier has been resolved in at least its general features, and how we may conceive— in terms of the best we know scientifically and religiously —how God can affect men's thinking and behavior, and give them faith and hope and worthy commitments, by noncoercively influencing the physical operations of their brains.

This scheme helps us to conceive also, and be grateful for, God's giving us our daily bread—and all other common gifts of life, be they physical or spiritual—without invoking or evoking ideas of magic. The uncommon ones may be thought of in similar fashion as gifts of nature and of God, for example, the utterly novel and unpredictable mutations or emergents of biological evolution, and the remarkable emergents of man's cultural evolution, the arts, sciences, philosophies, religions, social institutions, commerce, politics, and so on. We may include here also what faith likes to call "the mighty revelatory deeds of God"—such as the call of Abraham, the exodus, the giving of the Torah, the coming of the prophets, and the unprecedented cluster of Christ events. For the most part these seem to have been interpreted in the past as being interventions of the deus-ex-machina type. As traditional theism saw it, this did not seem undesirable. Process thought, however, objects that for post-modern man it is; and it proposes an alternative, namely, that they be regarded as exceptional events, not because they are basically different from others in character and origin but because they are remarkably paradigmatic and revealing as exemplifications of what is possible, and can become actual, in a universe all of whose occasions are brought forth by processes that spring from the subjective aims and causative activities of both God and nature. Far from denigrating the importance of these key concepts and events, this conceptuality enhances it—as the next section endeavors to show.

THE COSMIC CHRIST

This theism, modified in the vein of process thought, enhances in several ways the meaning of the great exceptional, miraculous, and revelatory events which have shaped the biblical faith. First, it gives them cosmic, more than only human or regional, significance. Not only its all-inclusive and basically cosmic stance but its very language tends to call forth the vision of a "cosmic Christ,"[12] an awareness that the remarkable mystery-reality Christians call "Christ"—which was so supremely and radiantly revealing of God in Jesus of Nazareth—is an eternal, all-pervading cosmic reality that is present creatively and remedially to all beings of the universe. The idiom of process thought with its emphasis on universality is in many respects reminiscent of that prevailing in the early church, which spoke of Christ as the alpha and omega of all existence, as the *logos*, and the light and the life of the world, which gave, and continues to give, existence, character, and meaning to all of it. As we have seen, it is fundamental to process thought that love, sensitivity, and tenderness are the potent forces of the cosmos, and operative internally at the core of all occasions. The reality that embodies these efficacies is, I take it, what Christianity means by the "Christ."

Second, this way of thinking leads inevitably to another important insight, namely, that faith in Christ must be understood ecumenically and as nonsectarian in the broadest sense, i.e., as being a part, consciously or unconsciously, of all genuine faith in God, be it explicitly Christian or not.[13] Wherever the creative and redemptive tender elements of life are at work among men of all cultures and religions, in shop or mart, the political arena or academic hall, there Christ is actively present, even though he may be incognito, and however he ("he" in the richest possible sense) may or may not be theologized formally. I, for one, believe that this personal-nonpersonal reality of love-power and mystery, named or unnamed, has today entered the minds of multitudes of men of all cultures and religions and has there become the motivating spirit for much of the life and work of the world.

A third point to be made here is that too often recent God-talk has given the impression, under the influence of an extreme existentialism, that the concepts of God, Christ, savior, and salvation have meaning only with respect to human beings, and particularly individual persons. This has greatly increased the difficulty of finding a solution to the problem of God's relationship to nature—by implying that any such relationship is unimportant in the first place. Biblical thought has, however, taken a broader view, as illustrated by another key passage from the writings of Paul: "For I reckon that the sufferings we now endure bear no comparison with the splendour . . . which is in store for us. . . . The universe itself is to be freed from the shackles of mortality. . . . Up to the present . . . the whole created universe groans in all its parts as if in the pangs of childbirth (Rom 8:18-23, NEB)." Whatever else may be affirmed there, this much certainly is, that God, Christ, and salvation or liberation are not only for men but for all of nature. All of creation is in pain and anguish (as we also noted, from a purely secular point of view, in chapters VIII and IX). But it is not suffering alone, unnoticed and pointless. God is there—its Christ—and he cares, and is unceasingly and with compassion acting upon the situation, transforming what would be *only* pain and senseless anguish into the no less painful, but gloriously meaningful, pangs and travail of giving birth to new life and reality—and eventually to a new world of unimagined splendor, in which nature will no longer be shackled. One can sense throughout this remarkable passage a cosmic dimension of Paul's thought. It is in this sense that for biblical faith Christ is God in the role of savior of the cosmos, not only of men.

XIV. Man Building the "New Earth" with God

THE SHIFT TO FUTURIST CONCERNS

There is one more aspect of biblical religion that needs consideration here, namely, that it is becoming much more future-oriented than formerly. It seems that when history is seen to be natural, and reality is seen to be developmental, and humanity becomes acutely aware of the power and responsibility that have come to it, there is likely to occur a shift in its concerns and preoccupations—and men tend to look relatively less to the past and more to the future. And this is precisely what is happening to biblical faith now.

Actually, of course, this faith has always been future-oriented, even though it has not always seemed so. Certainly when Abraham left the land of his fathers to seek another home and destiny, he was looking to the future. The story of Lot's wife, who looked backward with fatal results, indicates the importance faith has attached to the forward look. The great faith-chapter of the New Testament (Hebrews 11) portrays the ancient heroes of faith as men and women who trusted God for the unseen, mysterious future and stepped out into it adventurously. Moreover, as we have seen, the fundamental insight about the pattern of happenings in the world "for good" is essentially anticipatory, and a counting on the future.

In our time, however, there are new manifestations of this futurism, especially with regard to the "new humanity" and "new earth" now in the making, and to the religious community's responsibility for helping to plan and shape them for good. The question is, of course, two-fold: first, what specific characteristics that world should have, if it is to conform to the long-range cosmic trend—and divine intent—toward increased community and the more complete humanization of mankind; and second, what the possibilities or probabilities are for constructing that particular kind of world. What its general attributes should be we have discussed under the heading of principles of ethics derivable from the study of nature, in chapter XII. About these there seems to be a high degree of unanimity among thoughtful people. There arise, however, grave difficulties and disagreements when these are to be translated into the specifics of structuring and regulating society in its many aspects and enterprises nationally and internationally; of properly balancing the needs and rights of individuals and communities, and of present and future generations; and of establishing optimum relationships between the human and nonhuman components of the terrestrial ecosystem. It is here that the questions of possibility or feasibility arise with greatest urgency and poignancy.

There can be little doubt that man, with the tremendous power over nature he has achieved, can transform the world and himself for good. But *will* he? Though much is known about him and the working of his mind, and he is by no means wholly unpredictable, he is still the most significantly unpredictable causal factor to be taken into account in contemplating the future. What *will* he do? Will he turn out to be good for the cosmos? As far as our planet is concerned, will he continue to be the primary lethal factor in it? There is a very real possibility that he will go berserk and with his titanic strength completely wreck what has taken nature so long to build up. While faith is confident in its hope for a desirable outcome, it is unable to promise it, either to the world or to itself, with certainty. For one thing, it believes that man is *free* to go his own way, unconstrained by God in any way; and for another, its understanding of how God operates upon the causal system of the world to achieve his purposes is still far from being adequate enough to be helpful practically in developing either a satisfying prognosis of probabilities or a feasible plan of action for the future. And yet faith is acutely aware of being inescapably part of the entire determinative process and, at the same time, of having important, though not complete, responsibility for channeling or guiding it toward a worthy goal. Here, then, is real uncertainty and perplexity, and one important reason why faith has become so preoccupied with the future, which, it hopes and expects, will bring forth new insights and realities that will resolve them.

"GOD THE FUTURE OF MAN," AND "GOD THE EVER WHOLLY NEW"

It is in response to this pressing need that we hear such future-oriented voices as Leslie Dewart's and others' mentioned in the preceding chapter, and still others such as that of the distinguished Catholic theologian E. Schillebeeckx, who in his book, *God the Future of Man*, makes the following startling remarks: "The situation requires us to speak of God in a way quite *different* from the way in which we have spoken of him in the past."[1] He speaks of the "biblical primacy of the future over the present and the past" and counsels that we "not look back at the Bible, but rather forward with the Bible" and conceive "both the present and the past as open-minded, oriented towards a new reality—what is still to come," and oriented especially toward the God who is to come in perennial newness, "God the future of man."[2]

Then he proposes more specifically that the coming "new culture" be "the point of departure for a new concept of God,"[3] thus assuming the typically empirical stance of biblical faith. He sees that in that culture man will experience and conceive the world not as a static system in which the future depends deterministically upon the causal factors of the past only, but as a dynamic process (again we encounter process thought!), the future output of which is shaped quite as much by the causal consequences of utterly new possibilities and realities still to emerge and by man's management of, or creative intervention in, the operations of nature-history. It will be a culture in which men will sense that the future is something to be achieved, not simply accepted, and in which biblical faith will sense that the unprecedented possibilities that must be actualized by man for that future will be provided by God of the future. And Schillebeeckx senses that in such a situation men will intuitively conceive of God with a strong emphasis upon his meaning for the future.

Though biblical faith has—with Paul—seen God in a three-fold relationship to the universe, namely, as Source, Guide, and Goal, Western thought has instinctively stressed the first of these, as though God's primary function were obviously that of generating Source or First Cause. The idea of God as Guide has seemed less intuitively compelling, and that of God as Goal or End even less so. Now, however, comes the suggestion that in our time, and in the coming age, the most meaningful way of thinking about God may well be as Goal of the future-building process of the universe, as *the One who is to come* as our destiny. As Schillebeeckx suggests, this would represent a shift in conceptual emphasis from God as "the wholly other" to God as "the ever wholly new"—always beyond what he has been, and has been conceived to be, earlier.

Here is ultimate mystery in what is probably its existen-. tially most meaningful aspect, the mystery of the future. The mystery of origins and past existence has, of course, always seemed wondrous and fascinating; but it is the mystery of what has already happened—irrevocably. Men have faced it and, for good or ill, come to terms with it. What seems to matter most now, and probably will matter most in the coming culture, is the mystery of what has not yet happened and is always still to be faced—with dread or with hope. Perhaps it will be in facing this mystery of the future that biblical faith, and its conception of God as the God of the ever open future, will become most vital.

Schillebeeckx suggests too that in the new culture to come the idea of divine transcendence will become especially meaningful with reference to the future. As we have seen, the term has referred traditionally to levels of already existing reality beyond those directly perceivable by man. What is suggested now, however, is that it will refer also, and perhaps even more, to such levels of reality as do not yet exist—except potentially, as possibilities in God of the future—and are still to come.

GOD'S GRACE AND THE FUTURE

Let it not be supposed that the quest for new conceptions of God constitutes a cutting of the connections with past belief. Looking into the future of belief, or of anything else, is not a confronting of an infinity of possibilities unrelated to the past. By no means is *everything* possible in the future, even though it be "open." Both science and history have taught us that even the most unexpected emergence of novelty in nature-history can eventually be seen to fit into, and be dependent upon, patterns of relationships known in the past. So it is also with emergent beliefs.

Neither Dewart nor Schillebeeckx is cutting himself off from the past of Christian belief. Dewart, for example, speaking of the need for a solid foundation and a reliable guideline for future doctrinal development, pleads that "what is absolutely fundamental to the Christian experience is that which is conceptualized in the doctrine of *grace*."[4] This is the well-established Christian belief that all of life and the world is the gift of the God who is experienced "as friendly and benevolent pervasive presence in every reality which constantly manifests itself to us and which should normally produce the Christian's appreciation of existence, his enjoyment of life, and the consequent moral obligation of charity towards our fellow man."[5]

It seems most significant for present purposes that Dewart finds this doctrine of grace to be especially meaningful "in the light of contemporary understanding of the total contingency of nature,"[6] a subject we have considered earlier. Indeed, he sees it contributing so cogently to our understanding of God that the concept of the supernatural becomes for him quite superfluous. In this way man's consciousness of grace is an important link not only between future and past belief but also between the biblical consciousness and the post-modern world view, with its strong sense of the givenness of things, and of the cosmic giving-reality, which—or, better, whom—men can claim as God. Moreover, the scientific vision of an open, dynamic, creative world, conceived as a living, vibrant, spirited, societal organism in which relationship, event, and process have primary meanings, provides vivid imagery and potent concepts for conceptualizing the living, gracious giver-God in ways that may be truly meaningful for men of the future. And neither Dewart nor Schillebeeckx is about to relinquish this venerable old belief.

Now I cannot help feeling that this concept of divine grace—when joined with the insights of process thought regarding God's action in nature and those implied by the dual conception of God the Future of Man and God the Ever Wholly New—can have a tremendous impact upon biblical consciousness, and upon the contribution it can make to current thinking about the future. For surely its message is that *to build a "new earth" that will be in accord with the fundamental character of the universe and its God will not be as impossible as it may seem from analyses based only upon the past.* What all such analyses, and all predictions based upon them, do not, and cannot, take into account is what new causal factors will emerge in the future to change the situation—new realities lured into actuality by the novel possibilities provided by the God who is forever wholly new. For if the concept of "God the Future" is to be more than simply a pious phrase, it must refer to a future that is more than merely an elongation or extrapolation of the past, with its usual characteristics and possibilities, and must refer to a genuinely new future, with truly novel possibilities and actualities.

"MAN COME OF AGE"—
AND CREATING WITH GOD; SHALOM

To make my point quite clear I appeal once more to the thought of Dewart: "History is made by man, but in the presence of God. Conversely, God is personally present to man in history. *With* God indeed all things, all history, is possible to man."[7] Notice the language here: "with God" not "under God." What this implies is that man has become by grace the co-determiner with God of future reality in nature-history. He has "come of age" in the sense of having been given unprecedented creative and transformative power for building the world of the future. He has come to the age of responsibility and authority to be exercised "for good" in the presence of, and sensitively responsive to, God—from whom derive all the possibilities that are open to him. It is, of course, obvious that this is not the kind of assertion to be expected from classical theism. Nevertheless I, like many others, accept it as being utterly in harmony with the insights of basic biblical faith in our time.

There are two especially dangerous perils which confront men in this new status. The first is that they may exaggerate the power that has come to them, and come to feel that they are God—so that they would not in effect be "with God" at all as they labor toward a new world. This temptation to go it alone under false illusions of grand self-sufficiency is, of course, a perennial one—and one that is all too familiar to all of us. It would be stark tragedy if this were to be the way it turned out. The second peril is just the reverse of the first, namely, that men may underestimate and undervalue their God-given power, and will fail to realize how very much responsibility for creative and transformative endeavor such power calls for, and will fail to recognize and adequately exploit the tremendous new possibilities that God will be injecting into the situation from time to time. I suggest that it is the second of these perils that is to be feared more. Man has had more than ample experience in playing God—with tragic consequences —and has had countless warnings against doing it again in the future. Indeed, all too often this kind of warning is all that representatives of the church have had to offer at consultations about the coming new world, thus failing utterly to contribute positively to man's hope by calling attention to the powerful role that new possibilities and realities can play in determining the future—which unprecedented possibilities can be actualized only if man labors creatively *with* God. Herein lies our deadliest danger: that we may in our chronic shortsightedness fail to recognize the new doors that will be opening to us or, if we do recognize them, that we may not have the courage or will to enter them. What a tragedy that would be!

Can we imagine what some of such unprecedented world-transforming possibilities might be? Yes, I think so; although probably other still more potent and innovative ones are at present beyond human imagination. Illustrative of some I have in mind are the following few: As noted in chapter III, there may at any time break through to human consciousness dimensions or realms of physical reality that exist now but have not yet been encountered by man. Similarly, there may emerge new realities which do not yet exist. In either case there would become available to mankind hitherto unknown forces and processes of nature which would certainly alter the present terrestrial causal system and completely upset the current futurist calculations and predictions—which are for the most part no more than extrapolations of curves representing already familiar relationships and trends. Then, thinking about energy resources, it is not inconceivable that much sunlight that impinges upon our planet and is now going to waste can be harnessed for useful purposes. Third, we may even learn to unlock and make use of subnuclear energy (of which we spoke in chapter VI in connection with the ideas of John Wheeler). Fourth, it may be possible to develop novel forms of life and biological entities which may enable us to maintain the kind of distribution of the components of the atmosphere (e.g., a proper balance of oxygen and carbon dioxide) that is necessary for the continued existence of life on earth—thus combating some of the ominous consequences of air pollution. There is similar hope regarding water pollution.

Probably the most exciting and momentous possibility awaiting us is that science will soon discover and be exploring depths of the human psyche at levels far below—or, better, interior to—any now known, and certainly far beyond those uncovered by Freud, and that this will disclose the existence of human abilities, psychic forces, and energies of which we now have no inkling. Without doubt this will amplify tremendously man's potential for sensitivity and mutuality, wholeness and goodness, remediality and creativity, so that what now seems impossible will then become not only clearly possible but eventually concretely actual.

Most of the urgent problems that worry us as we contemplate the near future arise from the prospect of over-

population and from mankind's unwillingness to change its
ways of life accordingly. There is much evidence that
technology would be able to solve the technical aspects of
these problems—*if* we were willing, first, to foot the bill,
financially and otherwise; and second, to desist from making the unreasonable and wasteful demands we now make
for more and more and more of virtually everything, much
of which we don't actually need in order to maintain a
high quality of human and nonhuman existence. On both
counts what is needed to make this possible is a radically
different pattern of human attitudes and commitments,
and basic to this a further development of human consciousness, especially in the direction of increased altruism
and a keener sense of responsibility for the common good
—which could in turn lead to the kind of all-embracing
future-oriented ethic we considered in the last section of
chapter XII.[8]

As the result of such a revolutionary development in
altruistic consciousness, there may well emerge a radically
transformed ethos and mythos of technology, a new Gestalt
of understandings—of its proper function in society; of the
kind of ideals and ethical standards by which it should be
evaluated and governed; of ways by which it can contribute
best to the qualitative improvement of life and to the
achievement of peace and tranquility in their richest sense;
of how it can in practice confer supremacy upon organis-
mically unifying flower power rather than upon the virtually uncontrollable megapower-and-technics that now
dominate it to such an unfortunate extent; and, finally, of
the role mythical conceptions and imagery can play in this
transformation, and in determining the direction of technology's drives toward a new earth. Should such an emergence occur, it would be one of the unprecedented ones to
which I referred, which would introduce quite new causal
factors into the world situation and into futurist planning
and prediction.

Many people regard this kind of talk as utterly unrealistic, and as utopian in the worst possible sense. But to take
that position is to deny that nature-history, including mankind, is developmental and that the matrix of events, or

"the way things are," allows for, and even provides positively for, the emergence of genuinely new possibilities in terms of which to plan and shape the future. In any case, rejecting that denial, I confidently list among the reasonable expectations and probabilities for the foreseeable future a continuation of, and a big step forward in, the development of human consciousness following upon such disclosures and emergences as we considered above. Consciousness III will transform into Consciousness IV (followed by still other developments), which will, I believe, exhibit more conscious awareness of the realities, necessities, and potentialities of "practical" politics and statemanship in all aspects of social existence—as well as increased sensitivity to the transcendent-immanent-ultimate, which alone, as Roger Shinn suggests, can prevent human enslavement by institutions.

Throughout the history of the biblical tradition there has persisted, sometimes feebly and sometimes strongly, a dream and expectation symbolized by the ancient near-Eastern word "shalom," with a rich freight of futurist meanings and ideals, which may be summarized by the term "peace" conceived as the "harmony of harmonies," to use Whitehead's powerful conception.[9] This is the "peace on earth and good will among men" which, according to the Christmas story, was announced and promised by the celestial choir when the cosmic Christ first showed himself "visibly" in a newborn infant in a stable in Bethlehem long ago. Within the Christian tradition the shalom motif has been perpetuated by the symbol of "the second coming of Christ," the vision of a second—and this time universally experienced—powerful, charismatic manifestation of God's presence in the world, culminating eventually in the appearance on earth of a "new Jerusalem." However variously interpreted and understood, this hope has never died out in the CHRISTian community. This too is one of the powerful resources biblical faith can offer the culture now in the making.

APPENDIX: On the Meanings of "Mystery"*

The word mystery is used by many people and in many ways, but only rarely does anyone state explicitly what he means by it. Information about it is rather effectively hidden, because almost never is it indexed in a book, even if it is mentioned in the text, and systematic, comprehensive discussions of it are exceedingly scarce. Not one of ten major encyclopedias that I have consulted has an article on mystery in general—aside from pieces on mystery as religious rite, mystery and detective stories, the mystery play, and so on. The dictionaries offer little, even the Oxford, aside from a few common synonyms.

In view of the sparsity of definitive material on mystery, it is surprising how many meanings appear in the profusion of words that refer to it. A comprehensive list of such terms, ones that I have actually encountered in the literature of philosophy, anthropology, religion, and belles lettres, would be amazingly long. Some of these are presented herein, italicized and grouped so as to help in identifying what seem to be those major usages or meanings that are relevant for our study. In this appendix we are simply asking in general terms what the word mystery does in fact connote, thus laying a semantic foundation for our study of those aspects of nature, and of reality in general, in which men have sensed mystery so understood.

PSEUDO-MYSTERY
To begin with, there are three rather common usages that should not be regarded as signifying genuine mystery. I am

* This essay, first published in *The Iliff-Review* (Winter 1972, pp. 11–19), is republished here with the permission of that journal. The author's and publisher's thanks are expressed hereby.

designating them as pseudo-mystery. The first refers to *anything that arouses considerable curiosity:* the *problematic, as-yet-unexplained, not-yet-understood,* the *still-to-be-solved,* the *uncomprehended,* the *riddle,* the *puzzle,* or that which seems *as-yet-inconsistent* with what is known, the *as-yet-incongruous* or *temporarily paradoxical.* Here we have only provisional "mystery," i.e., until explanation is forthcoming, and usually an implication of particularity: *a* mystery, *the* mystery, or *these* mysteries. Gabriel Marcel[1] and others have urged that in such cases the term *problem* be used rather than mystery. This has been my practice throughout this book.

Next is the taboo concept: "mystery" as *forbidden secrets* declared to be inappropriate for human investigation, the preserve of the gods. One is reminded here of the familiar warnings heard even today in some religious circles: "This is not for man to know."

Finally there is the "mystery" taken to be superstition, *relegated to limbo, to-be-disregarded* as not worthy of serious study. In the nineteenth century this usage was fairly common, especially among "men of the enlightenment." The intent was: Let's not bother with it; it is only superstition anyway, without real significance.

MYSTERY AS "THE QUANTITY OF THE UNKNOWN"; THE INEXPLICABLE; THE INACCESSIBLE

Now we come to mystery proper, where we can recognize at least seven major meanings. First, there is the strong sense of the *inexplicable, unexplainable, unanswerable, insoluble, incomprehensible, unknowable.* Here presumably is permanent mystery. To illustrate, Milton Munitz employs this meaning in speaking of the *mystery of existence.* He asks, "Is there a reason-for-the-existence-of-the-world?" and argues persuasively that this is a legitimate question, that it does have meaning yet cannot be answered—and is therefore more than simply a problem.[2] Such mystery, like all genuine mystery, arouses not only curiosity but the realization that it cannot be satisfied completely.

The second meaning takes us one conceptual step further,

to what seems not only inexplicable, but even *impercep-tible, unperceivable-though-presumably-existent, unavail-able, unreachable, inscrutable,* and *unsearchable.* Thus Einstein has often been quoted as saying, "Existence in its profoundest depths is inaccessible to man."

At this point we introduce a break in the classification scheme. The two meanings just noted, the inexplicable and the inaccessible, have this in common, that they have an essentially *negative* connotation: the mysterious is that which *is not* and *cannot* be known or understood—the accent being on what we do *not* know. Pelikan has suggested therefore that mystery is conceived here as "the quantity of the unknown."[3] But there is more to mystery than that. As all the other usages, to be considered presently, imply, the term mystery has also a more positive connotation, namely, that wonder is evoked not only by the unknown but even more by the mysterious grandeur, meaningfulness, and power of the known.

MYSTERY AS "A QUALITY OF THE KNOWN"; THE INFINITE; THE INEFFABLE

This shift becomes apparent at once as we pass to the third category of mystery: the *limitlessness, unboundedness, in-finity, inexhaustibility,* and *unfathomability* of the reality we do perceive and have come to "know"—and is seemingly endless in its extension, content, range of qualities, and in its *depth dimension.* Here too we note the *ever-receding-horizon* of our knowledge and understanding; no matter how far we press the analysis of the known, the end of it remains out of sight. Always it has more to reveal of itself. Hence the strong sense of its utter unfathomability as to its content and meaning—even though there is no certitude of it. Clearly the accent of connotation here is on what is known or can be known. Pelikan speaks of this aspect of mystery as a "quality of the known."[4] I myself like to call it the glory aspect of mystery, in contrast to the unknowability aspect suggested by the first two usages. What the third usage refers to more specifically is the immensity or infinity aspect of mystery's glory. There is,

270

of course, a caution to be observed in this connection: While these distinctions between the negative and positive and between the quantitative and qualitative features of mystery are indeed cogent and helpful, they must not be delineated too sharply, for after all they are not actually separate or utterly distinct in man's awareness of mystery. As becomes abundantly clear in the body of the text, when we apply these rather abstract notions to the concrete realities of nature, mystery seems always to elicit a mixed response of wonder: wonder at how tremendous, and even boundless, is the unknown of anything we observe, and yet how incredibly and unfathomably wondrous and extensive is also the known of it. Without the recognition of both of these facets of mystery, our understanding of it would be disappointingly inadequate.

The distinction between them is made even more evident by the many terms that identify the fourth aspect of mystery. I am presenting these below in five subgroups, each to a line, to indicate how profusely varied are the mystery qualities of reality to which this particular sense of mystery responds, and how exquisitely differentiated are the shades of meaning that emerge from men's sensitivity to those qualities:

wondrous, awesome, glorious, radiant, illuminating,
    effulgent;
ineffable, nonconceptual, noncognitive;
nonrational, transrational, irrational;
elusive, tantalizing, enigmatic;
*fascinating, numinous, tremendous, fearsome.**

Clearly, each succeeding line discloses a different large-scale qualitative aspect of the known—from the wondrous to the ineffable to the nonrational, elusive, and fascinating—and each individual term a different facet of it.

This list gives vivid meaning to a perceptive remark by Hocking, that there is a "difference between the sense of ignorance and the sense of mystery" and that the latter may be thought of "as the discerning of something beyond the bounds of ignorance."[5] One may become conscious of

* Some of the terms of this fifth group appear frequently in the writings of Rudolf Otto, Friedrich Heiler, Mercia Eliade, and others, concerning the holy, sacred, and profane.

an absence or of a presence. It is not only the opacity or darkness of mystery that evokes awe but also its translucency, radiance, and glory. This is why this and the next meanings of mystery are for the most part noncognitive. They stem not from awesome knowing or not knowing but from an awesome awareness that somehow transcends both. Wheelwright says it this way:

> Now awe in the most adequate sense of the word, is a feeling appropriate to the presence of Mystery; and Mystery is no puzzling riddle with a solution to be published . . . it is a That which intrinsically and majestically transcends the possibility of finite comprehension. The mysterious—i.e., the radically enigmatic, not the temporarily puzzling—is that character or quality or relationship in things which, however much "explained," always transcends in its essence any totality of explanations given. The two elements are deeply interrelated, but analytically distinguishable.[6]

It is often said that as knowledge grows mystery is dissolved. Actually, however, with increased understanding genuine mystery deepens. Certainly that is what this fourth usage implies. The more we come to know, the more we sense of the mysterious ineffability and glory of that known.

No doubt, as all this implies, there is but one transcendent Mystery that envelops and imbues all of life and reality, even though it has different aspects. Much is known and much is not known. About both much can be said; but both comprehend more than can be known or said. This, then, is the fourth aspect of mystery: *the glory of the more than can be said or reasoned.* As Reinhold Niebuhr wrote recently, "a penumbra of mystery surrounds every realm of meaning."[7] No doubt this refers in part to the negative, unknowing side of mystery; but, suggests John H. Hayward, "the mystery itself is pregnant with potential meaning. It is a positive mystery, a power—not a void or empty cipher."[8] This is its positive, glory side. Bringing these together Niebuhr offers the following definition: "Mystery in short is the shadowy realm of twilight where both coherence and incoherence are known and intimated, as well as the threshold of glory which gives light but does not reveal its nature."[9]

THE EFFLUENT; THE PURPOSIVE

This reference to "the threshold of glory which gives light" introduces the fifth meaning of mystery—which comes from the sense of the *givingness,* the *creative future-directedness,* or the *becomingness* of being, or "life,"[10] or the world. It is this sense of mystery that seems to be articulated by the biblical concept of continuous creation—an ever-active bringing forth of reality. The perennial figure of the vast, bottomless abyss is transformed into that of the inexhaustibly effluent fountain or source whence comes all light, meaning, and reality. Perhaps, too, this is what has brought forth the symbols of "cosmic fire," "the burning fountain," and the "river of fire."[11]

There is here, however, not only a sense of the coming forth of the stream of life from the inexhaustible Source but of its ceaseless, inexorable flowing on into the mysterious future. This is, then, the glory-mystery of the perpetual dynamic effluence of known reality: its *giving, creating, bringing forth, outflowing, outpouring, pushing on, effluence, emanation, becoming.* This sense of the mysterious creative flow into the future seems to be coupled with a sense of the *glory of the open future.* There is power in this mystery, for, as Pelikan suggests, "To acknowledge that mystery means to open oneself to the unknown future."[12] When it is seen for what it is, it generates commitment to openness.

For many men mystery has yet another (sixth) dimension of meaning: *teleological purposiveness* in the overall scheme of things, as well as in some of its detailed features. They sense that the effluence and becomingness of reality has a preferred direction, indicating a cosmic pressure toward richer and more varied existence, i.e., toward increased possibilities for actualization of novelty in the future, toward enhanced interdependence, mutuality, community, and "goodness." This is for them of the profoundest significance, feeling that it reveals purpose in the *ground of being.* Moreover, the encounter with it may seem essentially personal in character, as evidenced, for instance, in its persistent and inescapable probing and searching and in the demands it makes. Some of the ancient psalmists were keenly aware of this, as may be seen so clearly in a psalm like Psalm 139. Not a few moderns sense this, too, and quite as keenly, I suspect.

Among them is Gabriel Marcel, who feels that the sensing of this personal element is crucial for his understanding of mystery. Munitz sees this clearly in Marcel's thought and expounds it as follows: "This contrast between 'problem' and 'mystery' is not a contrast between two kinds of questions that the human mind can raise. It is a contrast between what can be expressed, on the one hand, as a question, and what, on the other, has the form of faith in divine or human presence."[13] Hocking takes a similar position. Thus, in the passage quoted in part earlier, he says, "Religion is bound up in the difference between the sense of ignorance and the sense of mystery: the former means, 'I know not'; the latter means 'I know not; but *it is known.'* . . . 'I know not; but He knows.' "[14]

Such sensing of mystery often leads to a theistic philosophy or theology, i.e., one that postulates a person-God. Julian Huxley represents those who do not sense any personal dimension of mystery—though, as I interpret his writings, he is keenly conscious of the others, including those of the numinous, nonrational, and of the directional bias in the development of the world (yet without actual "purpose").[15] Hence his consistent espousal of a nontheistic and humanistic position. It is possible, of course, to assume a stance that is nontheistic and nonhumanistic, as did Paul Tillich, who certainly discerned all dimensions of mystery in history and all save the personal in nature. He repeatedly disavowed theism, at least in its traditional form; yet some theologians regard him as a theist in its best and most fundamental sense.

However it may be in regard to a possibly personal element in the overall scheme of things, the sense of direction and purposiveness we have considered provides the basis for a confident sense of *the glory of a good and open future* and of an adequate, personal orientation toward it. Again we may refer with profit to a remark by Pelikan:

It would be a mistake to conclude that faith looks upon the future as mysterious merely because it is inscrutable. . . . The deepest meaning of the divine mystery is not insight into the future, but openness toward the future. . . . The future now becomes one dimension of the mystery disclosed in the past and operative in the present.[16]

It may well be, therefore, as suggested recently by Harvey Cox, Michael Novak, and others, that the most potent approach to an adequate conception of "God" may be through the sense and concept of the open future and of the mystery-reality that brings it into being.

It has been asserted that without the recognition of a personal element in this component of mystery it is impossible to make any sense out of a large group of others that are more specific, such as the *mystery of creation, of redemption, of Christ, of the Scriptures, of the Eucharist,* and others related to them (not to speak here of those encountered in non-Christian religions). May it not be too that it was the awareness of this aspect of mystery that led early translators to render the New Testament Greek *mystèrion* into the Latin *sacramentum?*

THE RADICALLY QUESTIONABLE
The last, and seventh, usage of the term mystery that I have encountered is that of *radical questionableness (radikale Fraglichkeit)*, which introduces certain overtones of connotation that seem not to have been intended by any of the terms mentioned earlier. There are apparently at least two aspects and depths of this. To begin with, while we have insisted that problems are in themselves not genuine mystery, it is one of the remarkable characteristics of real mystery that it does arouse amazement, and curiosity, and the desire to ask questions and to solve problems. To him who senses it at all adequately, mystery—far from repelling or forbidding investigation of it—perpetually invites the quest and then is inexhaustibly rewarding, yielding answer after answer, allowing solution after solution of problems or so-called myster*ies,* while yet itself remaining unmoved, unfathomable mystery. While it lures and beckons, the more insight it yields, the more gloriously mysterious it seems. Every question answered simply leads to

others, and still others. Surely this is what de Lubac meant when he asserted that "it is one of the forms of the fruitfulness of the mystery that it gives birth in man's mind to a movement which can never end."[17] While he is talking here specifically about the mystery of God, I dare say he would not deny that all genuine mystery is infinitely questionable and fruitful in this way.

Second, as Gerhard Ebeling sees it,

> The understanding of what the word "God" means has its place within the sphere of radical questionableness. The question how God is actually experienced, how it can actually become clear what God means in the context of the reality that encounters me, can be answered in the first instance only by the pointer: God is experienced as a question. In the context of the reality that encounters me God encounters me as the questionableness of that encountering reality. . . . The man who does not venture to ask questions is closed to the meaning of the word "God." To him the word "God" says absolutely nothing.[18]

Jürgen Moltmann puts it this way, after asserting that a comprehensive analysis of reality must recognize and take into account its radical questionableness: "In the radical questionableness of reality there appears the problem of transcendence, or simply the *question of God,* in the face of which the Christian affirmation of God must prove and authenticate itself." However, he explains, *this* "question of God" is not primarily about the existence and character of God but about how and why the question of God arises so compellingly. He then observes, "What the name 'God' means can be intelligibly shown only when it is related to a radical, and therefore necessary, questionableness of reality. 'God' is what we are talking about in and with this questionableness of reality."[19]

This is, of course, a tricky theological point with much chance for misunderstanding, and this is not the place for an exposition of it. At least this much should be said, however, namely, that one of the fundamental mystery-attributes of reality is its "radical questionableness," and that the meaning of the terms "God" and "transcendence" is inextricably enmeshed with it. There are at least three reasons for designating this questionableness as *radical.*

First, it invokes a querying and questing toward the ultimate root or ground of being. Second, reality is taken to be fundamentally (radically) questionable in the sense that it will never be otherwise than questionable; no supposedly final formulation of answers could stop the flow of questions; the questioning leads forever to new formulations of both question and answer. Third, the questionableness is radical because it relates not only to objective reality but also, and especially, to personal existence, that of the questioner. Clearly this refers to genuine mystery, indeed, ultimate mystery, infinitely evocative of radical questioning, infinitely fruitful of experience and insight, yet never ground for claims of finality therein.

This, then, brings to a close our survey of the major meanings of "mystery" of which I have become aware. We have been able to identify seven clearly distinguishable ones, the first two pertaining primarily to the extent of the unknown, and the others to the glory of the known. They are (1) the *inexplicable*, (2) the *inaccessible*, (3) the *infinite*, (4) the *ineffable*, (5) the *inexhaustibly effluent*, (6) the *ultimately purposive*, and (7) the *radically questionable*. There are also three common usages we have declined to attribute to genuine mystery: (a) the *problem*, (b) the *forbidden* (taboo), and (c) what is taken to be *superstitutious nonsense*. It should be emphasized that these distinctions are valid for analysis only. Surely mystery and the experience of it are unitary even though many-sided.

Notes

Chapter I. New Sensitivities and Sensibilities

1. Herbert Butterfield, *The Origins of Modern Science* (London: George Bell & Sons, 1949), pp. 104ff.
2. Karl Jaspers, *The Origin and Goal of History* (New Haven, Conn.: Yale University Press, 1953), pp. 1–3.
3. Ibid., p. 102.
4. Ibid., pp. 116ff.
5. Ibid., p. 117.
6. Marshall McLuhan, *Understanding Media: The Extensions of Man* (New York: McGraw-Hill, 1964), pp. vii, 7.
7. Jaspers, op. cit., pp. 126ff.
8. Ibid., p. 117.
9. Ibid., p. 139.
10. Alfred North Whitehead, *Science and the Modern World* (New York: Macmillan, 1926), p. 286 (also paperback).
11. Theodore Roszak, *The Making of a Counter-Culture* (Garden City, N.Y.: Doubleday—Anchor Books, 1969).
12. Charles A. Reich, *The Greening of America: The Coming of a New Consciousness and the Rebirth of a Future* (New York: Random House, 1970; also paperback). Reich portrays the consciousness of "the new generation" accurately and predicts that "the coming American revolution" will be a "revolution by consciousness."

Chapter II. Sensitivity to Mystery in Science and Religion

1. I have discussed this at length in my *Science and Religion: An Interpretation of Two Communities* (New York: Charles Scribner's Sons, 1962). See also William G. Pollard, *Physicist and Christian* (New York: Seabury Press, 1961), and Michael Polanyi, *Science, Faith and Society* (Chicago: University of Chicago Press, 1964) and *Personal Knowledge: Towards a Post-Critical Philosophy* (London: Routledge & Kegan Paul, 1958).
2. John Compton, "Natural Science and the Experience of Nature," *Journal of Existentialism*, Winter 1965–66.
3. Harlow Shapley, *Beyond the Observatory* (New York: Charles Scribner's Sons, 1967).

4. As to the distinction between knowing and understanding, I follow the usage and meanings of Edwin A. Burtt in his profound book, *In Search of Philosophic Understanding* (New York: New American Library, 1965).

5. Loren Eiseley, *The Immense Journey* (New York: Random House, 1946); *The Firmament of Time* (New York: Atheneum Publishers, 1960); *Darwin's Century* (New York: Atheneum Publishers, 1958).

6. Michael Polanyi, *Science, Faith and Society* (Chicago: University of Chicago Press, 1964); *Personal Knowledge* (London: Routledge & Kegan Paul, 1958).

7. John R. Platt, *The Excitement of Science* (Boston: Houghton Mifflin Co., 1962).

8. Philipp Frank, *Einstein: His Life and Times* (New York: Knopf, 1947).

9. René Vallery-Radot, *The Life of Pasteur* (Garden City, N.Y.: Doubleday, 1923).

10. Theodore Roszak, *The Making of a Counter-Culture* (Garden City, N.Y.: Doubleday—Anchor Books, 1969), p. 253.

11. Quoted by Robert S. Mulliken in "Spectroscopy, Quantum Chemistry and Molecular Physics," *Physics Today*, April 1968, p. 56.

12. Lucien Price, *Dialogues of Alfred North Whitehead* (Boston: Atlantic-Little, Brown and Co., 1954), p. 131. Used by permission.

13. Robert A. Millikan, *Evolution in Science and Religion* (New Haven, Conn.: Yale University Press, 1935), p. 11.

14. Ibid., pp. 10–11.

15. Alfred North Whitehead, *Science and the Modern World* (New York: Macmillan, 1926), p. 275.

16. *A New Catechism, Catholic Faith for Adults* (New York: Herder & Herder, 1967). Used by permission.

17. See, for instance, Alban G. Widgery, *Living Religions and Modern Thought* (New York: Roundtable Press, 1936) or, more recently, Bernard E. Meland, *The Secularization of Modern Cultures* (New York: Oxford University Press, 1966).

18. Michael Foster, *Mystery and Philosophy* (London: SCM Press, 1957), pp. 54, 55.

19. Lewis Mumford, *The Myth of the Machine: The Pentagon of Power* (New York: Harcourt Brace Jovanovich, 1970), pp. 395ff. Used by permission.

Chapter III. The Depth Dimension of Physical Reality

1. L. L. Foldy, "The Structure of Nucleons," *Physics Today*, September 1965, p. 26. Used by permission.

2. Max Born, *The Restless Universe*, 2nd ed. (New York: Dover, 1951), p. 231. Used by permission.

3. Lincoln Barnett, *The Universe and Dr. Einstein* (New York: New American Library—Mentor Books, 1952), p. 73.

4. A. S. Eddington, *Space, Time and Gravitation* (New York: Cambridge University Press, 1921).
5. George Gamow, *The Birth and Death of the Sun* (New York: New American Library—Mentor Books, 1953), chap. 12.
6. Fred Hoyle, *The Nature of the Universe* (New York: New American Library—Mentor Books, 1955), pp. 111ff.
7. Lawrence Lessing, "The Exploding Universe of Quasars," *The Physics Teacher*, March 1966.
8. William G. Pollard, *Science and Faith: Twin Mysteries* (New York: Thomas Nelson & Sons, 1970), p. 31.
9. Gamow, op. cit., chap. 5.
10. George Wallerstein, "Astronomical Evidence for Nucleosynthesis in Stars," *Science*, Vol. 162, 8 Nov. 1968, p. 625.

Chapter IV. The Symphonic Character of Matter-Energy: Its Particle-Wave Features

1. Donald H. Andrews, *The Symphony of Life* (Lee's Summit, Mo.: Unity Books, 1968), chaps. 2 and 3. Used by permission.
2. Max Born, *The Restless Universe*, 2nd ed. (New York: Dover, 1951), chap. IV. Used by permission.
3. Andrews, op. cit.
4. Edwin M. McMillan, "Nobel Laureate in Physics," *Science*, 8 Nov. 1968, p. 645.
5. Andrews, op. cit.
6. Gerald Holton and Duane H. D. Roller, *Foundations of Modern Physical Science* (Reading, Mass.: Addison-Wesley Publishing Co., 1958), part VIII, "The Quantum Physics of Light and Matter."
7. David Bohm, *Quantum Mechanics* (Englewood Cliffs, N.J.: Prentice-Hall, 1951), p. 90.
8. Born, op. cit., p. 233.
9. From *Nature and God*, by L. Charles Birch. Published in the U.S.A. by The Westminster Press, 1965. © SCM Press Ltd., 1965. Used by permission.
10. Born, op. cit., p. 233.
11. Henry Margenau, *Open Vistas* (New Haven, Conn.: Yale University Press, 1961), p. 141.
12. Born, op. cit., p. 265.

Chapter V. Complexity and Simplicity in Nature and Science

1. C. P. Snow in Ralph E. Lapp, *Matter*, "The Life Science Library" (New York: Time-Life Books), p. 7. © 1963 Ralph E. Lapp and the Editors of Life. Used by permission of Time Inc.
2. Lapp, ibid., p. 9.
3. Ibid., pp. 99ff.
4. Herman F. Mark, *Giant Molecules*, "The Life Science Library" (New York: Time-Life Books), p. 11.
5. Ibid., p. 56.

6. Cyril S. Smith, "Matter versus Materials: A Historical View," *Science*, Vol. 162, 8 Nov. 1968, p. 639. Copyright 1968 by the American Association for the Advancement of Science. Used by permission of the publisher and author.
7. Ibid., p. 637.
8. Ibid., p. 638.
9. Ian Barbour, *Issues in Science and Religion* (Englewood Cliffs, N.J.: Prentice-Hall, 1966), pp. 156–61.
10. Victor F. Weisskopf, *Knowledge & Wonder* (Garden City, N.Y.: Doubleday, 1962), p. 85; also plate IV.
11. Nelson Goodman, "Science and Simplicity," booklet 16, Philosophy of Science Series, Voice of America Forum, Lectures, U.S. Information Agency, Washington, D.C.
12. Quoted in John R. Platt, ed., *New Views of the Nature of Man* (Chicago: University of Chicago Press, 1965), p. 93.
13. Smith, op. cit., pp. 643, 644.

Chapter VI. Nature's Reality Open or Closed? Its Relationality

1. A. Pais, "The Particles Jungle," *The Rockefeller University Review*, Jan.-Feb. 1966, p. 3. Used by permission.
2. Gerald Holton, reprinted from the May 30, 1966 issue of *Christianity and Crisis*, p. 114, copyright © 1966 by Christianity and Crisis, Inc.
3. David Bohm, *Causality and Chance* (New York: Harper & Row —Harper Torchbook, 1961), pp. 133, 139.
4. Walter Sullivan, "Smallest of the Small," *New York Times*, 5 February, 1967. © 1967 by The New York Times Company. Reprinted by permission.
5. Jeoffrey F. Chew, "Hadron Bootstrap: Triumph or Frustration?" *Physics Today*, October 1970. Used by permission.
6. David Bakan, *The Duality of Human Existence* (Skokie, Ill.: Rand McNally & Co., 1966), pp. 5, 9. Used by permission.
7. Victor F. Weisskopf, *Knowledge & Wonder* (Garden City, N.Y.: Doubleday, 1962), pp. 100ff.
8. Kenneth E. Boulding, *The Meaning of the Twentieth Century* (New York: Harper & Row, 1965), p. 155.
9. Louis Rosen, "Meson Factories," *Physics Today*, Dec. 1966, p. 36.
10. Paul Tillich, *Systematic Theology*, vol. III (Chicago: University of Chicago Press, 1963), p. 88.

Chapter VII. The Depths of Time; the Developmental Character of Reality

1. Philipp Frank, *Philosophy of Science* (Englewood Cliffs, N.J.: Prentice-Hall, 1957), pp. 158ff.
2. P. W. Bridgman, *The Logic of Modern Physics* (New York: Macmillan, 1927), p. 69.
3. Max Born, *The Restless Universe*, 2nd ed. (New York: Dover, 1951), p. 233. Used by permission.

4. Carl F. von Weizsäcker, *The Relevance of Science: Creation and Cosmogony*, Gifford Lectures 1959–60 (New York: Harper & Row, 1964), chap. 7.
5. G. M. McKinley, *Evolution: The Ages and Tomorrow* (New York: Ronald Press, 1956), pp. 55ff.
6. Harlow Shapley, *On Stars and Men* (Boston: Beacon Press, 1958), p. 112. Walter Sullivan, *We Are Not Alone*, rev. ed. (New York: New American Library, 1966).

Chapter VIII. Nature's Unity and Disunity, Creativity and Destructiveness

1. Schilling, *Science and Religion* (New York: Charles Scribner's Sons, 1962), pp. 22, 23.
2. See L. Charles Birch, *Nature and God* (Philadelphia: Westminster Press, 1965), pp. 36ff., and Harlow Shapley, *On Stars and Men* (Boston: Beacon Press, 1958), p. 24; in Sol Tax, ed., *The Evolution of Life* (Chicago: University of Chicago Press, 1960), see Hans Gaffron, "The Origin of Life," pp. 39ff.; and in Sol Tax, ed., *Issues in Evolution* (Chicago: University of Chicago Press, 1960), see panel discussion, "The Origin of Life," pp. 69ff.
3. Teilhard de Chardin, *The Phenomenon of Man* (New York: Harper & Row, 1959): see "The Advent of Life," p. 77; "The Transit to Life," pp. 79ff.
4. Birch, op. cit., p. 45; Theodosius Dobzhansky, "Evolution as a Creative Process," *Proceedings of the Ninth International Congress Genetics* (Caryologia, Suppl.) 1954, pp. 435–48.
5. Paul Tillich, *Systematic Theology*, vol. III (Chicago: University of Chicago Press, 1963), chap. I; John Habgood speaks of "the untidiness of life" in his *Truths in Tension* (New York: Holt, Rinehart & Winston, 1965), chap. 1.
6. Roger L. Shinn, *Tangled World* (New York: Charles Scribner's Sons, 1965).
7. Loren Eiseley, *The Firmament of Time* (New York: Atheneum Publishers, 1960), especially chaps. I–IV.
8. Ibid., chap. VI, then V.
9. Peter L. Berger, *A Rumor of Angels: Modern Society and the Rediscovery of the Supernatural* (Garden City, N.Y.: Doubleday, 1969), pp. 81ff.
10. Hudson Hoagland, "Some Biological Considerations of Ethics," in *Technology and Culture in Perspective*, an occasional paper (booklet) published by The Church Society for College Work, Cambridge, Mass., 1967.

Chapter IX. The Flowering of Mind and Spirit

1. Edmund W. Sinnott, *The Bridge of Life: From Matter to Spirit* (New York: Simon and Schuster, 1966), p. 95. Copyright 1966 by Edmund W. Sinnott.

282

2. John R. Platt, "1966 Nobel Laureate in Chemistry: Robert S. Mulliken," *Science*, 11 Nov. 1966, pp. 745–47.

3. Sinnott, op. cit.

4. Gilbert Ryle, *The Concept of Mind* (London: Hutchinson, 1949).

5. Sol Tax, ed., *The Evolution of Man* (Chicago: University of Chicago Press, 1960); of special interest is Leslie White, "Four Stages in the Evolution of Minding," pp. 239ff. See also Sol Tax, ed., *Issues in Evolution* (Chicago: University of Chicago Press, 1960), panel discussion "The Evolution of Mind," pp. 175ff.; Teilhard de Chardin, *The Phenomenon of Man* (New York: Harper & Row, 1959); see "The Birth of Thought" and "The Deployment of the Noosphere," pp. 163–211; Sir Russell Brain, "Body, Brain, Mind and Soul," in Julian Huxley, ed., *The Humanist Frame* (New York: Harper & Row, 1961), especially "The Evolution of Mind," pp. 59ff.; and L. Charles Birch, *Nature and God* (Philadelphia: Westminster Press, 1965), "Mind and Matter," pp. 66ff.

6. From *The Immense Journey*, by Loren Eiseley, pp. 186ff. Copyright © 1955 by Loren Eiseley. Reprinted by permission of Random House, Inc.

7. Joseph L. Grucci, *Time of Hawks* (Pittsburgh, Pa.: Mayer Press, 1955), p. 11. Used by permission of the author.

8. Walter Sullivan, *We Are Not Alone*, rev. ed. (New York: McGraw-Hill, 1966), p. 245.

9. Alfred North Whitehead, *Science and the Modern World* (New York: Macmillan, 1926), p. 275.

10. Loren Eiseley, "Man: The Lethal Factor," *American Scientist*, Vol. 15, March 1963, pp. 71–83.

11. Loren Eiseley, *The Firmament of Time* (New York: Atheneum Publishers, 1960), p. 123. Used by permission.

12. Eiseley, "Man: The Lethal Factor," pp. 78–79. Used by permission of author and publisher.

13. John Baillie, *The Belief in Progress* (New York: Charles Scribner's Sons, 1951).

14. Karl A. Menninger, *The Crime of Punishment* (New York: Viking Press, 1968).

15. Teilhard, op. cit., p. 265.

16. Edwin A. Burtt, *In Search of Philosophic Understanding* (New York: New American Library, 1965), chap. 9, "Love, Creation, and Reality," especially pp. 225–30.

17. Kenneth E. Boulding, *The Meaning of the Twentieth Century* (New York: Harper & Row, 1965). Lancelot L. Whyte, *The Next Development in Man* (New York: New American Library— Mentor Book, 1962); John R. Platt, *The Step to Man* (New York: John Wiley & Sons, 1966), especially the last chapter.

18. This phenomenon of men's universal sharing of experience, and of their unification in this way, has been discussed at length

by Marshall McLuhan, *Understanding Media: The Extensions of Man* (New York: McGraw-Hill, 1964).

19. William G. Pollard, *Physicist and Christian* (New York: Seabury Press, 1961), chap. III, "The Reality of Spirit," pp. 64ff.

Chapter X. The Mystery of Transcendence-Immanence

1. Robert Frost, *Poems* (New York: Modern Library, no. 242).
2. From an article by Philipp Frank, "Contemporary Science and the Contemporary World View," reprinted by permission of *Daedalus*, Journal of the American Academy of Arts and Sciences, Boston, Mass., Winter 1958, *Science and the Modern World View.*
3. Kent Bendall and Frederick Ferré, *Exploring the Logic of Faith* (New York: Association Press, 1962), p. 177.
4. Ian T. Ramsey, *Models and Mystery* (New York: Oxford University Press, 1964), pp. 21, 20.
5. Alfred North Whitehead, *Science and the Modern World* (New York: Macmillan, 1926), p. 286.
6. Henry Margenau, *Yale Alumni Magazine*, Feb. 1963.
7. Philip Wheelwright, *The Burning Fountain* (Bloomington, Ind.: Indiana University Press, 1954), chap. 1.
8. Peter L. Berger, *A Rumor of Angels: Modern Society and the Rediscovery of the Supernatural* (Garden City, N.Y.: Doubleday, 1969), pp. 81ff.
9. Paul Tillich, *Systematic Theology*, vol. III (Chicago: University of Chicago Press, 1963), p. 88.
10. See Edwin A. Burtt, *In Search of Philosophic Understanding* (New York: New American Library, 1965), on the meaning of *understanding* as distinguished from *knowledge.*
11. Bernard E. Meland, *The Secularization of Modern Cultures* (New York: Oxford University Press, 1966), p. 117.
12. Bernard E. Meland, *Realities of Faith* (New York: Oxford University Press, 1962), p. 222.
13. Tillich, op. cit., part IV, "Life and the Spirit," p. 21.
14. See Meland, *Realities*, p. 241, and *Secularization*, especially the chapter "The Significance of Religious Sensitivity and Wonder in Any Culture"; in *Realities*, see chapters entiltled "The Encounter with Spirit" and "The Reality of Spirit."
15. Berger, op. cit., pp. 65ff. Copyright © 1969 by Peter L. Berger. Reprinted by permission of Doubleday & Company, Inc.
16. Ibid.
17. Meland, *Realities*, pp. 276ff.
18. Tillich, op. cit., vol. III, p. 359.
19. Albert C. Outler, *Who Trusts in God: Musings on the Meaning of Providence* (New York: Oxford University Press, 1968), p. 37.

Chapter XI. Today's Biblical Religious Consciousness

1. Roger Shinn, *Life, Death and Destiny* (Philadelphia: Westminster, Press, 1957), p. 27.
2. H. Richard Niebuhr, *Radical Monotheism and Western Culture* (New York: Harper & Row, 1960), p. 38.
3. Ibid., pp. 119, 120, 122.
4. This similarity has been described at length in my *Science and Religion* (New York: Charles Scribner's Sons, 1962).
5. Antony Flew and Alasdair Macintyre, *New Essays in Philosophical Theology* (New York: Macmillan, 1955), chap. 6, "Theology and Falsifiability."
6. Robert L. Calhoun, *God and the Common Life* (New York: Charles Scribner's Sons, 1935), republished by The Shoe String Press (Hamden, Conn., 1954), p. 238. Used by permission.
7. Ibid., p. 237.
8. Roger Shinn, *Perspective*, Winter 1972, pp. 76ff. Used by permission.
9. Ibid.
10. Ibid.

Chapter XII. The Developmental Character of Biblical Religion

1. In Walter H. Horton, *Christian Theology: An Ecumenical Approach* (New York: Harper & Row, 1958), alternative views are expounded with great clarity.
2. Daniel D. Williams, *The Spirit and the Forms of Love* (New York: Harper & Row, 1968), pp. 4, 5.
3. John Dillenberger, *Contours of Faith: Changing Forms of Christian Thought* (Nashville: Abingdon Press, 1969), pp. 35, 36. Used by permission.
4. Ibid., p. 83.
5. Ibid., p. 58.
6. Ibid., pp. 84, 85.
7. See my discussion of creeds and their development in *Science and Religion* (New York: Charles Scribner's Sons, 1962), pp. 28, 114, 121; especially chap. 7. See also Roger L. Shinn and Daniel D. Williams, *We Believe* (Philadelphia: United Church Press, 1966). This is an interpretation of the United Church Statement of Faith.
8. See paper by Walter Ong in *Technology and Culture in Perspective: Report of a Seminar at MIT, 1966*, published by the Church Society for College Work, Cambridge, Mass.
9. Paul Tillich, *Systematic Theology*, vol. I (Chicago: University of Chicago Press, 1952), pp. 116ff.
10. Loren Eiseley, "Man: The Lethal Factor," *American Scientist*, Vol. 51, March 1963. Used by permission of author and publisher.

Chapter XIII. Difficult Perplexities for Today's Faith

1. Leslie Dewart, *The Future of Belief* (New York: Herder &

Herder, 1966). Used by permission. Its subtitle is suggestive: *Theism in a World Come of Age.*

2. Gabriel Fackre, *Humiliation and Celebration* (New York: Sheed & Ward, 1969).

3. Gabriel Moran, *Commonweal*, 10 Feb. 1967, p. 503.

4. Dewart, op. cit., pp. 173, 185, 196, 206.

5. L. Charles Birch, *Nature and God* (Philadelphia: Westminster Press, 1965); Richard H. Overman, *Evolution and the Christian Doctrine of Creation* (Philadelphia: Westminster Press, 1967).

6. W. Norman Pittenger, *Process Thought and the Christian Faith* (New York: Macmillan, 1968).

7. Peter Hamilton, *The Living God and the Modern World* (Philadelphia: United Church Press, 1967).

8. Ian Barbour, *Issues in Science and Religion* (Englewood Cliffs, N.J.: Prentice-Hall, 1966).

9. Pittenger, op. cit., pp. 44, 46–48.

10. Ibid.

11. Ibid.

12. The concept of the cosmic or "universal Christ" was central in the thought of Teilhard; see many references to it in Claude Cuénot, *Teilhard De Chardin* (Baltimore: Helicon Press, 1965).

13. See, for instance, Raymond Panikkar, *The Unknown Christ of Hinduism* (London: Darton, Longman & Todd, 1964).

Chapter XIV. Man Building the "New Earth" with God

1. From *God the Future of Man* by Edward Schillebeeckx, O.P., translated by N. D. Smith, p. 53, © Sheed & Ward Inc., 1968.

2. Ibid., pp. 35, 36.

3. Ibid., p. 178.

4. Leslie Dewart, *The Future of Belief* (New York: Herder & Herder, 1966), p. 207. Used by permission.

5. Ibid.

6. Ibid., p. 209.

7. Ibid., p. 197.

8. See also my chapter, "The Whole Earth Is the Lord's: Toward a Holistic Ethic," in Ian Barbour, ed., *Earth Might Be Fair* (Englewood Cliffs, N.J.: Prentice-Hall, 1972); and Ralph Wendel Burhoe, ed., *Science and Human Values in the Twenty-First Century* (Philadelphia: Westminster Press, 1971).

9. Alfred North Whitehead, *Adventures of Ideas* (New York: New American Library—Mentor Book, 1955), last chapter, "Peace."

Appendix: On the Meanings of "Mystery"

1. Gabriel Marcel, *The Mystery of Being.* Gateway ed., 2 vols. (Chicago: Henry Regnery Co., 1960).

2. Milton K. Munitz, *The Mystery of Existence* (New York: Appleton-Century-Crofts, 1965).

3. Jaroslav J. Pelikan, *The Christian Intellectual* (New York: Harper & Row, 1966), pp. 69ff.
4. Ibid.
5. William E. Hocking, *The Meaning of God in Human Experience* (New Haven, Conn.: Yale University Press, 1912), pp. 235–36.
6. Philip Wheelwright, *The Burning Fountain: A Study in the Language of Symbolism* (Bloomington, Ind.: Indiana University Press, 1954), pp. 295, 74.
7. Reinhold Niebuhr, *Christianity and Crisis*, 13 June 1966, p. 127.
8. John H. Hayward, *Zygon*, March 1966, p. 32.
9. Niebuhr, op. cit.
10. In this context the term "life" is used in Paul Tillich's sense, as in the third volume of *Systematic Theology* (Chicago: University of Chicago Press, 1963).
11. Wheelwright, op. cit., chap. XIV.
12. Pelikan, op. cit., p. 79.
13. Munitz, op. cit., p. 31.
14. Hocking, op. cit., pp. 235–37.
15. Julian Huxley, *Religion Without Revelation* (London: Parish, 1957); also "The Humanist Frame" in book of same title (New York: Harper & Row, 1962).
16. Pelikan, op. cit., p. 78.
17. Henri de Lubac, *The Mystery of the Supernatural* (New York: Herder & Herder, 1967), p. 216.
18. Gerhard Ebeling, *Word and Faith* (Philadelphia: Fortress Press, 1963), p. 347. Used by permission.
19. Jürgen Moltmann, *Theology of Hope* (New York: Harper & Row, 1967), p. 272.